Gracious Beaufort

GRACIOUS BEAUFORT

EDITED BY WILLIAM P. BALDWIN

LOST PHOTOGRAPHS FROM THE
HISTORIC AMERICAN BUILDINGS SURVEY

Charleston London
History
PRESS

Published by The History Press
Charleston, SC 29403
www.historypress.net

Cover image: Dr. Johnson House. *Photographer Charles N. Bayless.*

First published 2007

Manufactured in the United Kingdom

ISBN 978.1.59629.365.6

Library of Congress CIP data applied for.

Notice: The information in this book is true and complete to the best of our knowledge. It is offered without guarantee on the part of the author or The History Press. The author and The History Press disclaim all liability in connection with the use of this book.

For Selden "Bud" Hill

PREFACE

Almost every photograph included here was taken from the HABS collection—the Historic American Buildings Survey catalogue found in the Library of Congress. Beginning in 1934, photographers, professional and otherwise, were sent out across the country to record the nation's buildings. Like the vast majority of Americans during the Depression, these men and women needed a salary and were meant to earn it simply by some useful documenting. Still, like those of the better-known FSA (Farm Security Administration), they were professionals, skilled photographers or at least earnest amateurs, and the best of them were creating art. They still are. This Depression-age survey is still going on, and tucked away in the Library of Congress vaults (and computers) are over thirty-six thousand HABS buildings (350,000 images) from which we drew the contents of this book.

These photographs are like old friends of mine—friends I'd like to introduce to you. My first glimpse of the HABS came in 1983, and even then I wondered if a book were possible. In 1996 I actually spent a week in the Library of Congress and made a list of about one hundred South Carolina images I'd like to use and then returned a second time in 2003 and expanded my search. Satisfied that the project was feasible, I began to visit the Library of Congress's HABS site online and downloaded a handful of images. Looking over this random sampling, my son Aaron suggested I structure the book around a particular portion of architecture or locality and use that framework to discuss the South. Sifting through the HABS digital records of every Southern state (often twice), I came up with thirteen hundred photographs, which Aaron helped me cull to seven hundred. Georgia photographer Elizabeth Turk reduced those to about two hundred and placed them in close to their present order. Then I inserted a dozen or so rejects that I couldn't live without. Elizabeth shuffled those in and my neighbor Gary Bronson converted the result to a computerized format for the publisher. That gave us the original *Mantelpieces of the Old South*, which The History Press published in 2005. For the present book, *Gracious Beaufort*, I worked alone, but the process remained pretty much the same, and naturally I'm in the debt of the three above mentioned.

The photographs can stand on their own, and except for the location, photographer's name, the date taken and a few minimal comments, they do. But before you turn the page, you should understand there's a progression to what follows. In the earlier book Elizabeth explains:

> *When editing you look for visual rhythms. Shape, shadow, quality of light, subject matter and yes, emotional content. In a single photo all that makes an impact. By itself that photo might be "nice" but place it next to another and you have a relationship. Two photos can be taken by different people and fifty years apart, but put them together and a connection is made. Perhaps a romance starts or even an antagonism. Whatever happens, you have a narrative, and it's one you usually can't put into words.*
>
> *Of course, this means the arrangement of the entire book has to also work as a sequence. That is, it has to present a dramatic progression just as you'd find in an essay—or a novel. You don't just have all the mantels going off to the right or all the mirrors grouped together. You manipulate on a deeper level. And even if people don't get the connections, they can still bring their own. There's a tension in the sequencing that you want the viewer to sense. A logic that can't necessarily be verbalized—a visual logic.*
>
> *Just look at the images. Let the images lead you—and don't be too quick to judge them. Some are strong images. Some aren't. The light's not good, or the focus soft. But that, too, can add a dramatic edge to the photograph and make you think about the past—and the present.*

Fearlessly (I won't say foolishly) I've attempted to follow this plotting in the present book as well. And again I invite you to turn the pages and listen with your eyes. Enjoy.

Credits & Acknowledgements

The HABS Photographers:

Charles N. Bayless
James E. Boucher
Gilford Photography
C.O. Greene

A special thanks to Kirsty and her pals.

Introduction

Beaufort's handsome old houses:

> *Designed primarily for coolness, with high basements and spacious verandas, they are set in old fashioned gardens where yellow jessamine, moss, and wisteria intermingle; where oleanders, camellias, and evergreens grow riotously. Architecture presents a combination of the Classical Revival and an adaptation of the smaller plantation house, with here and there a touch of semitropical Spanish and more formal Georgian. Peculiar to the Low Country are the houses of "tabby," a composition made of crushed oyster shells.*

That's the account of the 1940 WPA guidebook, and it is hard to improve on. "Turbulent" is the word they use for the town's history, and that suits as well. In the sixteenth century the Spanish colonized here without success, and so did French Huguenots. The Scots tried a settlement in 1685. The English came around 1711 and three years later the Yemassee drove them from the site. Rebels and Tories fought it out in the surrounding neighborhoods. In the next war the Union forces took the town and only partly gave it back. And today the entire region is enjoying the mixed benefits of a "land boom." I suppose a bit of all that activity has found its way into the architecture. There's definitely a Beaufort style: large double piazzas, some with strong Classical Revival columns and others with porches stacked upon the smaller columns of superimposed orders. But architecture buffs should be on guard, for to comply with this "Beaufort style" a variety of existing houses have been refaced with double porticos. The use of tabby is another local adaptation. With clay for making bricks scarce, builders mixed oyster shell with lime (burnt shell) and poured the mixture into board frames that could be built higher and higher. The majority of these houses are built on tabby foundations and several of them are made completely of tabby. Note, too, the frequency of the T shape in these houses. By extending the back rooms slightly out, the occupants there could enjoy the breeze. And finally, I should mention the Adam brothers. During the eighteenth century these two Scotsmen brought a lightness to both interior and exterior design that was welcomed in Beaufort even before it was accepted in Charleston. The John Mark Verdier House is a good example of this Adamesque, or Federalist, refinement, but there are dozens of others.

I can't think of a better town or city to walk in. Beaufort's older and better-known sisters (Charleston and Savannah) can't begin to compete in that category. Here's a final bit from the WPA guide:

> *Seldom is the day that the sun does not shine on Beaufort, and flowers are always in bloom. Scarlet poinsettias are framed against tabby walls; an avenue of palmettos line Boundary Street. Great spreading live oaks, festooned with Spanish moss, weave shifting patterns on the narrow crooked streets; these still bear their original names, although in some cases their former oyster-shell whiteness has surrendered to progress and modern cement. Beneath the trees a carpet of lush grass slopes down to ancient sea walls, and through green vistas gleams the gray-green tidal river, with little fleets of sailboat in the bay beyond.*

True in 1940. Still true today.

All but two of these Beaufort houses and most of the church photographs included here were taken by Charles N. Bayless in 1978. Out of respect for his abilities and to maintain clarity, I've repeated his name with each house. With so much kinship, keeping the occupants of these entries straight was a bit tricky. Hopefully I've done it. If not: apologies.

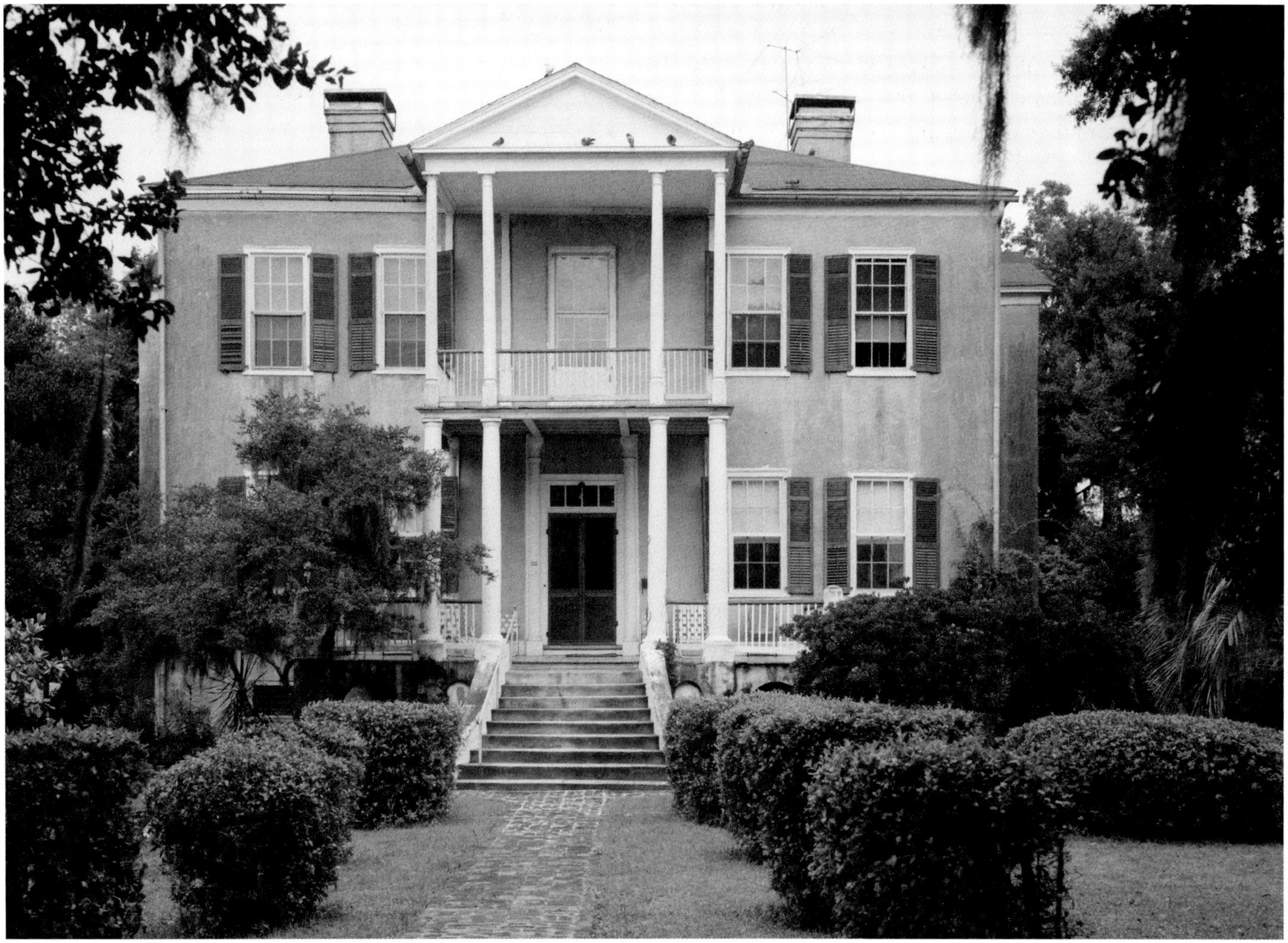

THOMAS FULLER HOUSE — Charles N. Bayless, 1978 (photo series)

Cotton planter Thomas Fuller built this tabby house on the bay in 1786.

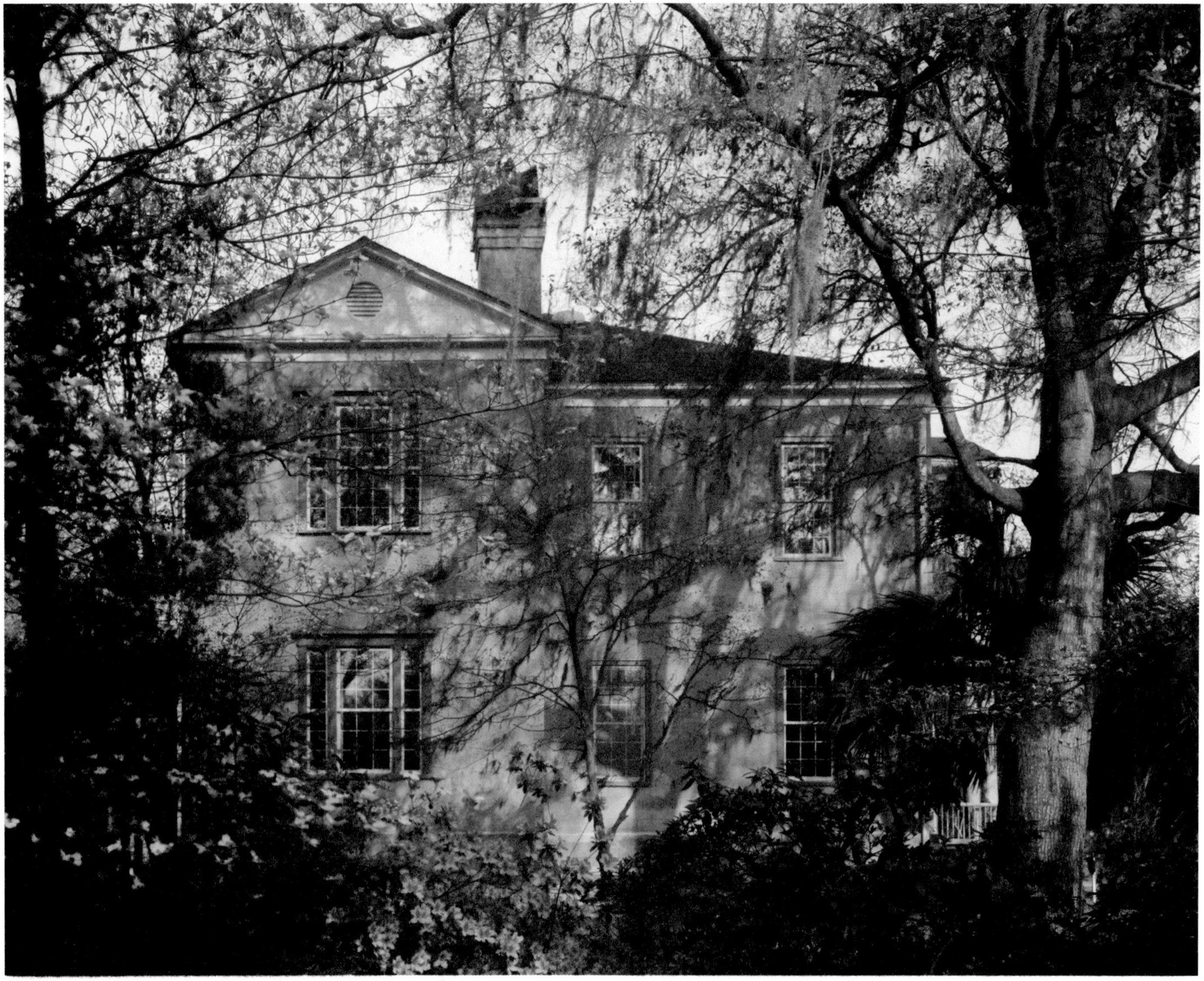

Thomas Fuller House

The T-shaped bays to the rear guaranteed that each room would have exposure to the breeze.

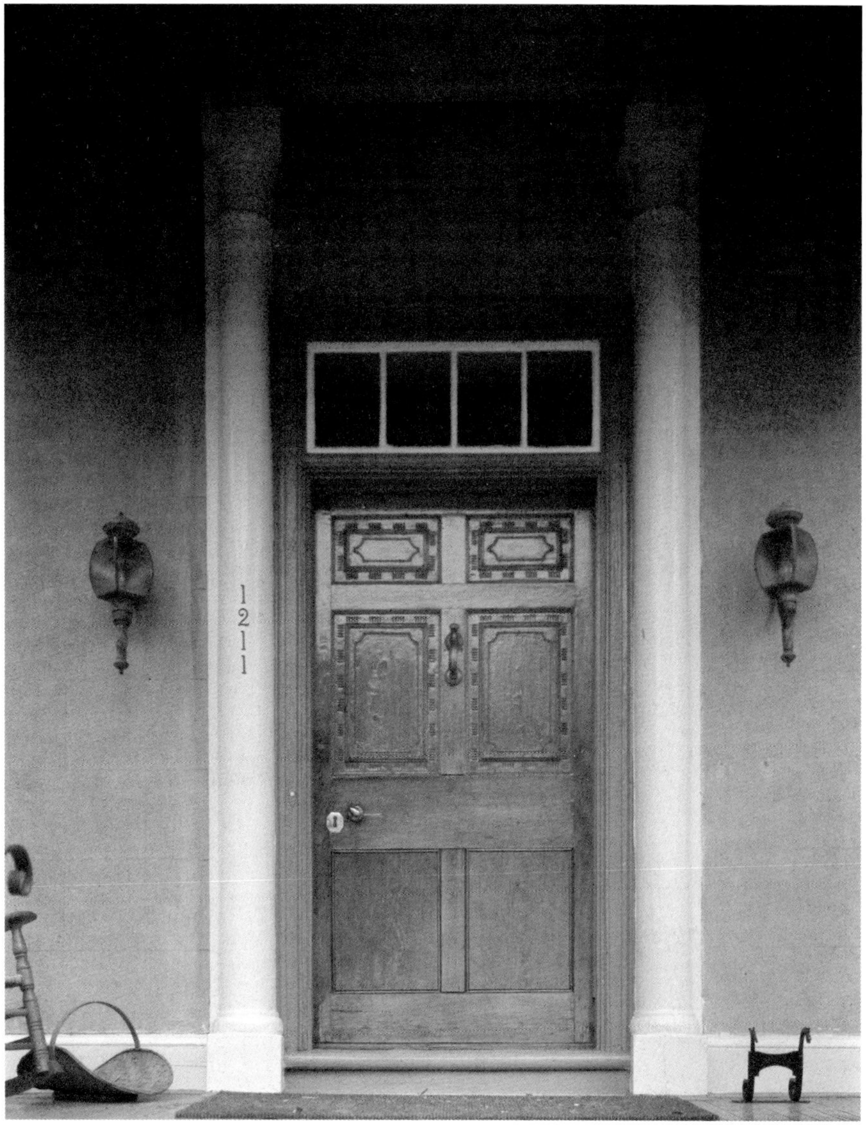

Thomas Fuller House

The door is from another era, but the boot scraper isn't.

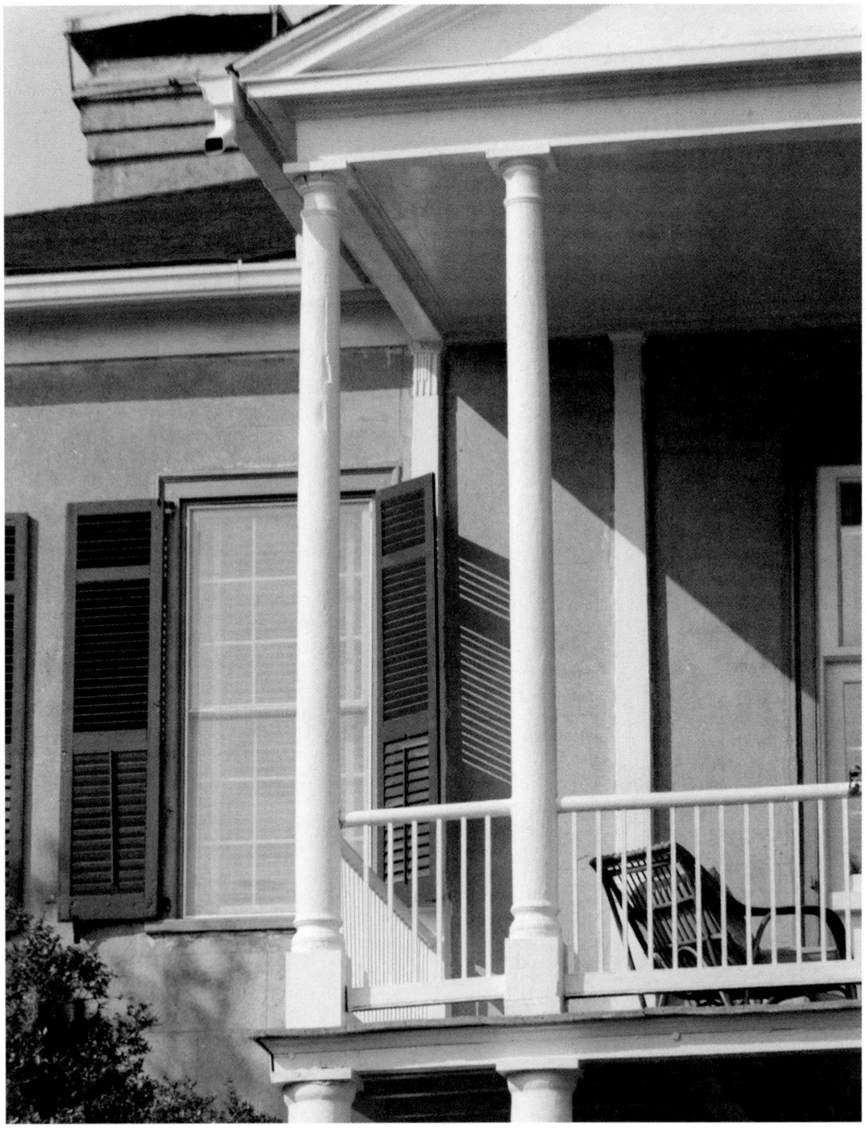

Thomas Fuller House

A good and graceful Federalist design that's gone untouched.

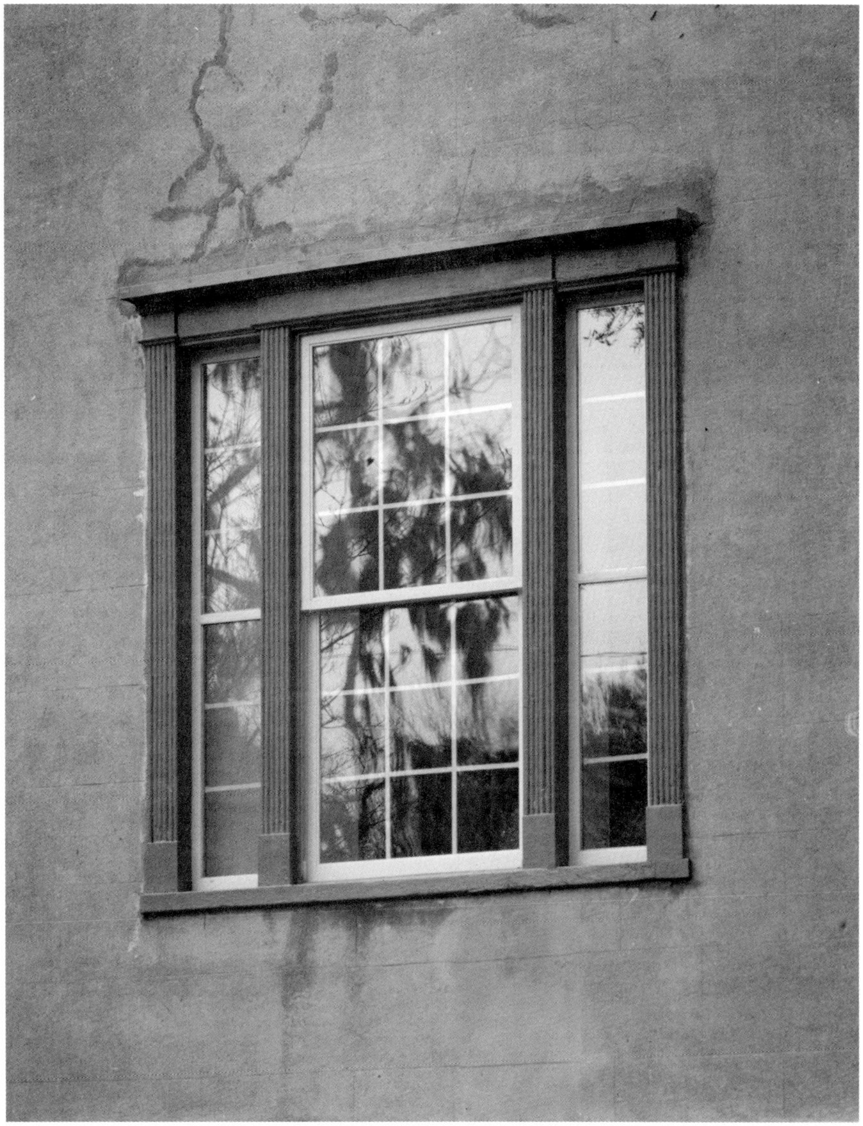

Thomas Fuller House

A "typical triple window" reflecting a typical moss-draped oak.

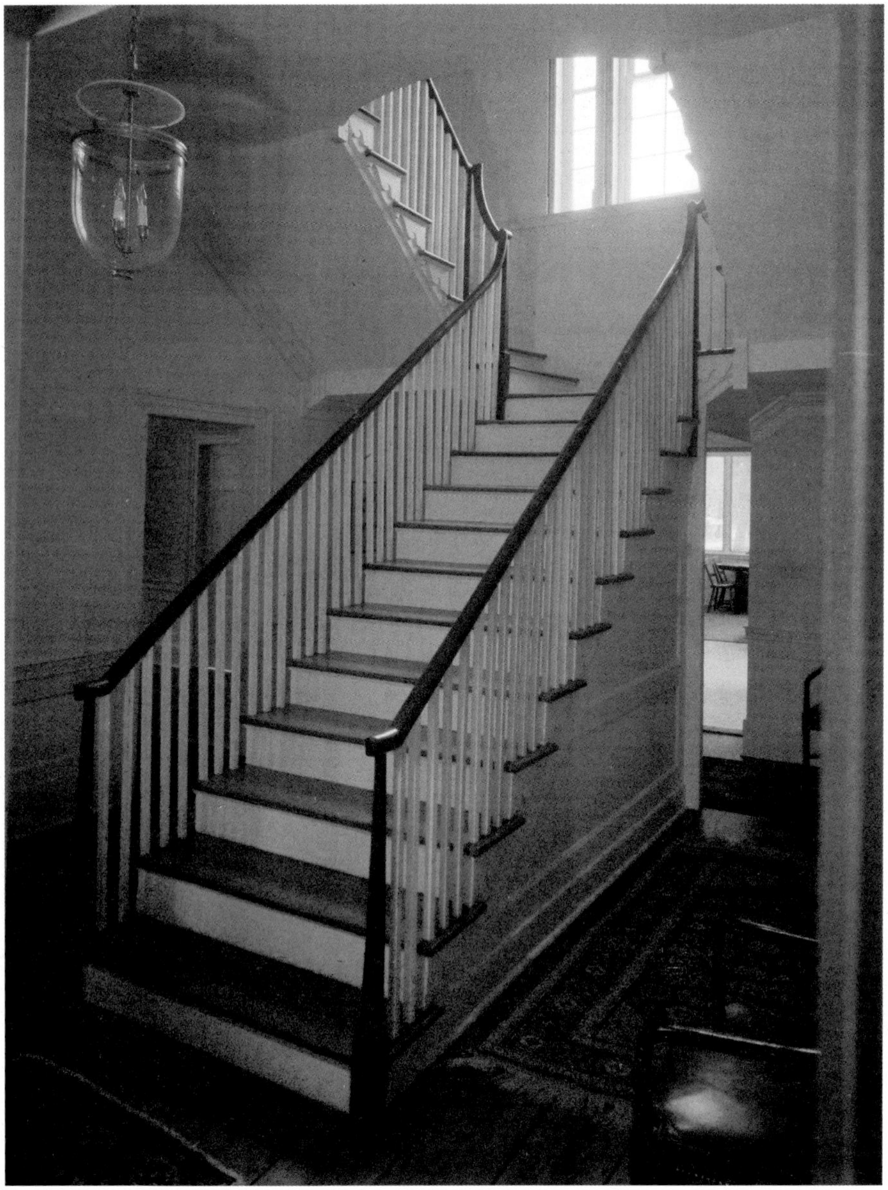

Thomas Fuller House

The main stair.

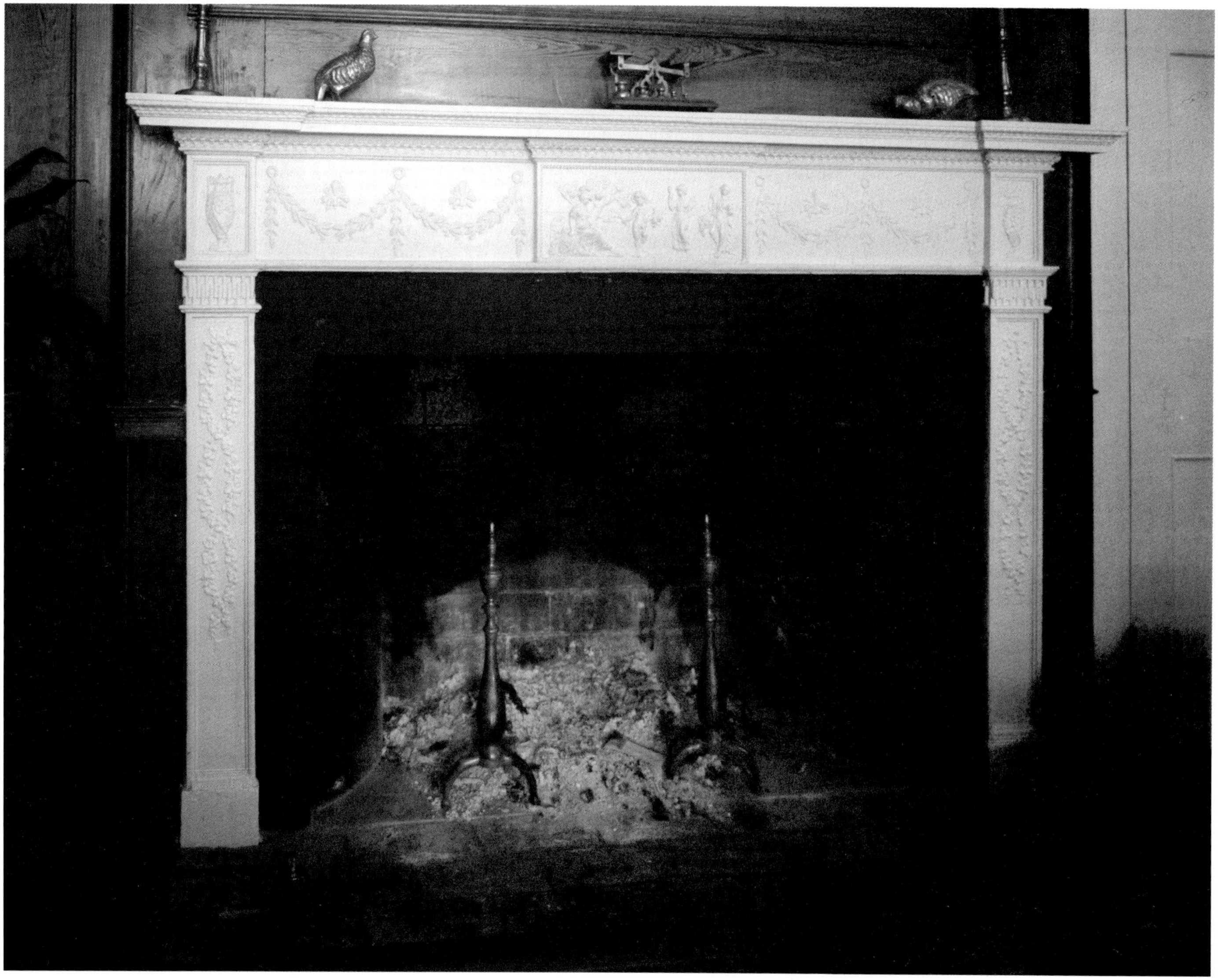

Thomas Fuller House

An Adamesque, or Federalist, mantel.

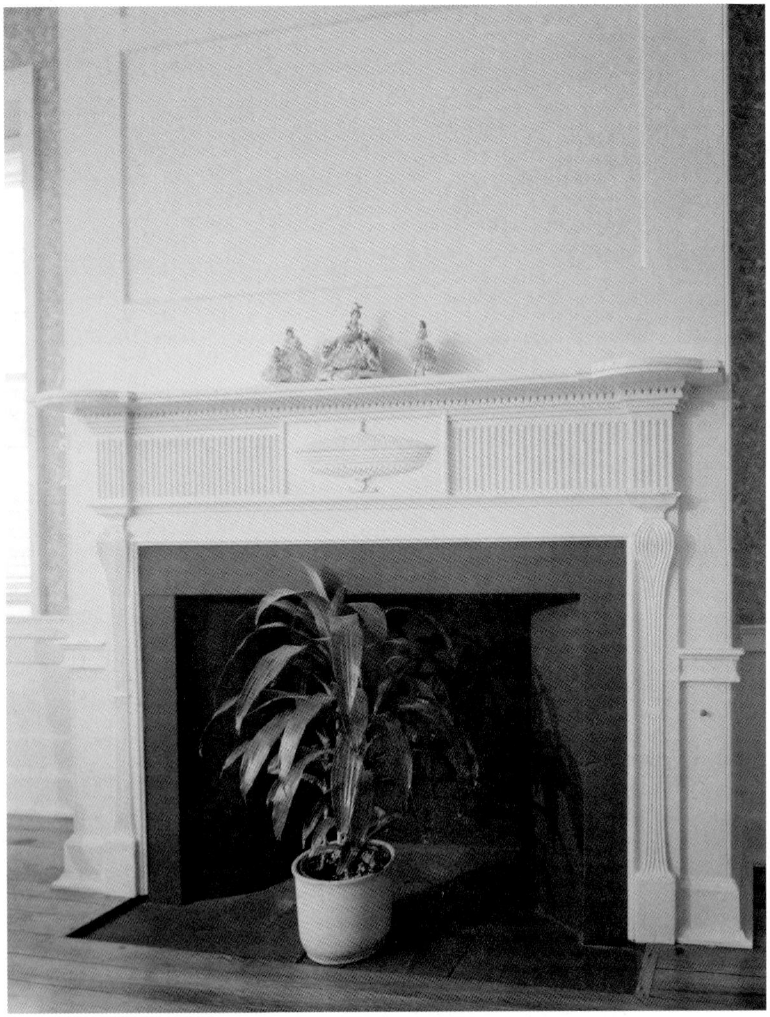

Thomas Fuller House

And a mantel of a later style.

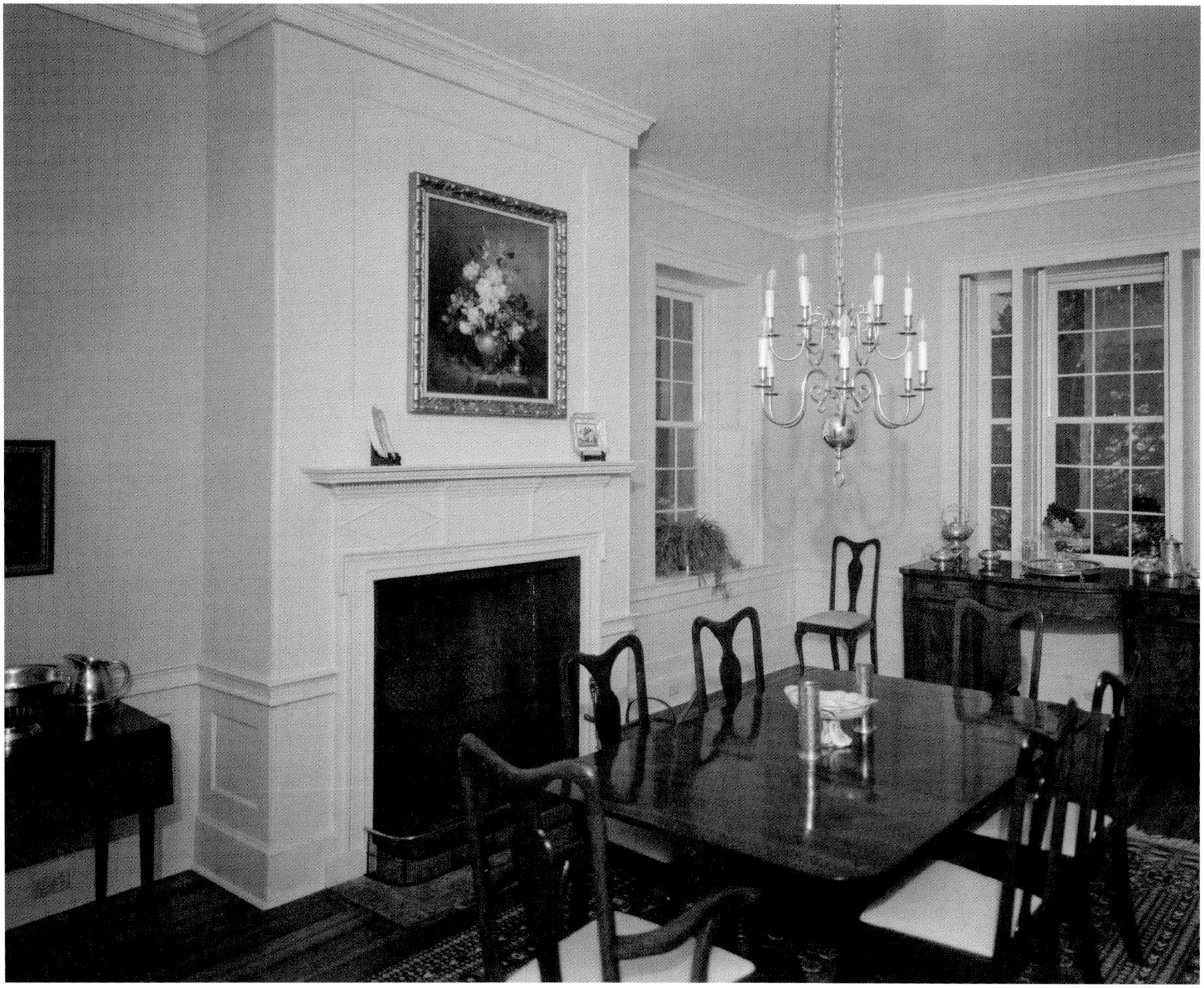

Thomas Fuller House

Dining room with floral arrangement.

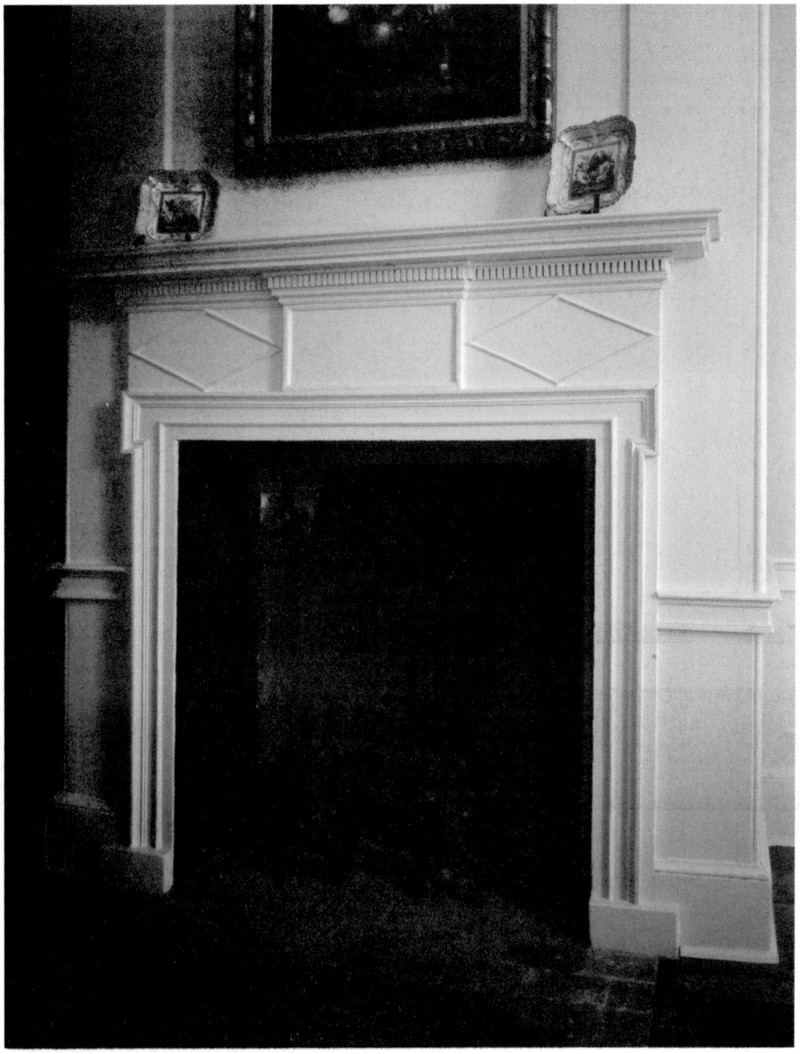

Thomas Fuller House

Detail of mantel.

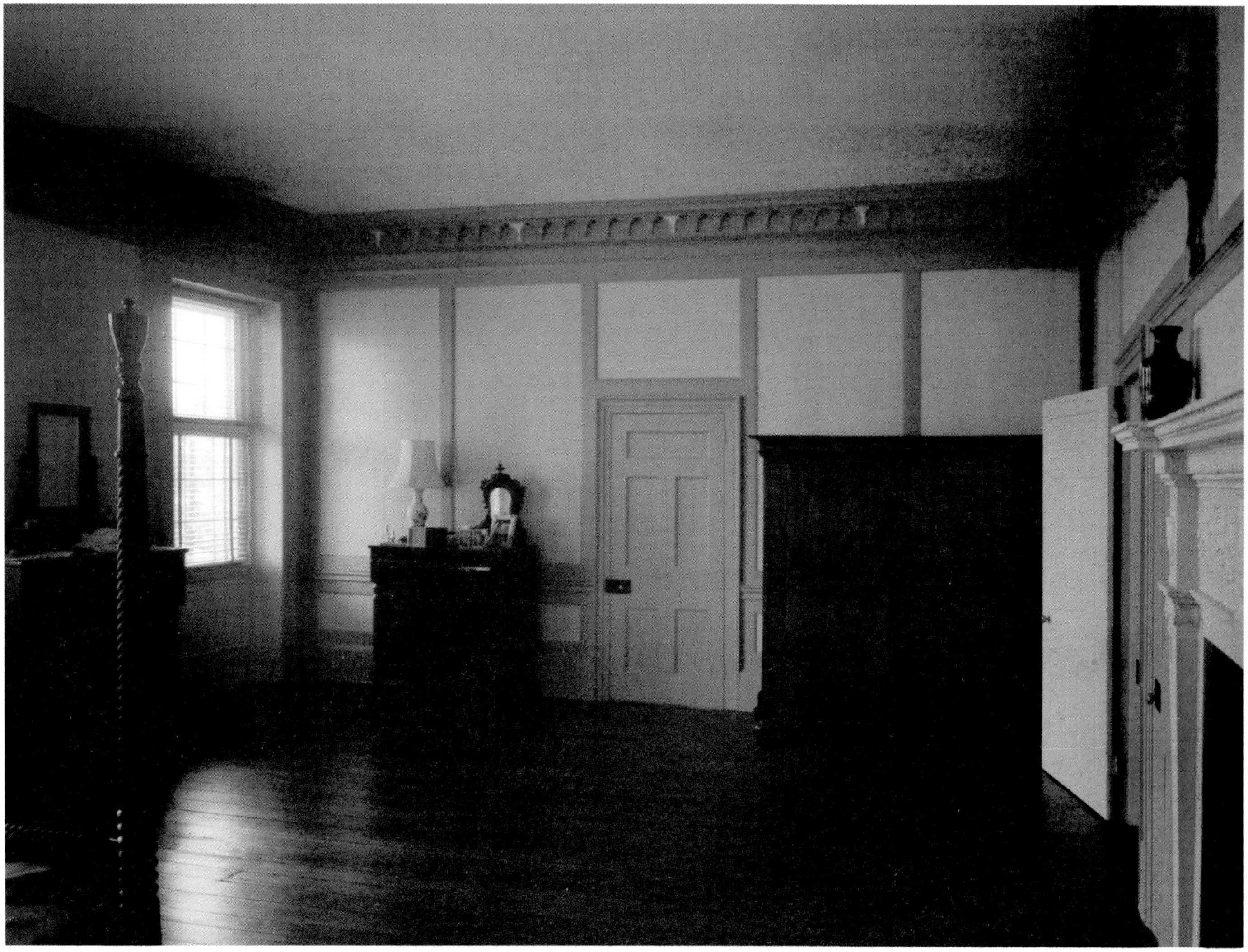

Thomas Fuller House

Second-story bedroom.

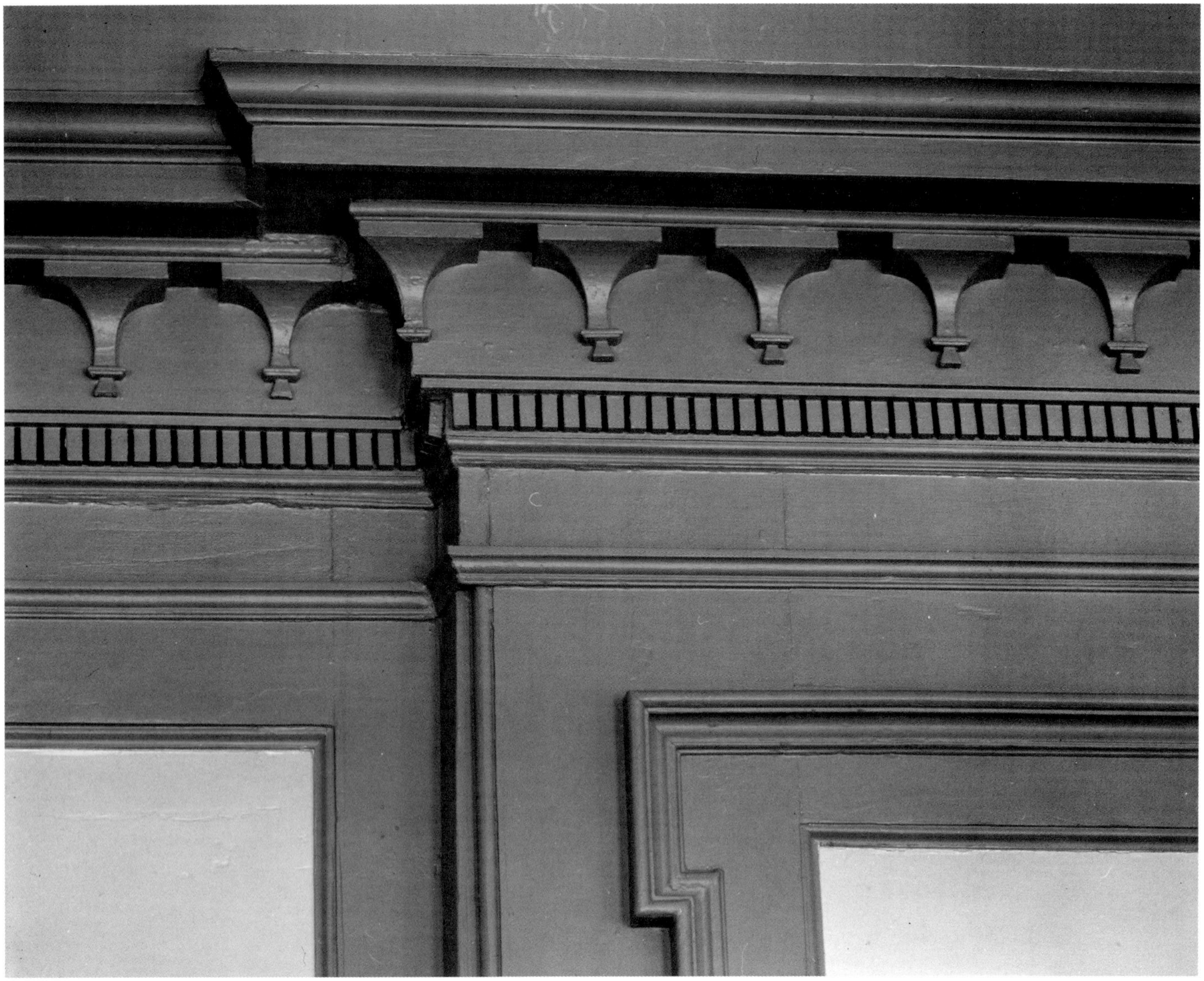

Thomas Fuller House

Cornice detail.

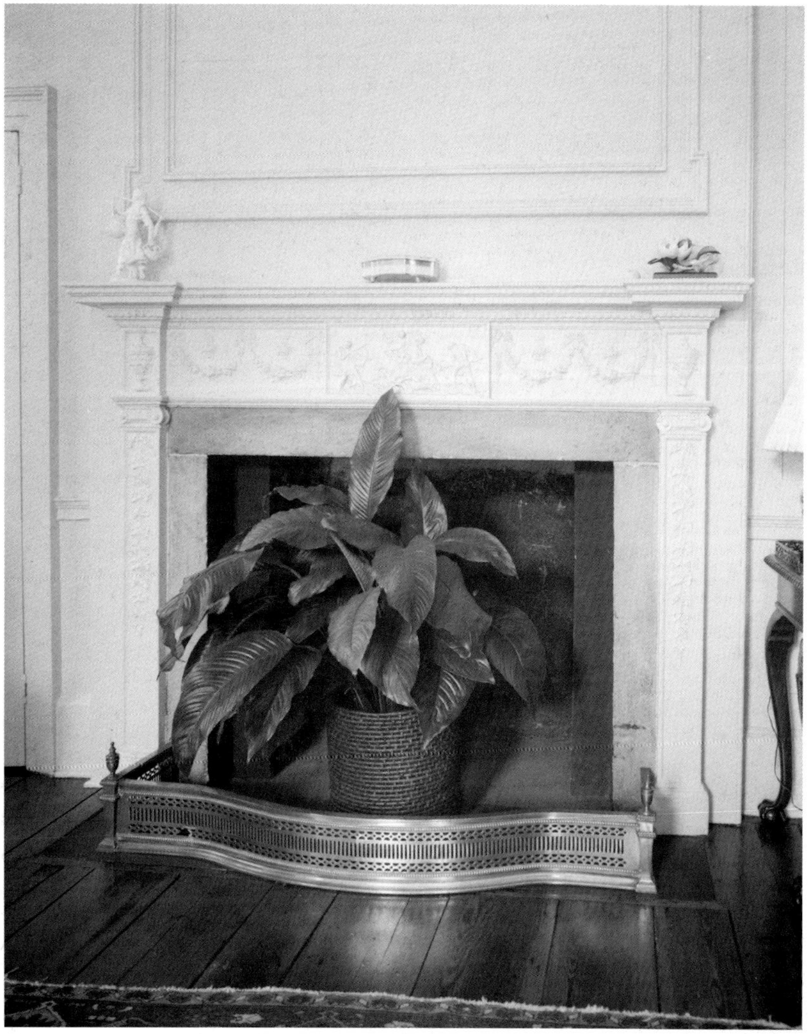

Thomas Fuller House

A second Adam brothers' mantel.

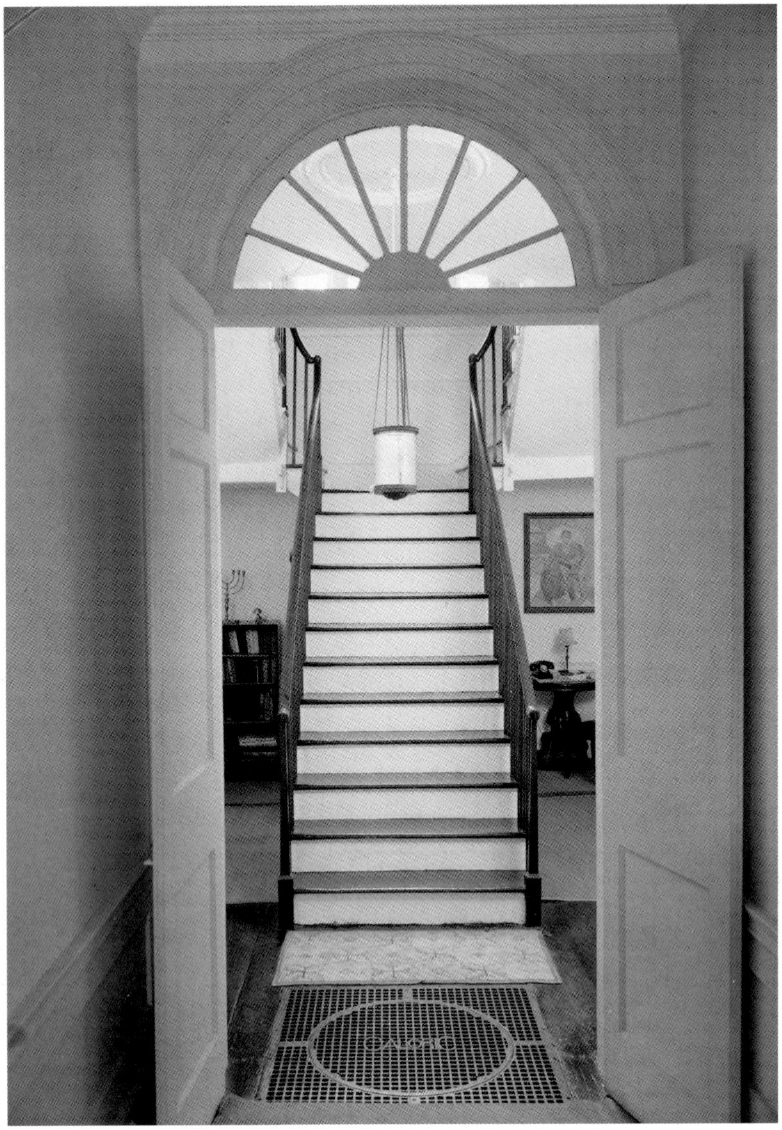

Thomas Fuller House

The central stair.

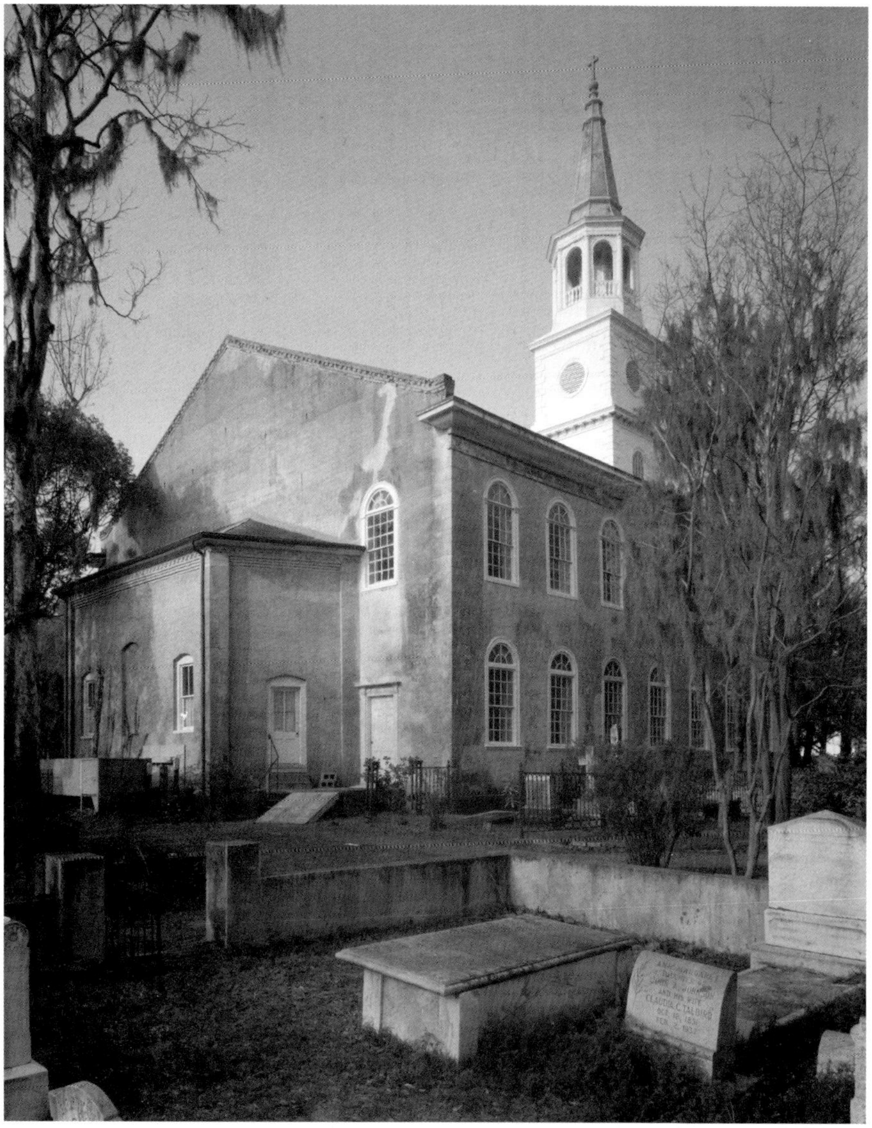

St. Helena's Episcopal Church Charles N. Bayless, 1978 (photo series)

A tabby structure dating from 1724 was expanded into this handsome church. Town founder and Indian fighter "Tuscarora Jack" Barnwell is buried here.

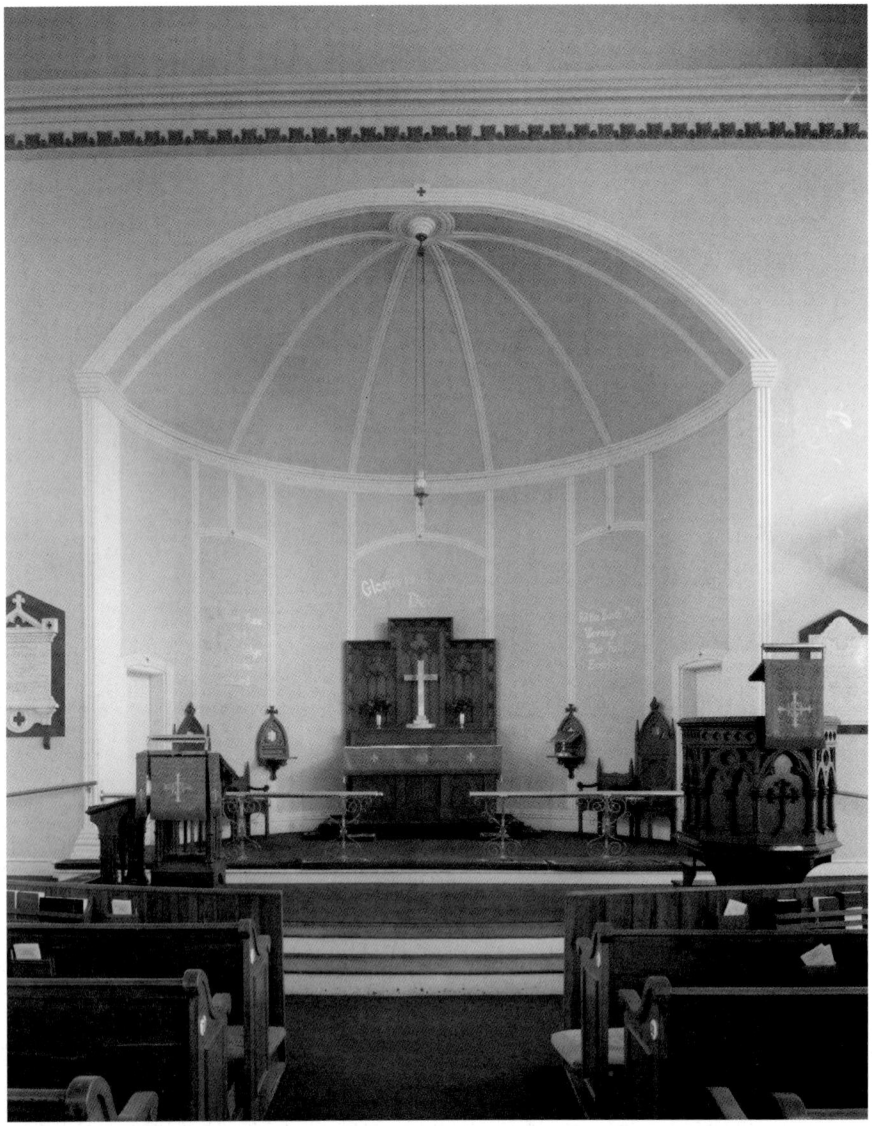

St. Helena's Episcopal Church

The altar was given to the church by occupying Union officers.

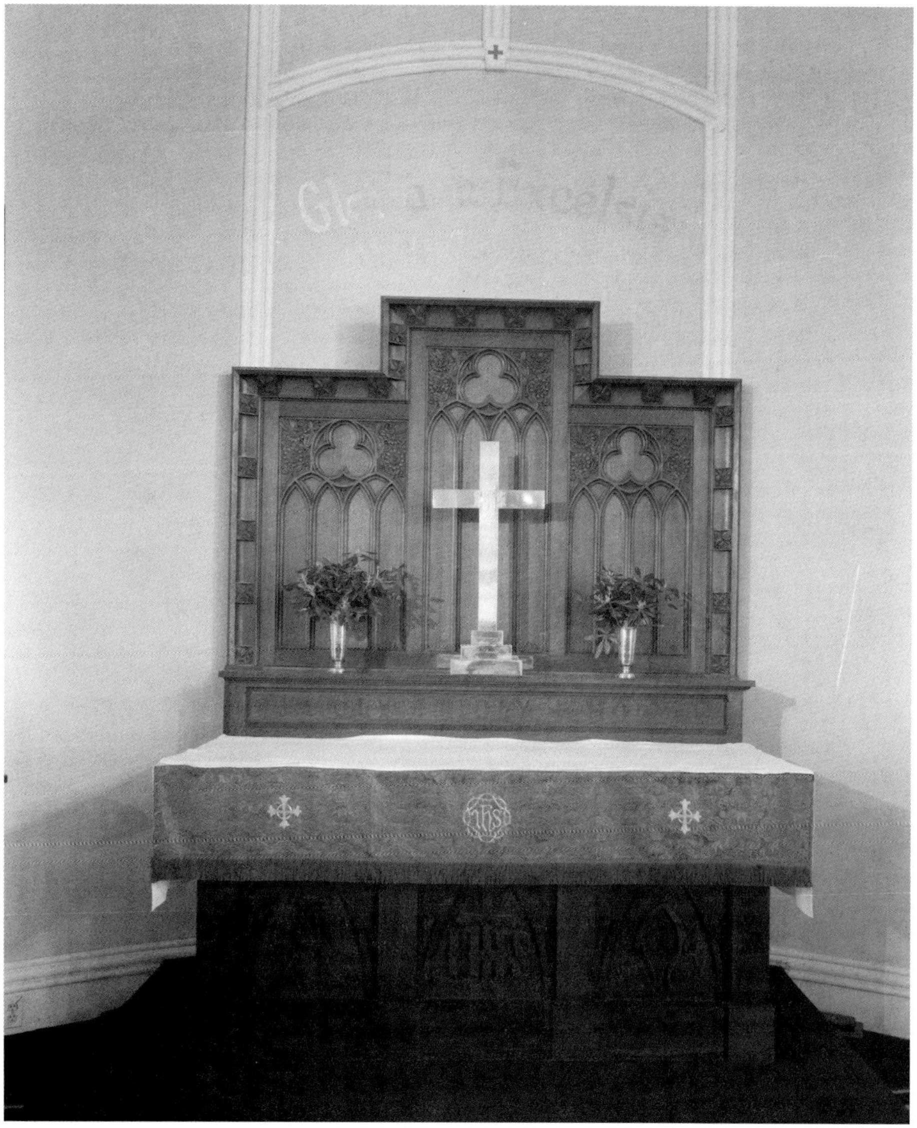

St. Helena's Episcopal Church

Detail of altar.

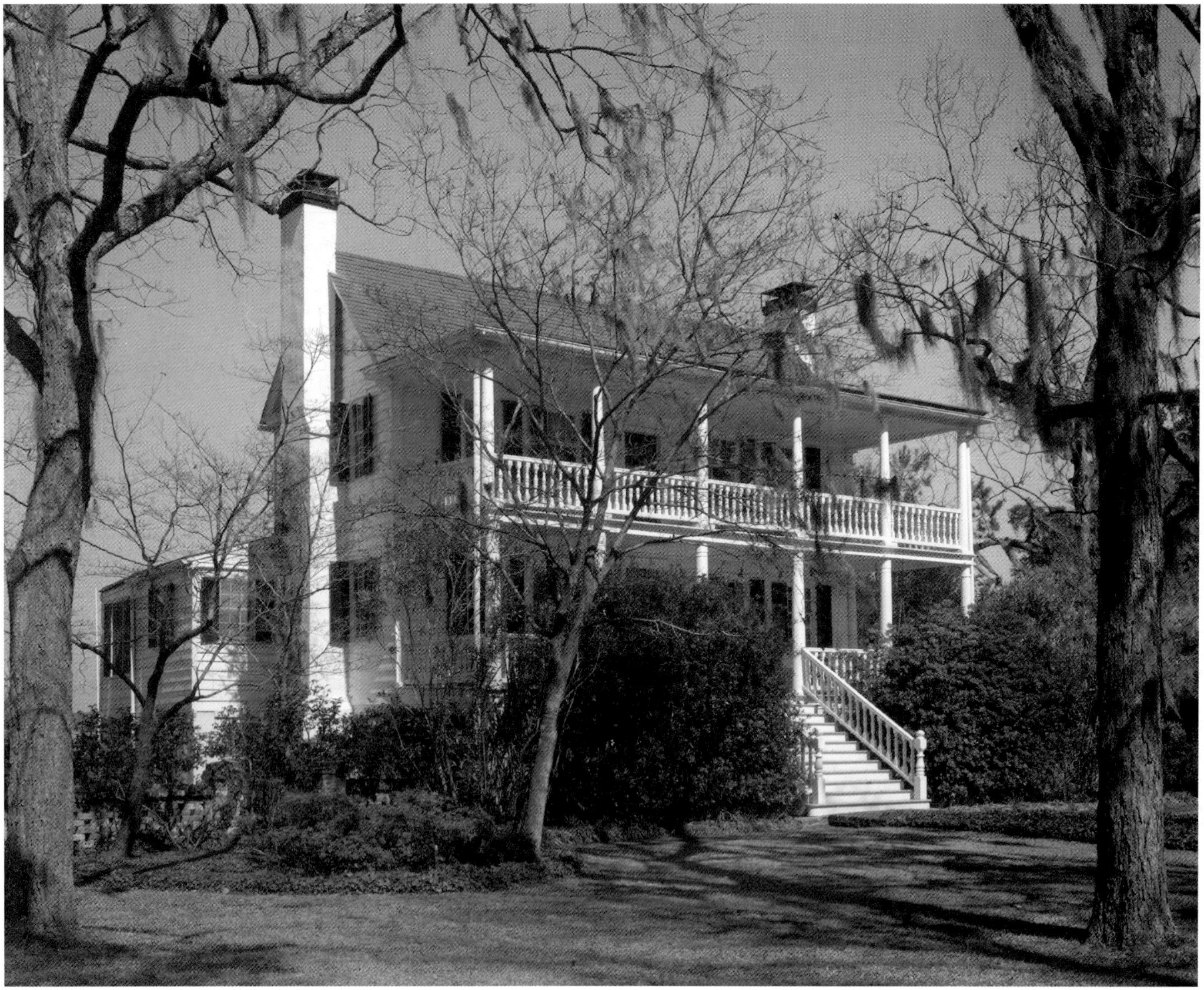

Elizabeth Hext House — Charles N. Bayless, 1978 (photo series)

Hext house exterior: a familiar tabby foundation below and a commonly pitched roof above. When built, this house was "in the country."

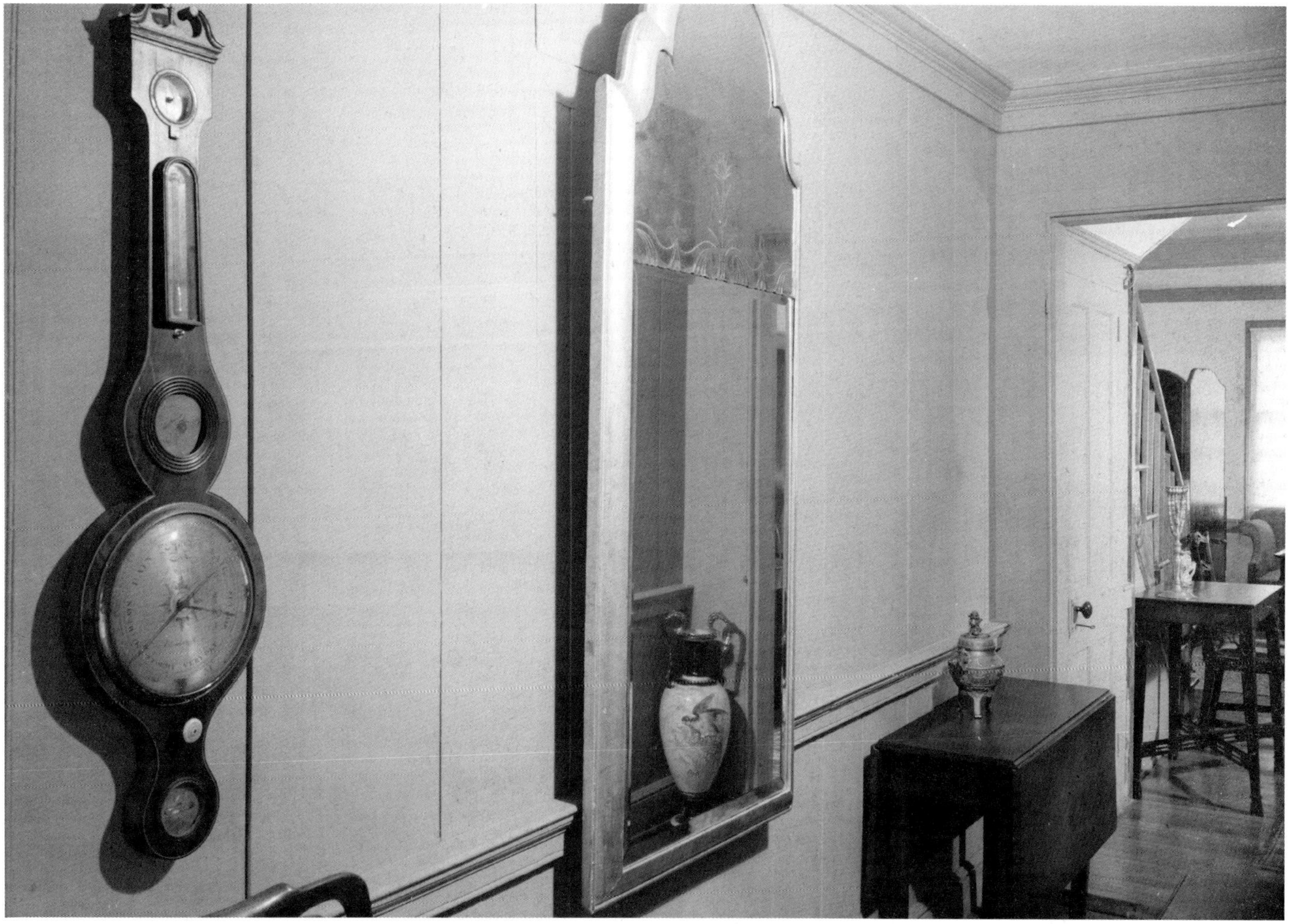

Elizabeth Hext House

Wood-paneled walls and low ceilings for this 1765 home of Elizabeth Hext. The daughter of a founding family, she married a grandson of Tuscarora Jack Barnwell.

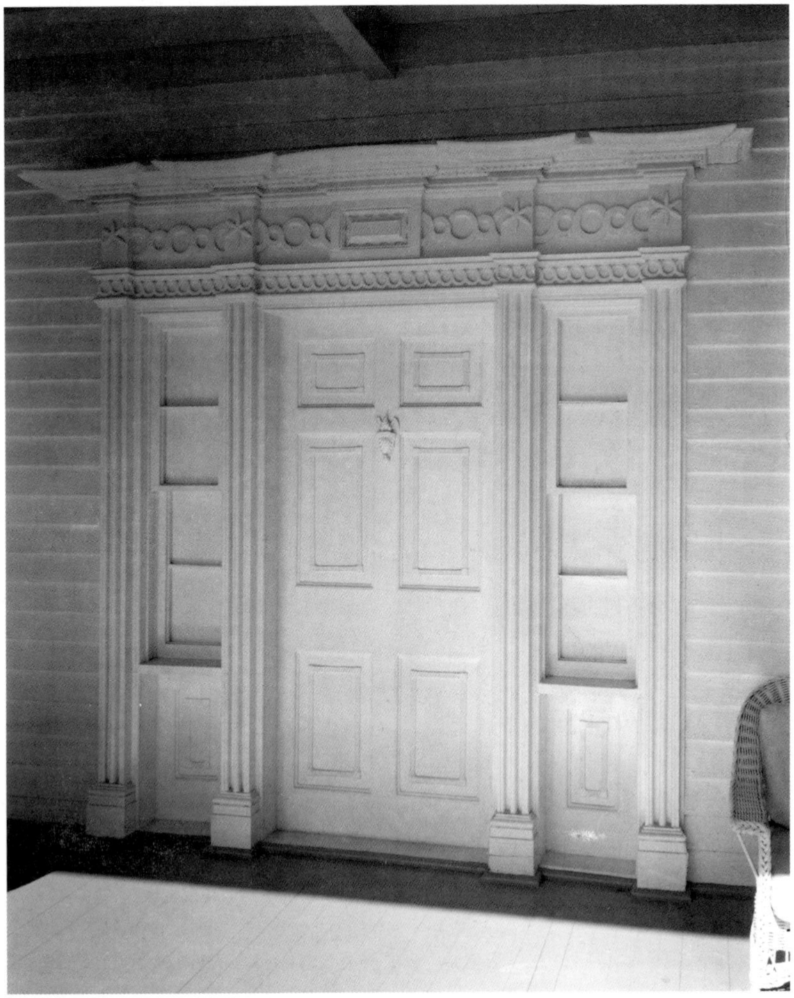

Joyner Smith House — Charles N. Bayless, 1978 (photo series)

A false entry on the south side. The house seems to be a Bay Street residence, but the front door is actually on Wilmington.

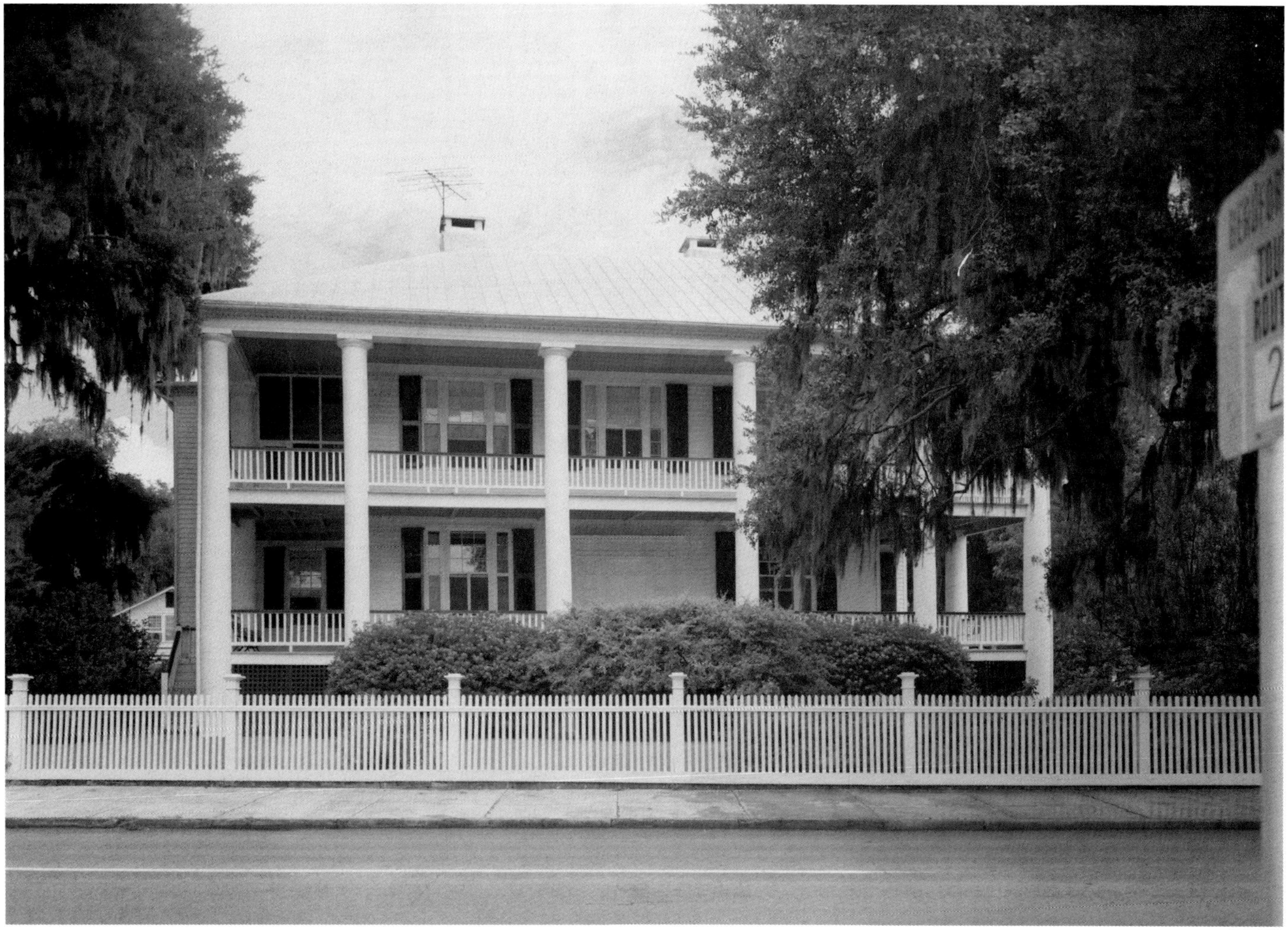

Joyner Smith House

Built around 1850 by John Joyner Smith, the house has had many occupants, including Union officers.

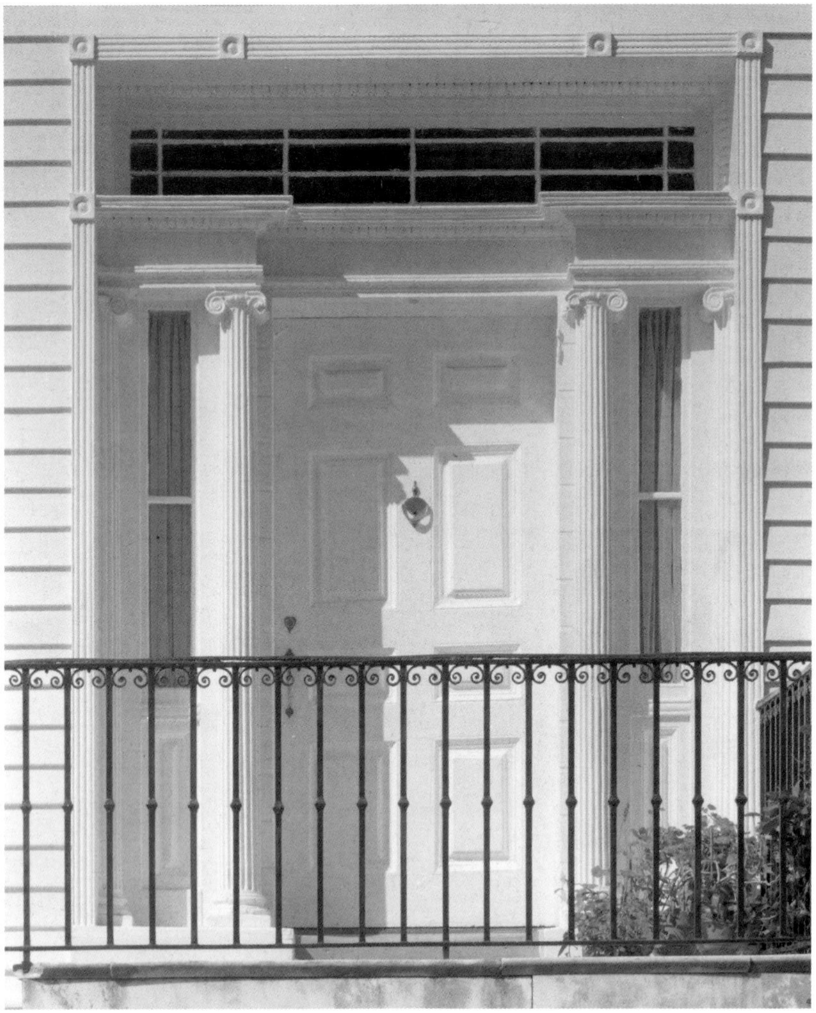

Joyner Smith House

"Two Greek Ionic columns," says the HABS write-up. The filigree of the railing caught my eye.

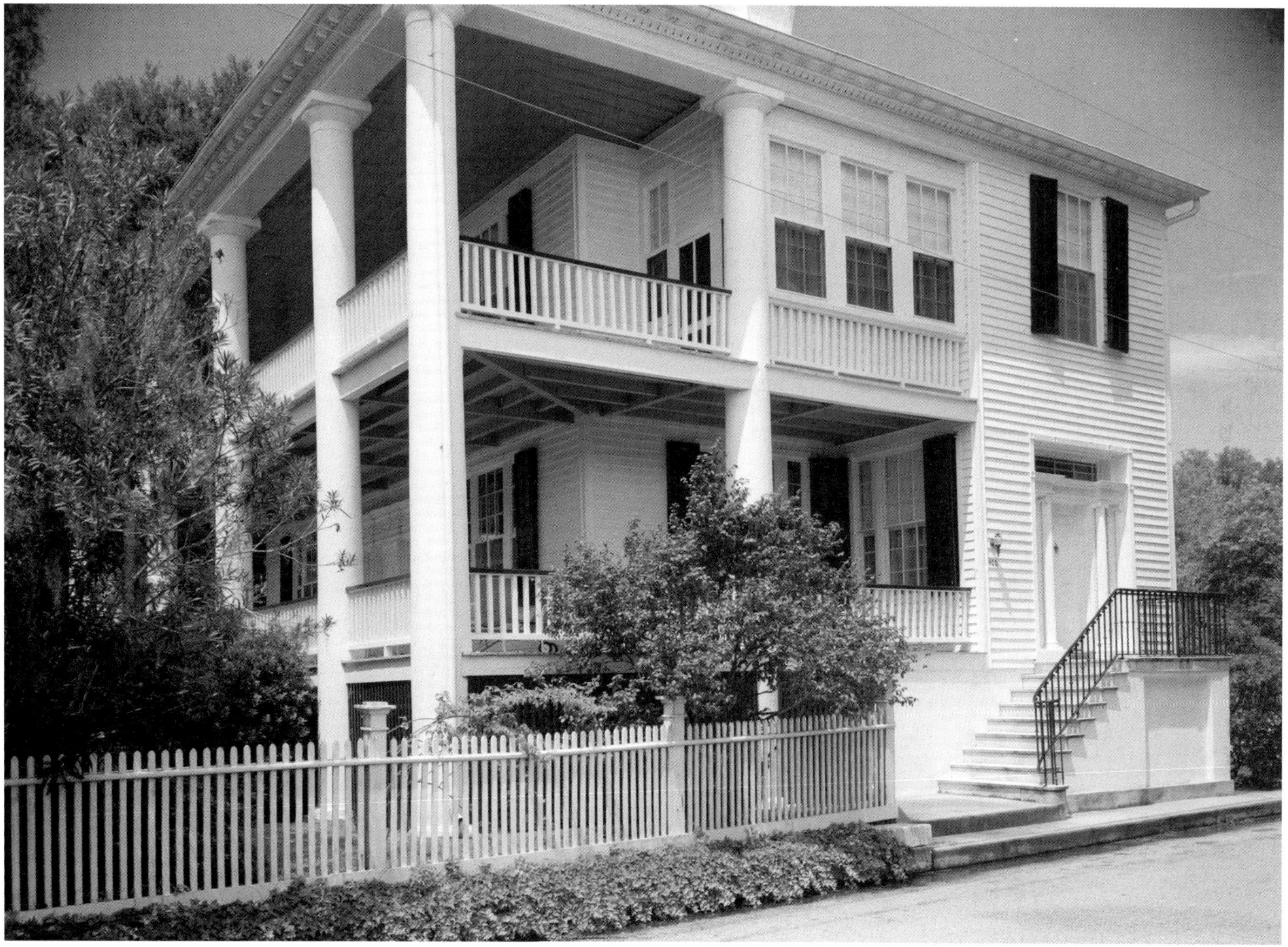

Joyner Smith House

The true entry.

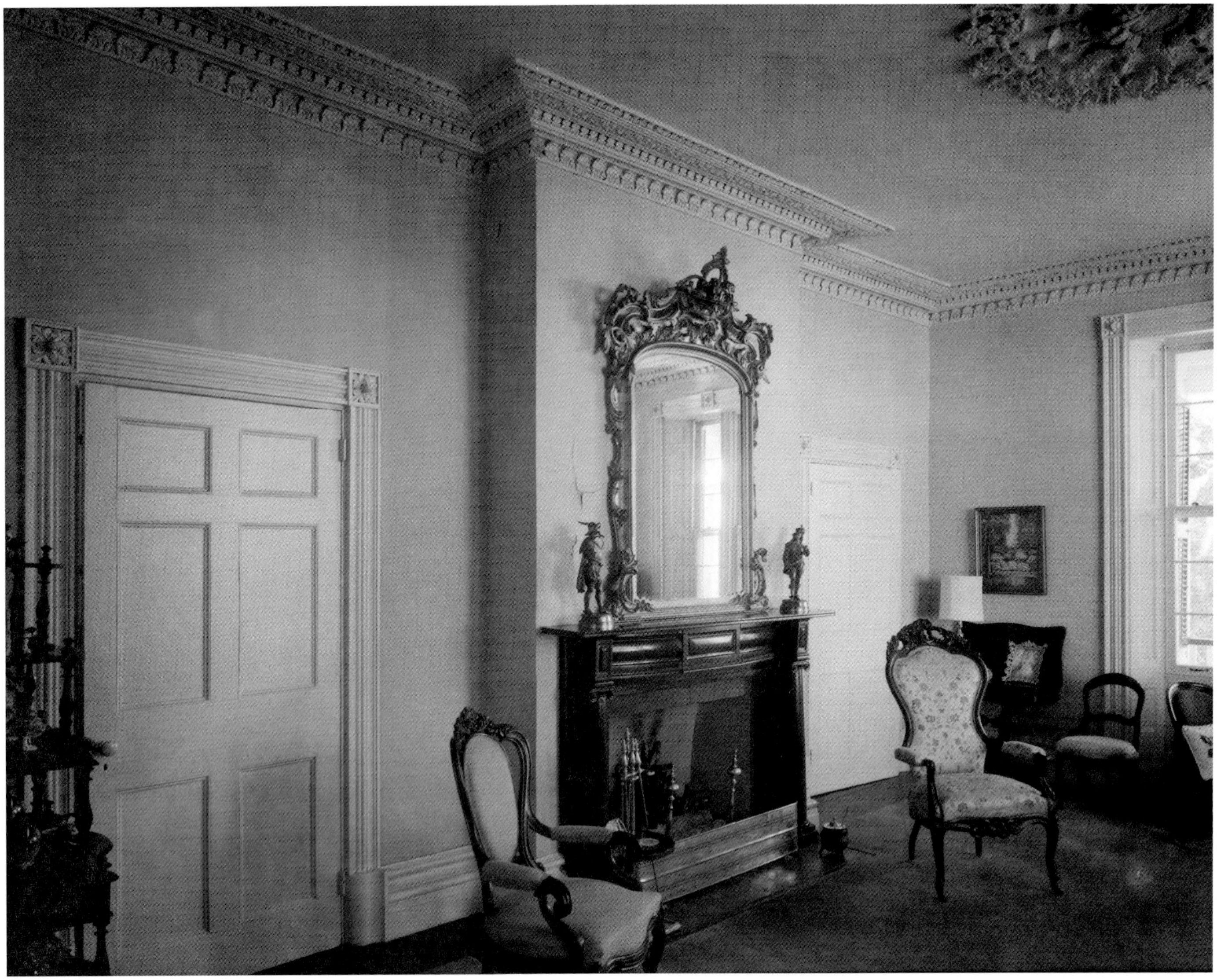

Joyner Smith House

Mantelpieces of black marble.

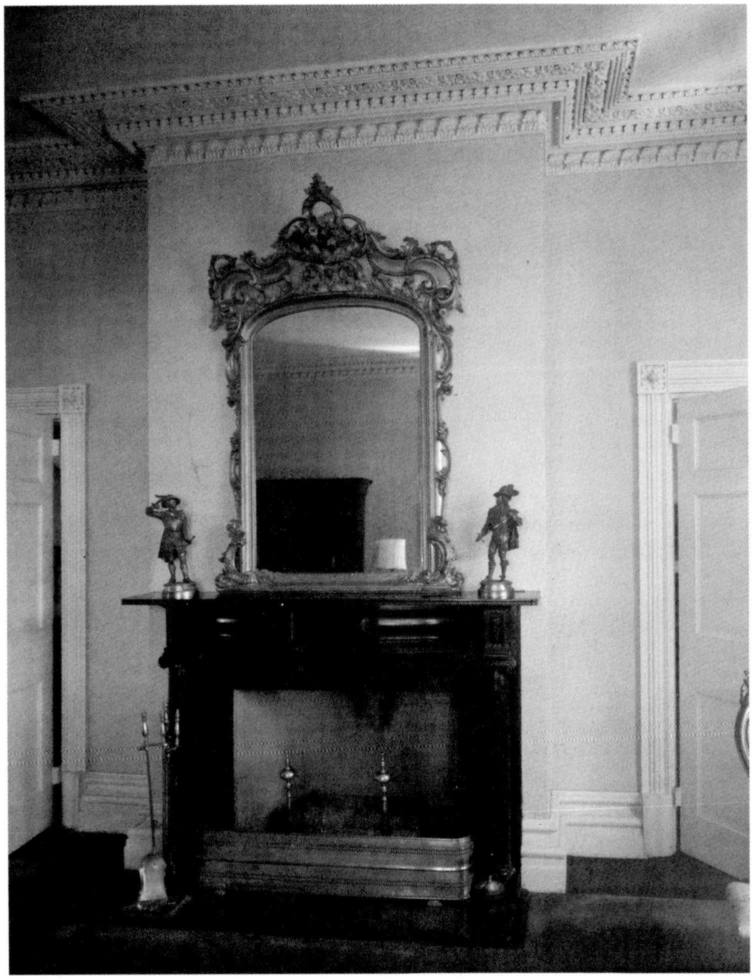

Joyner Smith House

A detail of the mantel. "Free standing Ionic columns," says the HABS, "over which the entablature breaks out."

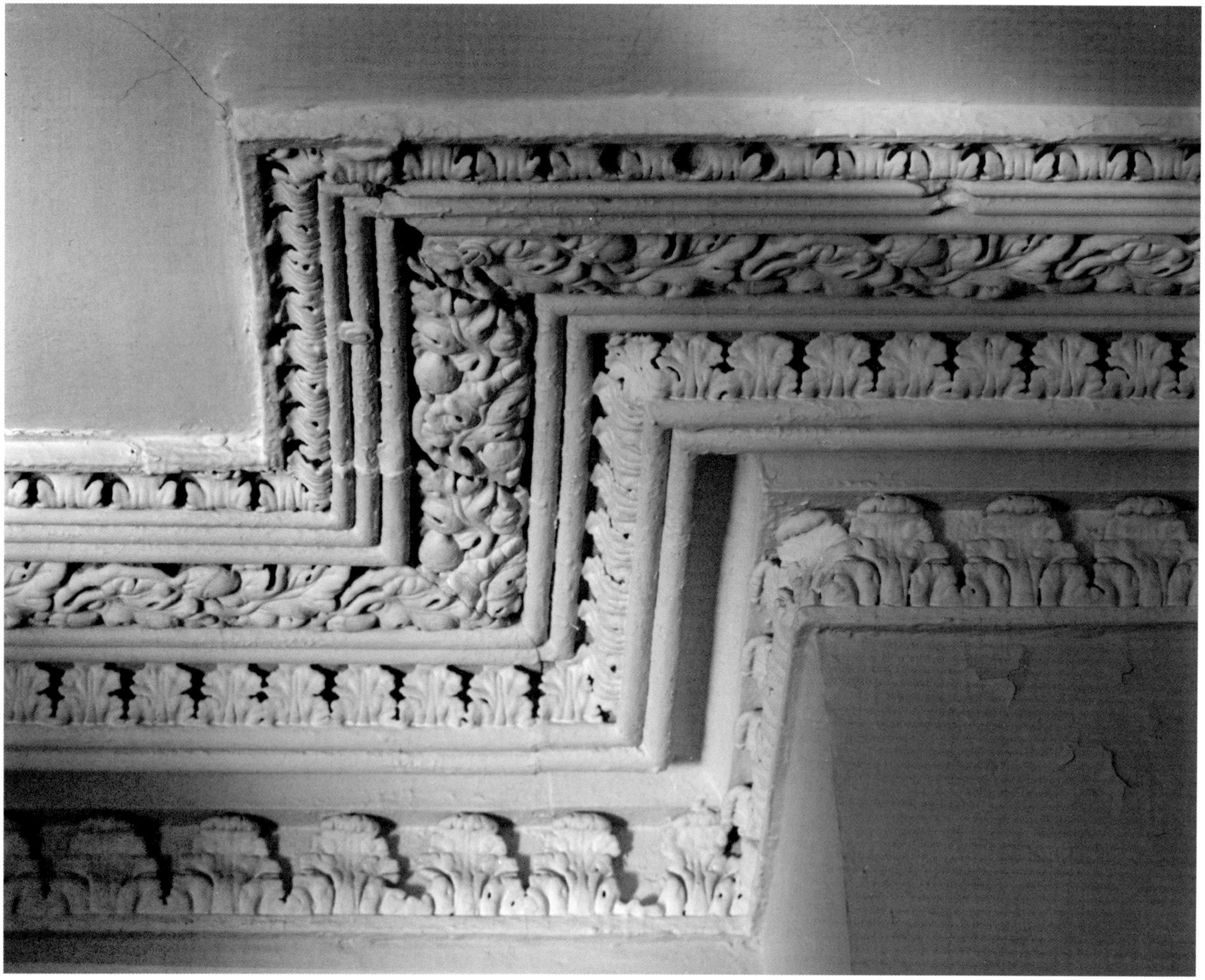

Joyner Smith House

A complex cornice: upright acanthus leaves, plain moldings, a band of smaller leaves, a band of oak leaves, acorns and then a small band of acanthus leaves.

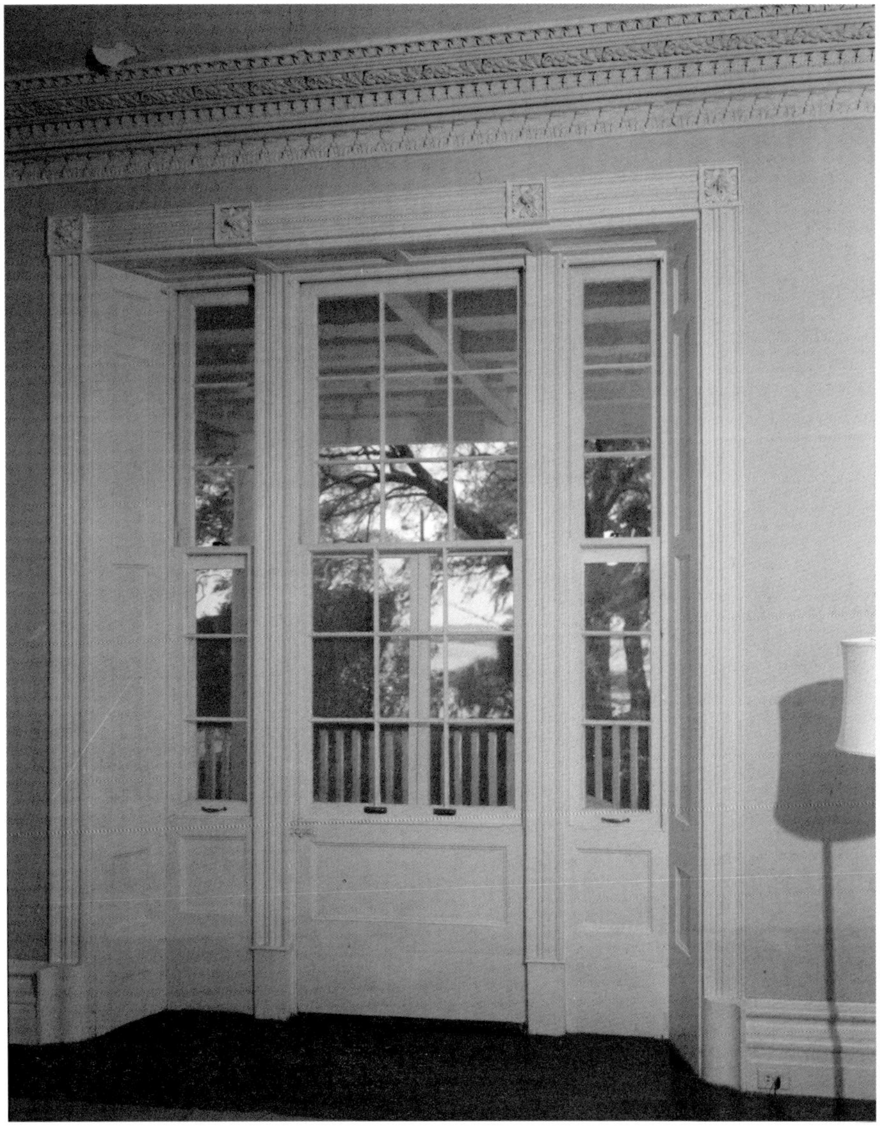

Joyner Smith House

A jib door gives access to the porch.

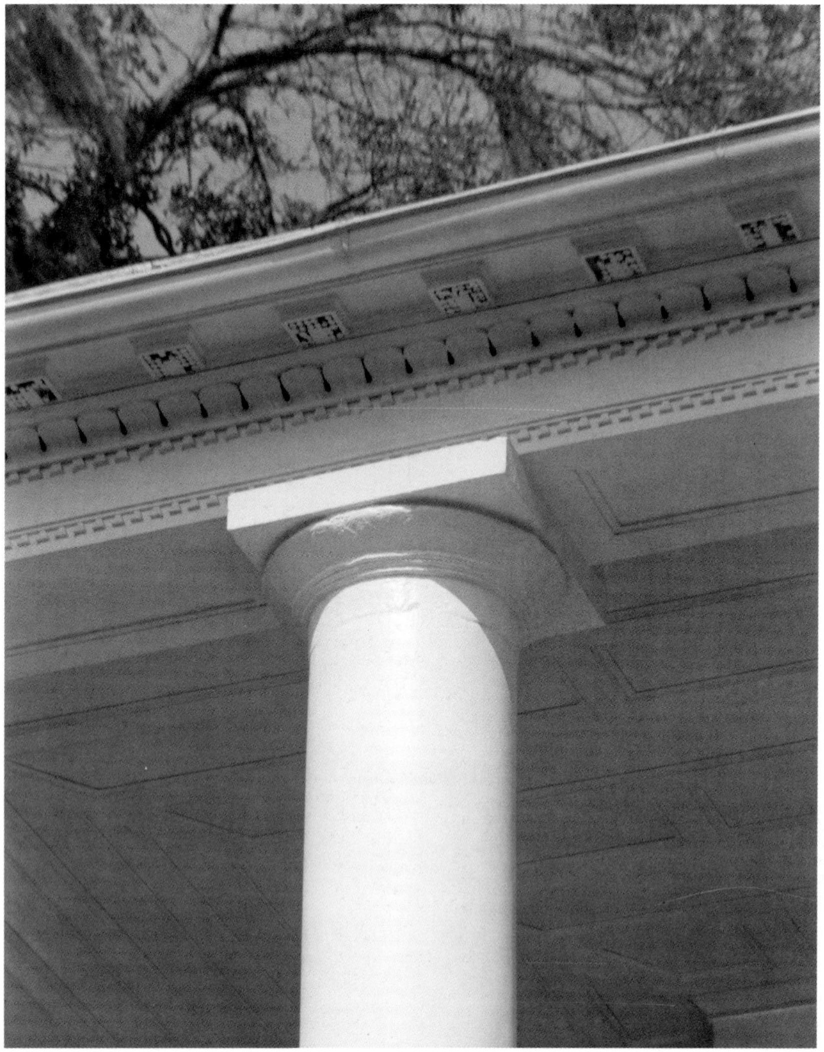

Joyner Smith House

A simpler column but a delicate cornice.

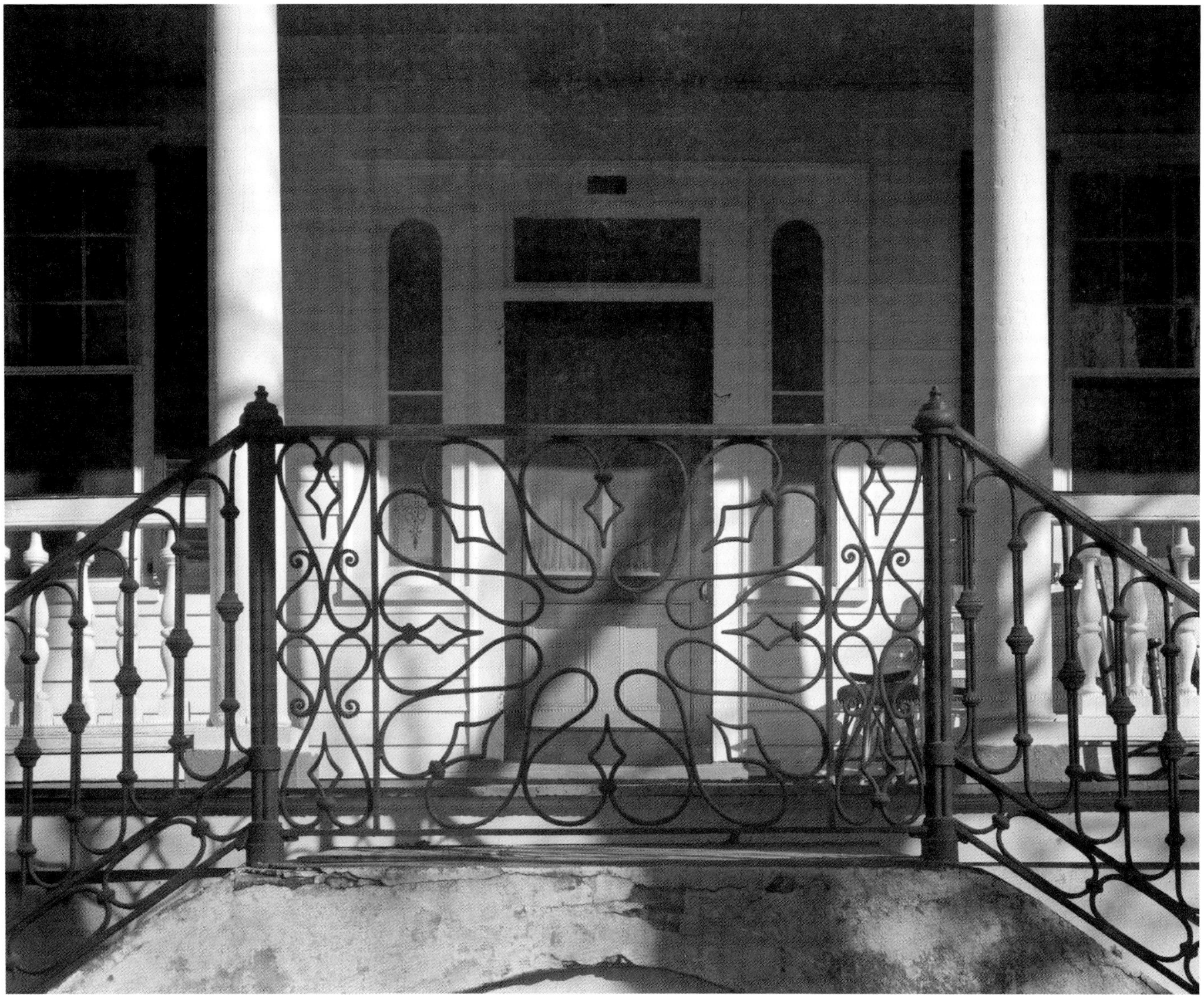

Dr. William Jenkins House — Charles N. Bayless, 1978 (photo series)

Tradition says Dr. Jenkins built the house in 1845, but it may be of the earlier Federalist period. Distinctive ironwork greets the visitor.

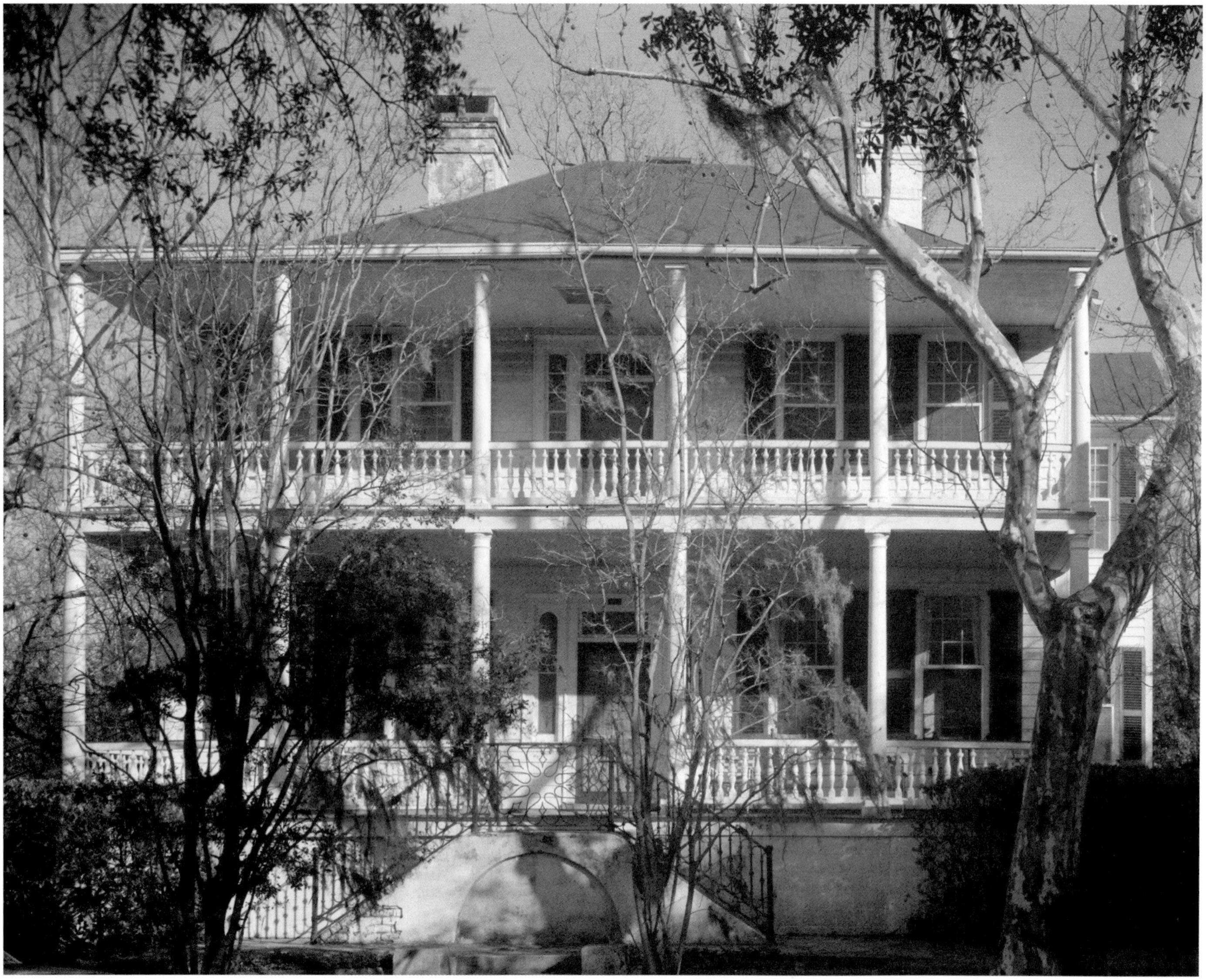

Dr. William Jenkins House

Here again, a simple double portico has given way to Beaufort piazzas.

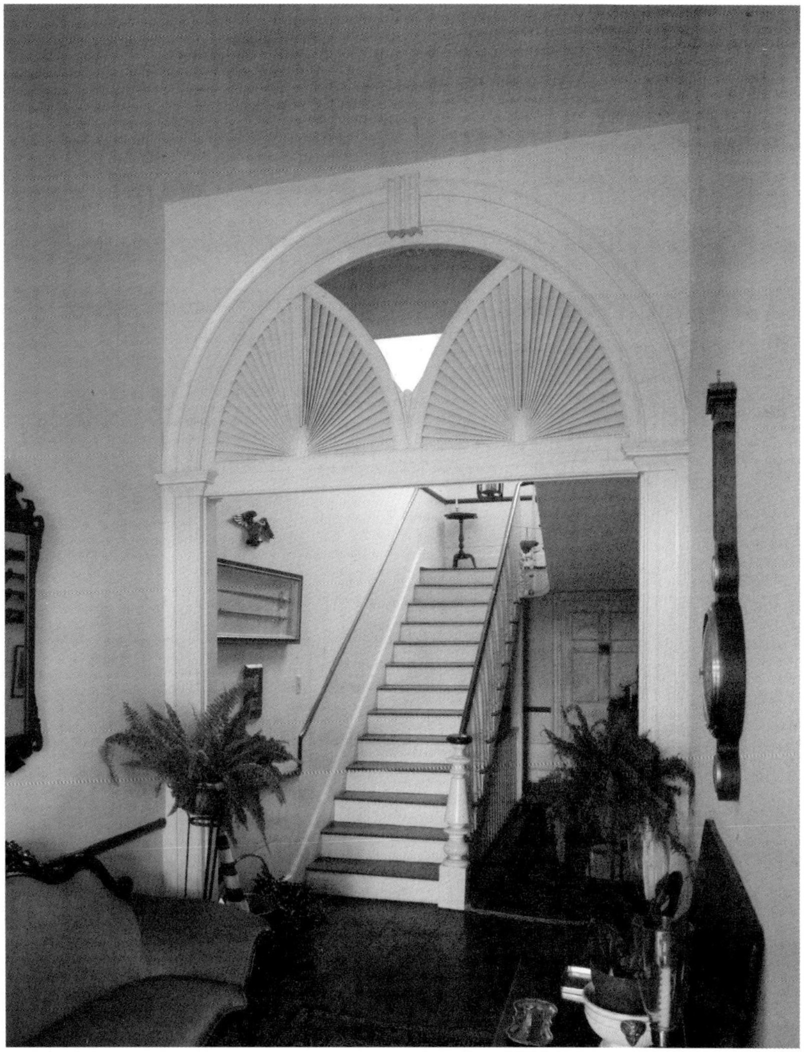

Thomas Rhett House Charles N. Bayless, 1978 (photo series)

Delicate fan work of the entry hall.

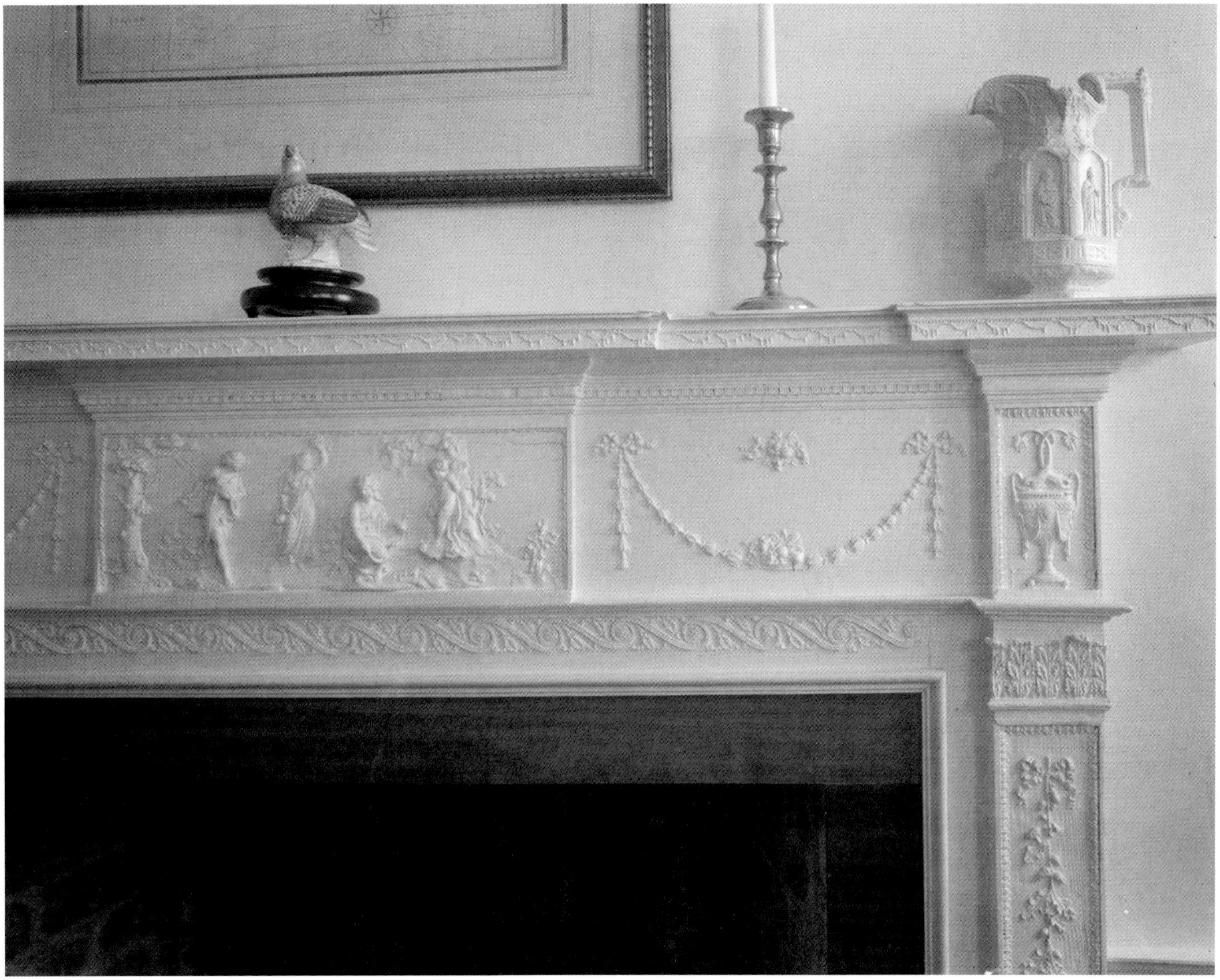

Thomas Rhett House

An Adamesque mantel.

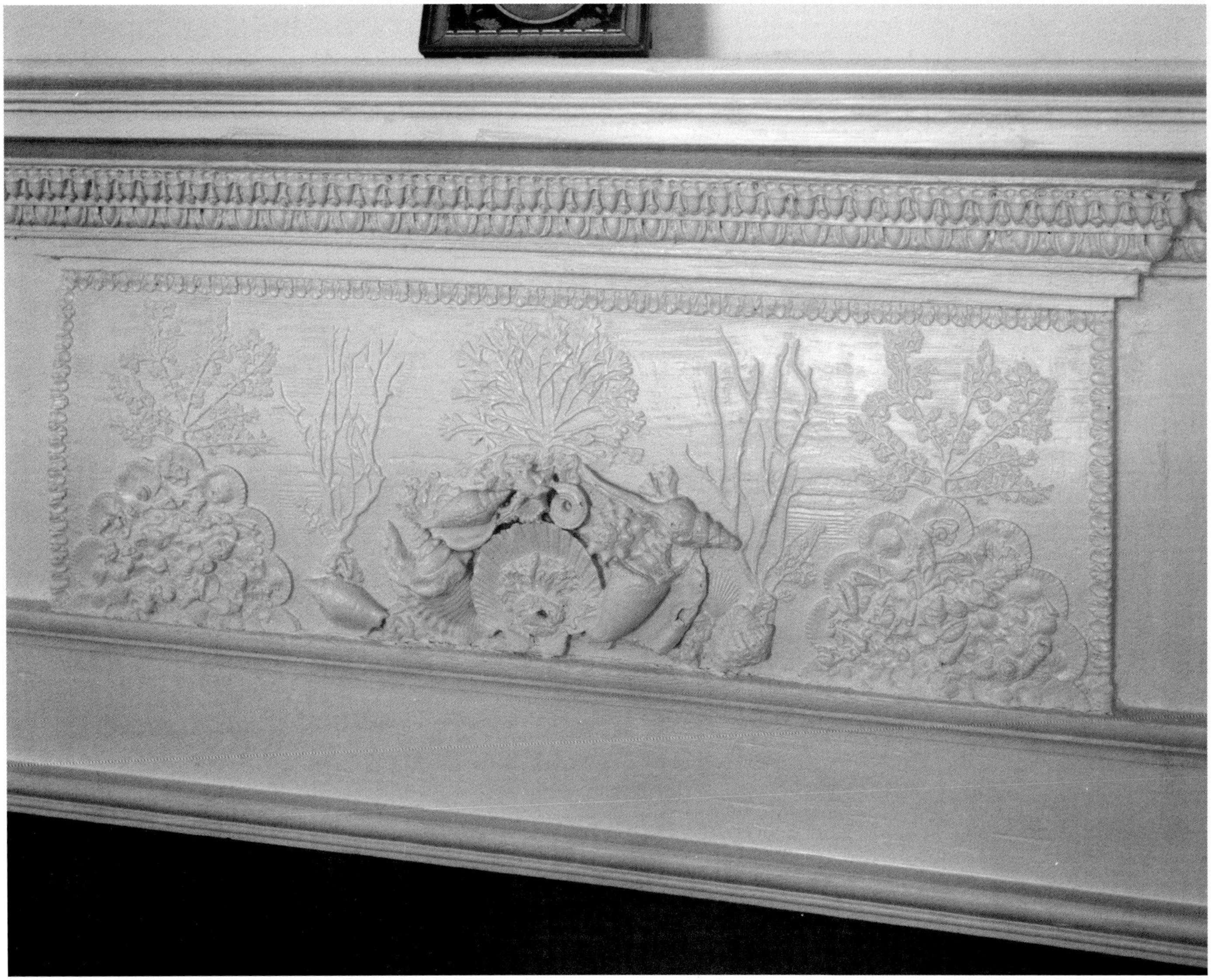

Thomas Rhett House

Detail of an exceptional mantel.

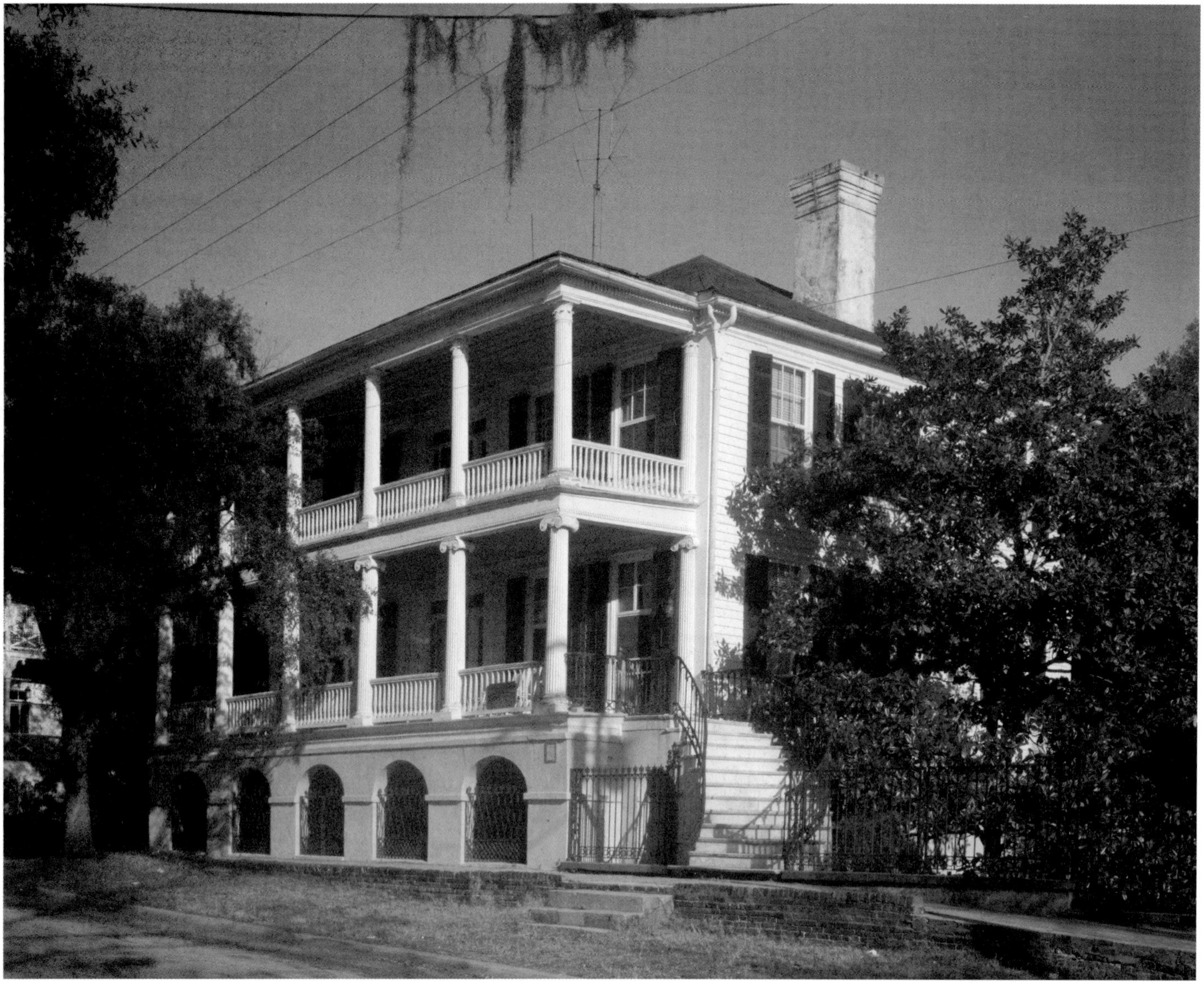

THE SECESSION HOUSE — Charles N. Bayless, 1978 (photo series)

Using an earlier tabby foundation, Milton Maxcy of Massachusetts built this house in 1813. Edmund Rhett bought it just before the war and remodeled in the Beaufort style.

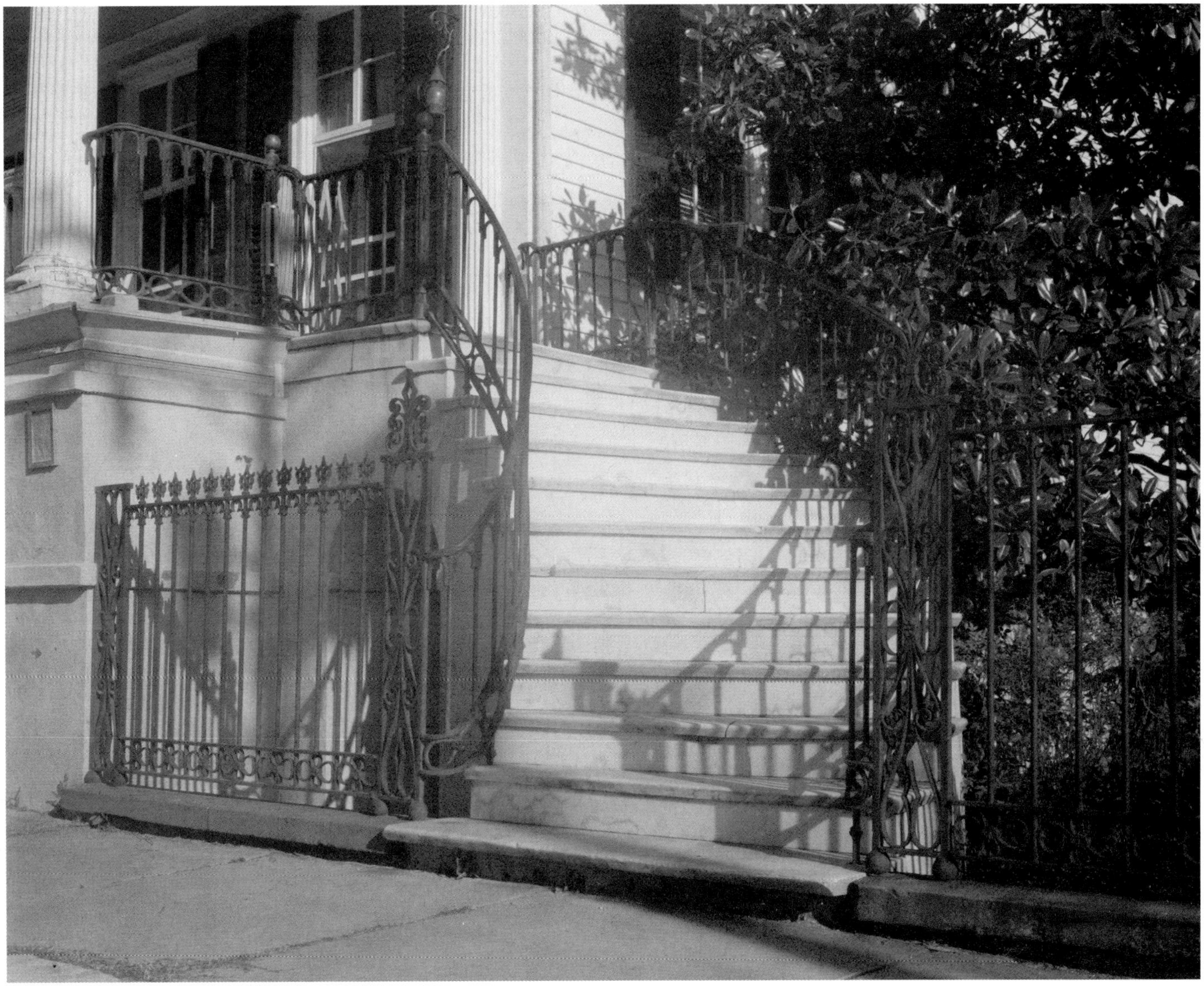

The Secession House

Curved marble steps with wrought-iron balustrade. It is said that secession from the Union began here. "The first house to leave the Union." That's what I wrote in a 1993 guidebook. "And judging by the closeness of the Bay, probably one of the first to get back in." Ho, ho.

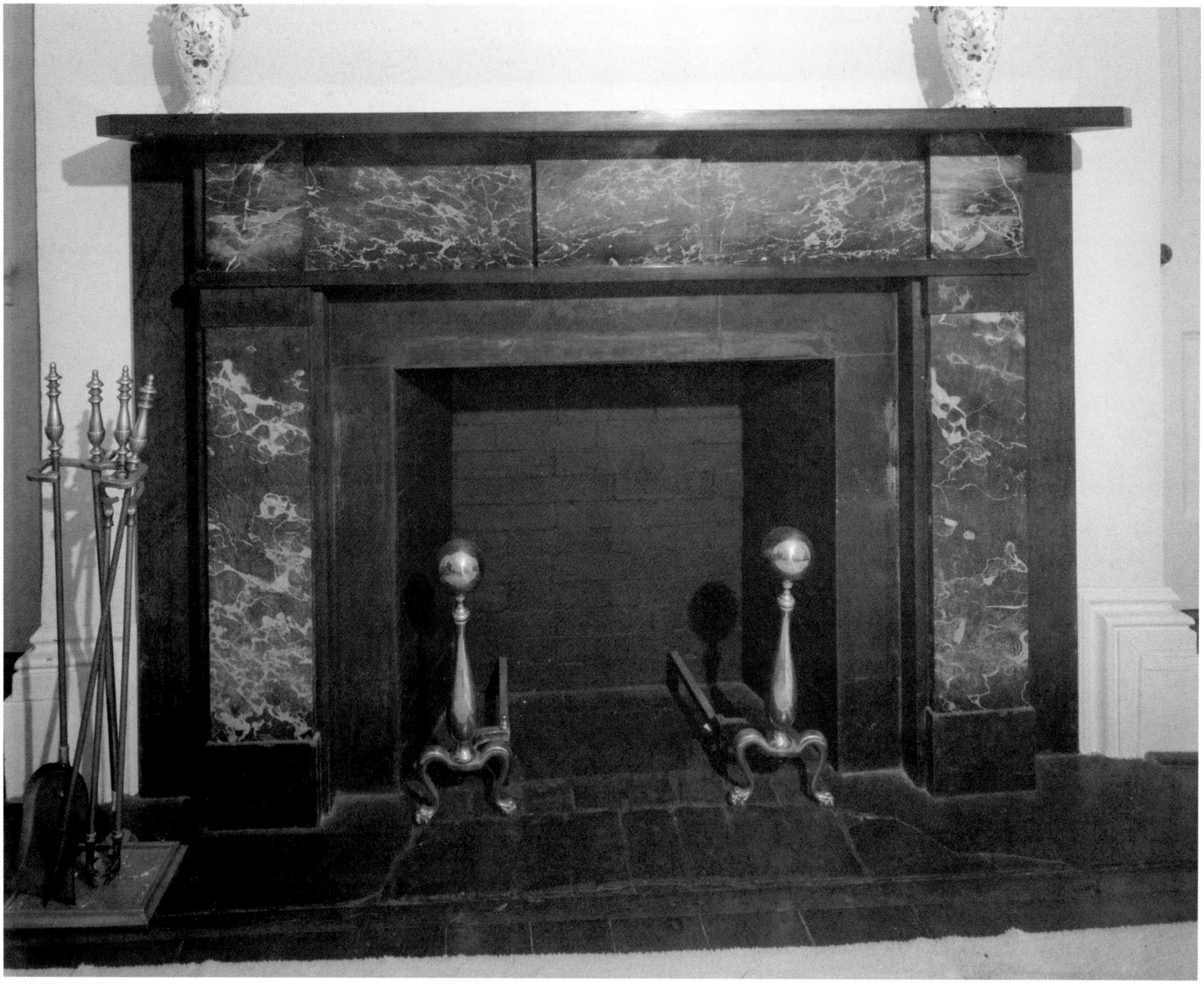

The Secession House

Marble mantels.

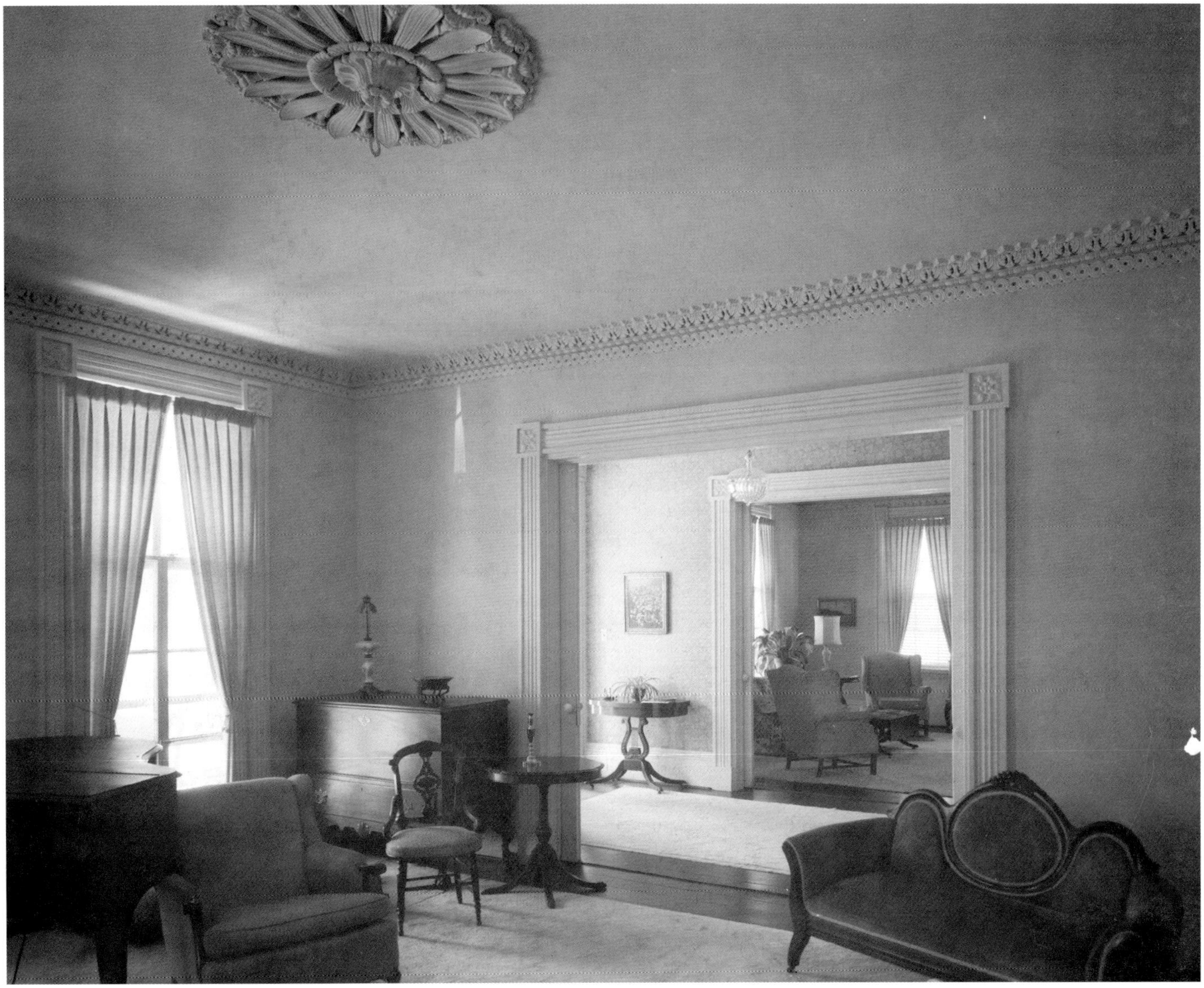

THE SECESSION HOUSE

First-floor sitting rooms.

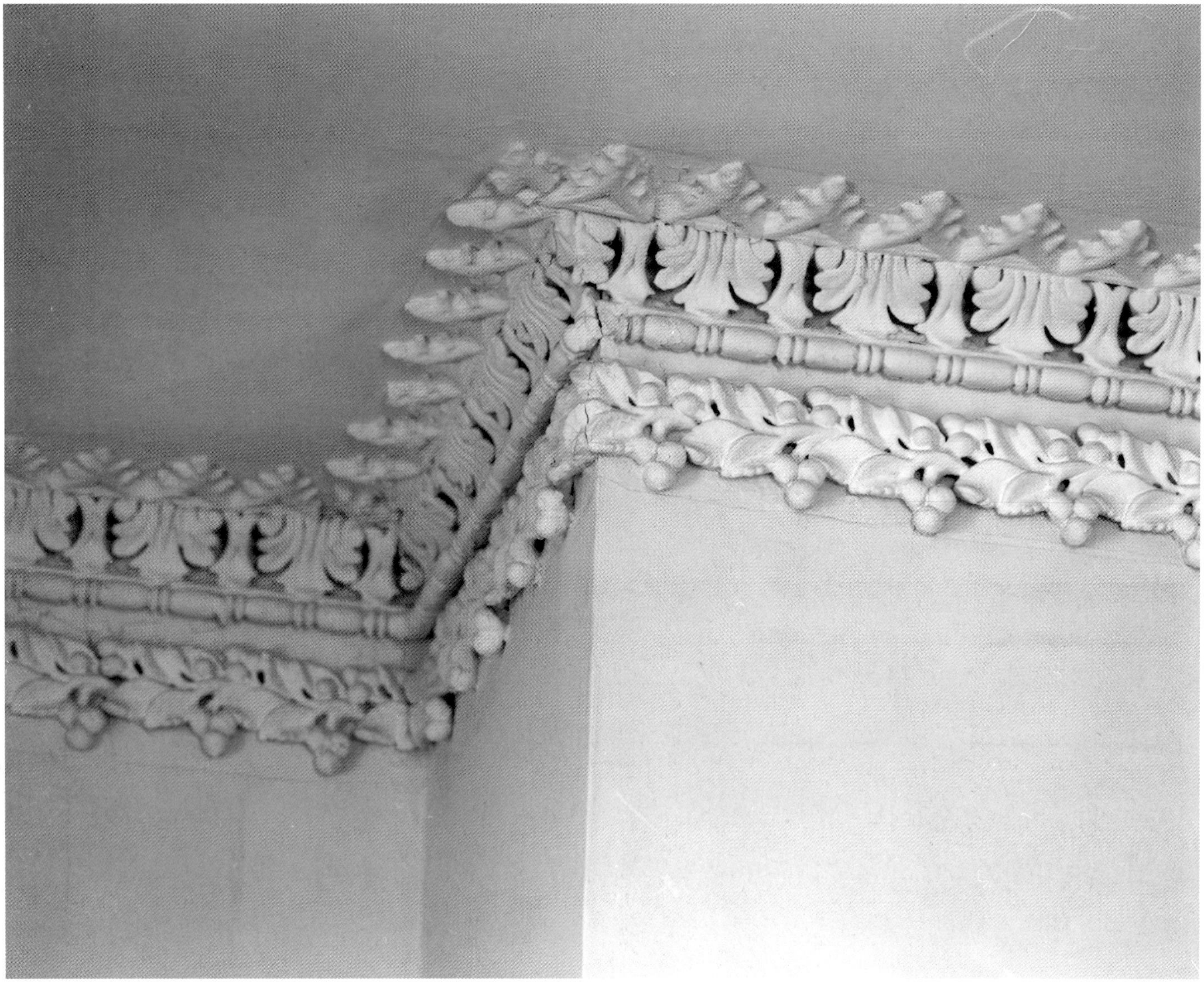

The Secession House

An intricate cornice. The usual suspects: acanthus leaves and acorns among them.

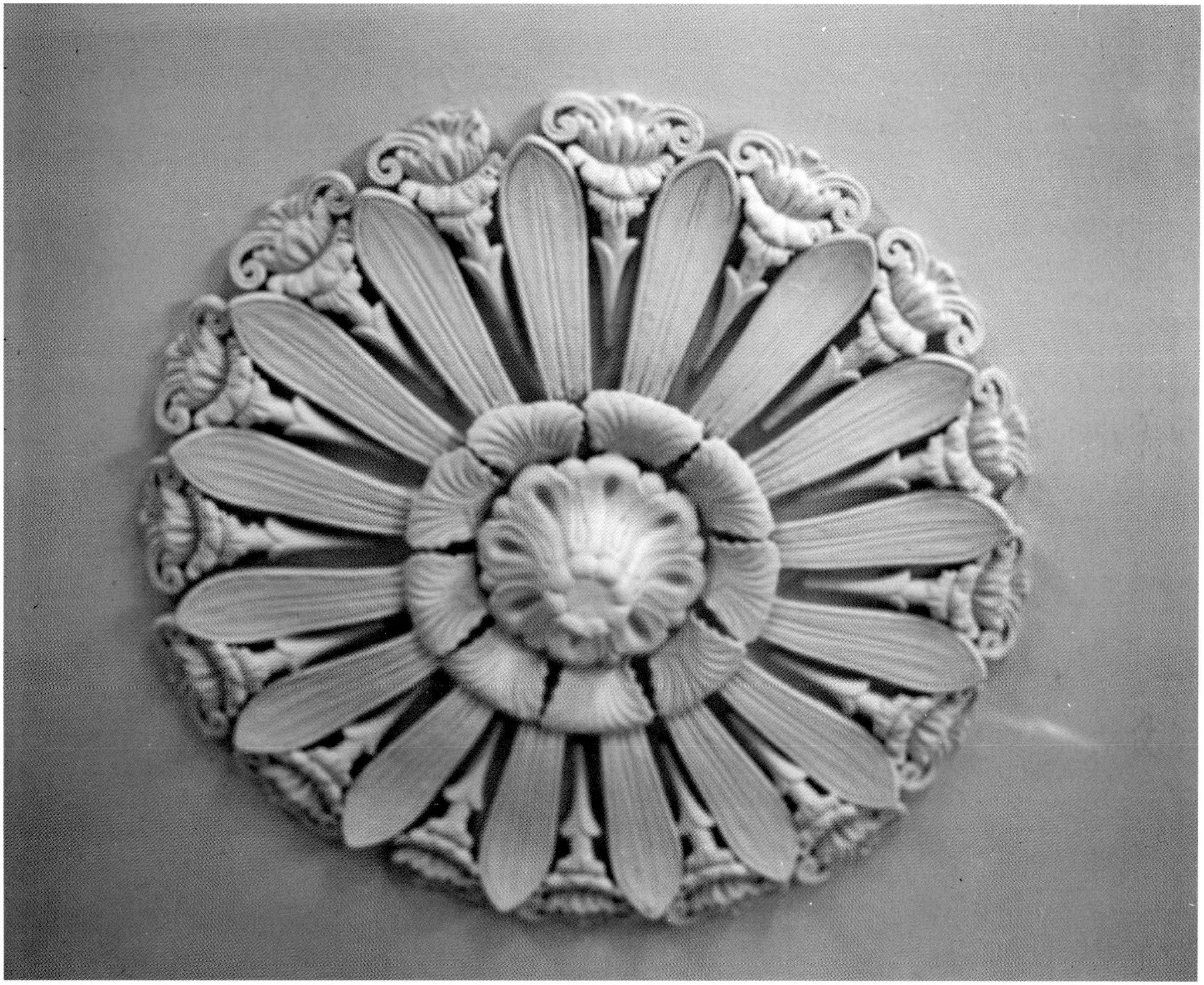

The Secession House

And a ceiling medallion to match.

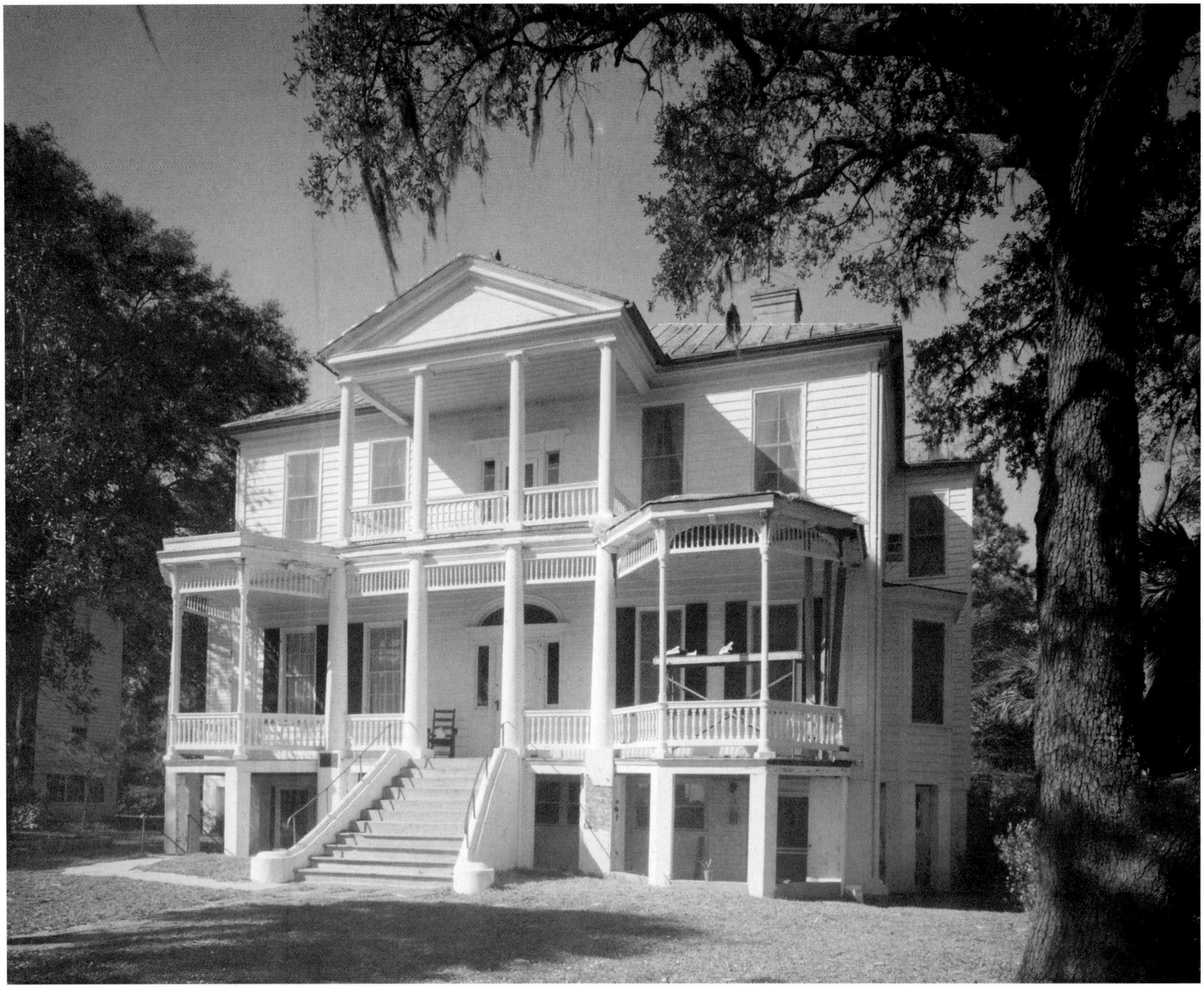

John Cuthbert House — Charles N. Bayless, 1978 (photo series)

John built this house for his bride, Mary, in 1811. The porch was extended after the Civil War.

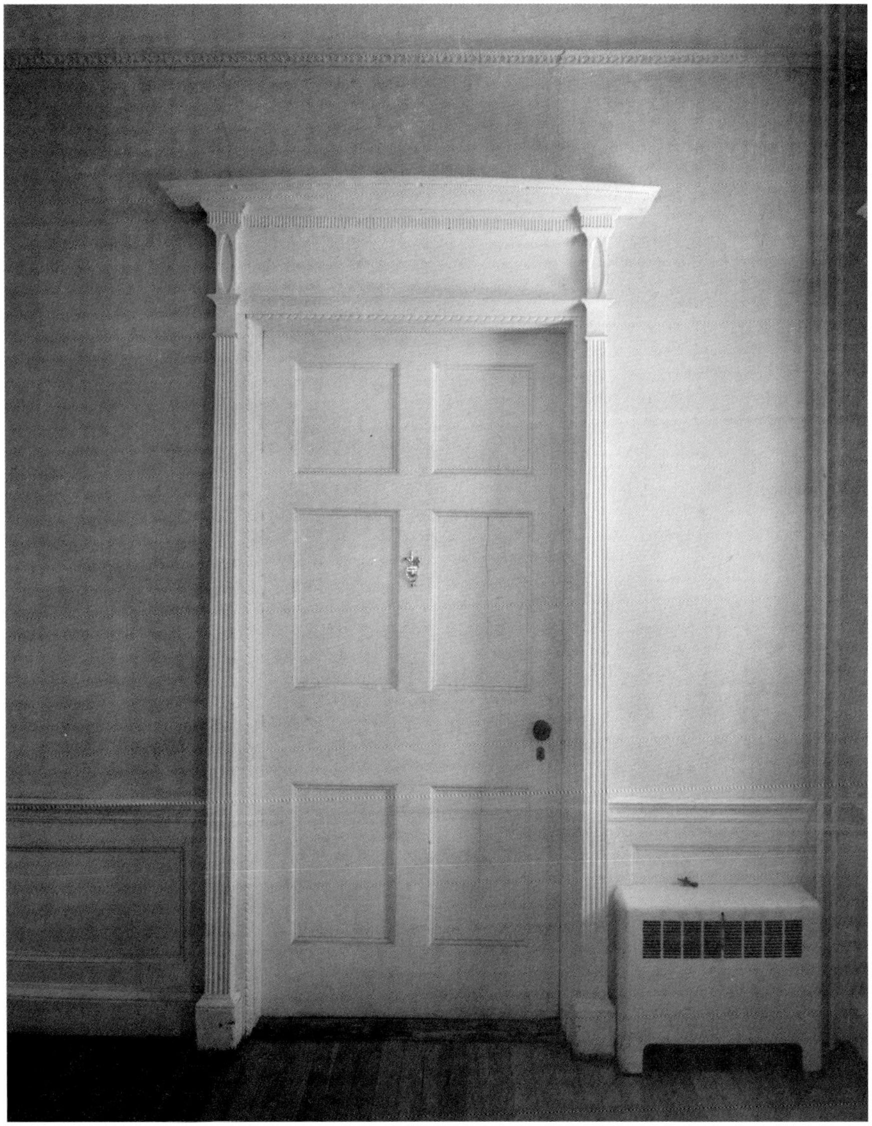

John Cuthbert House

A typical door and casement.

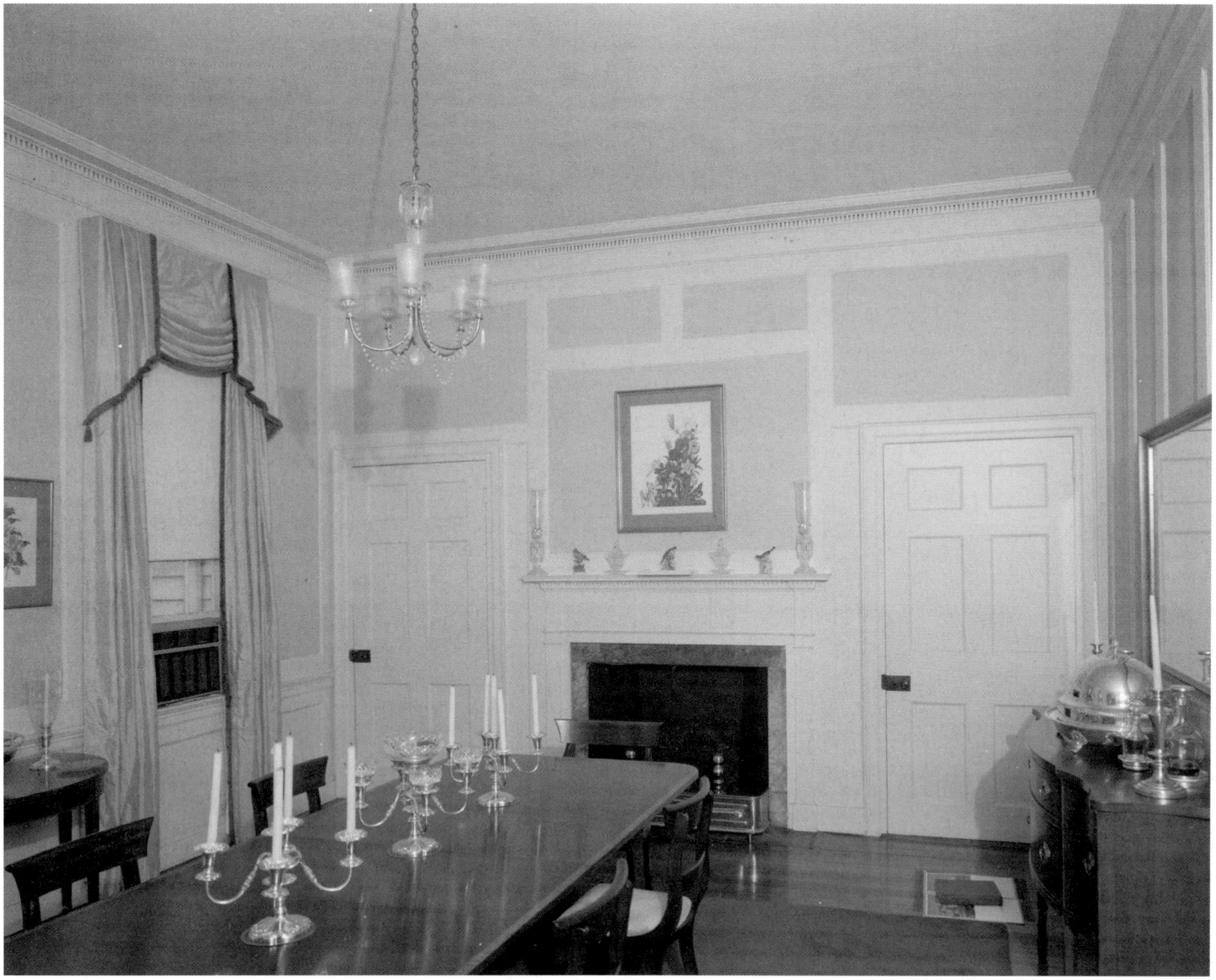

Robert Means House

Charles N. Bayless, 1978 (photo series)

Dining area with simple wall treatment.

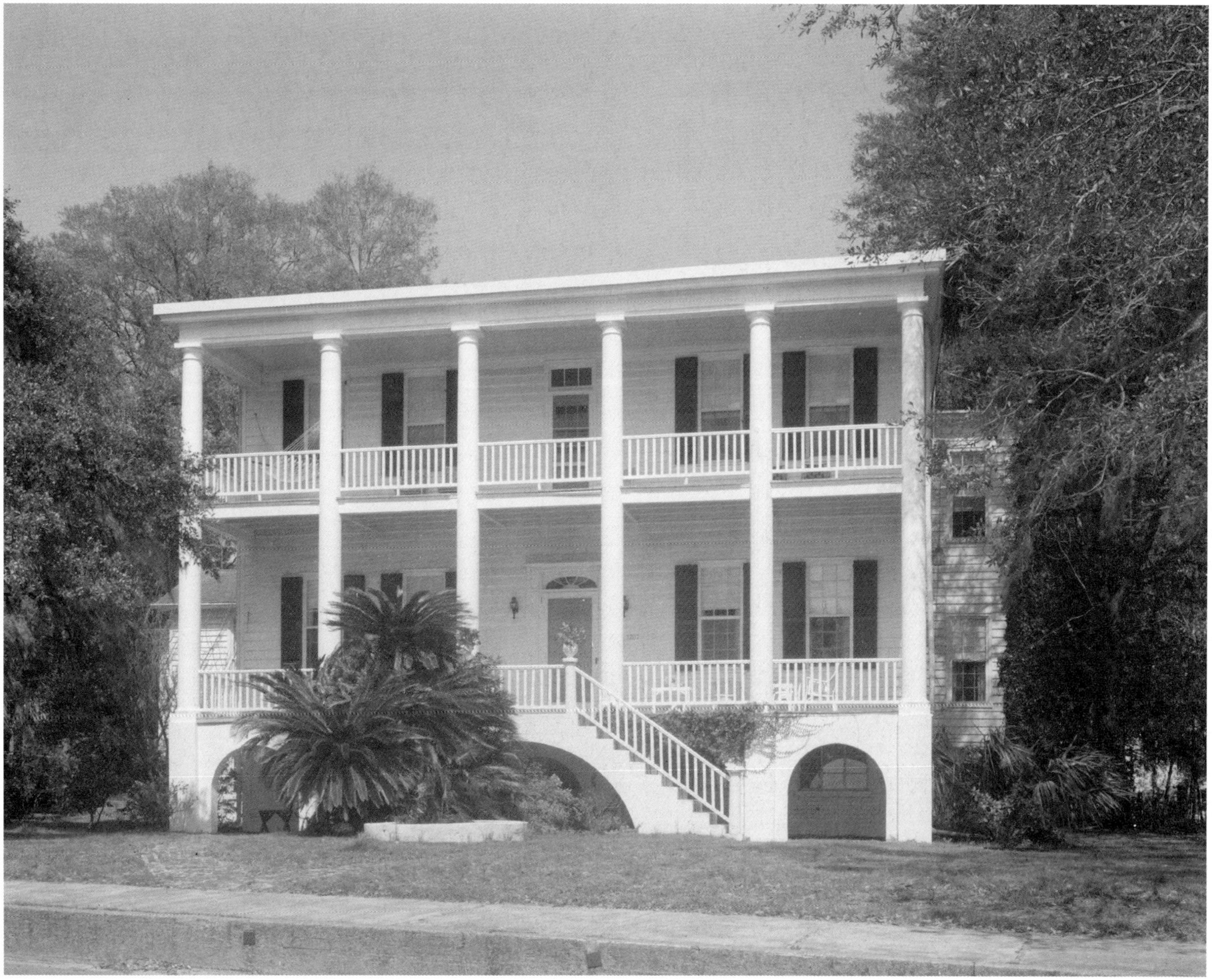

Robert Means House

A familiar Beaufort-style façade.

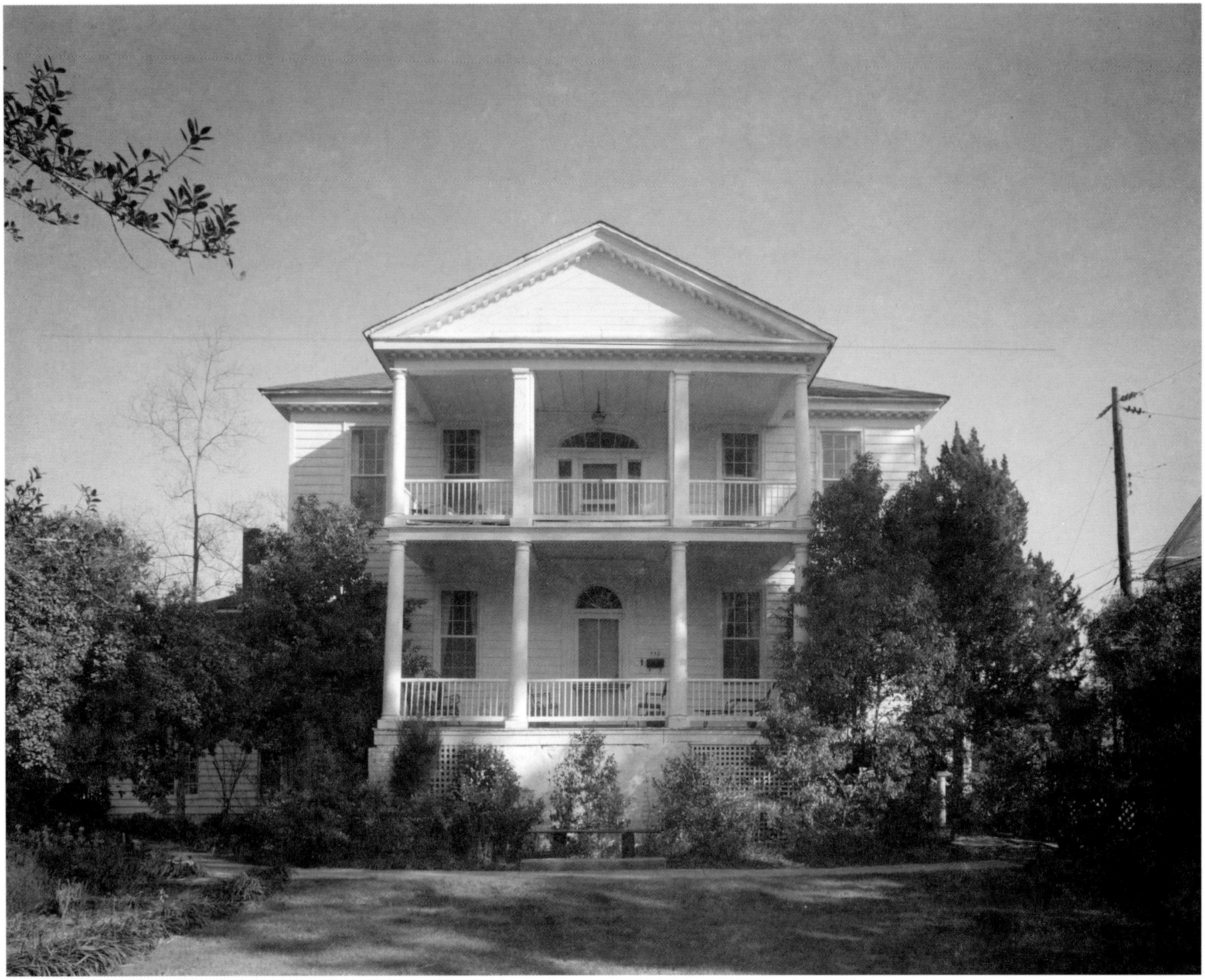

Henry Farmer House — Charles N. Bayless, 1978 (photo series)

A tabby foundation with two Federalist stories above. Farmer built it in 1800 and sold it soon after to Reverend Richard Fuller.

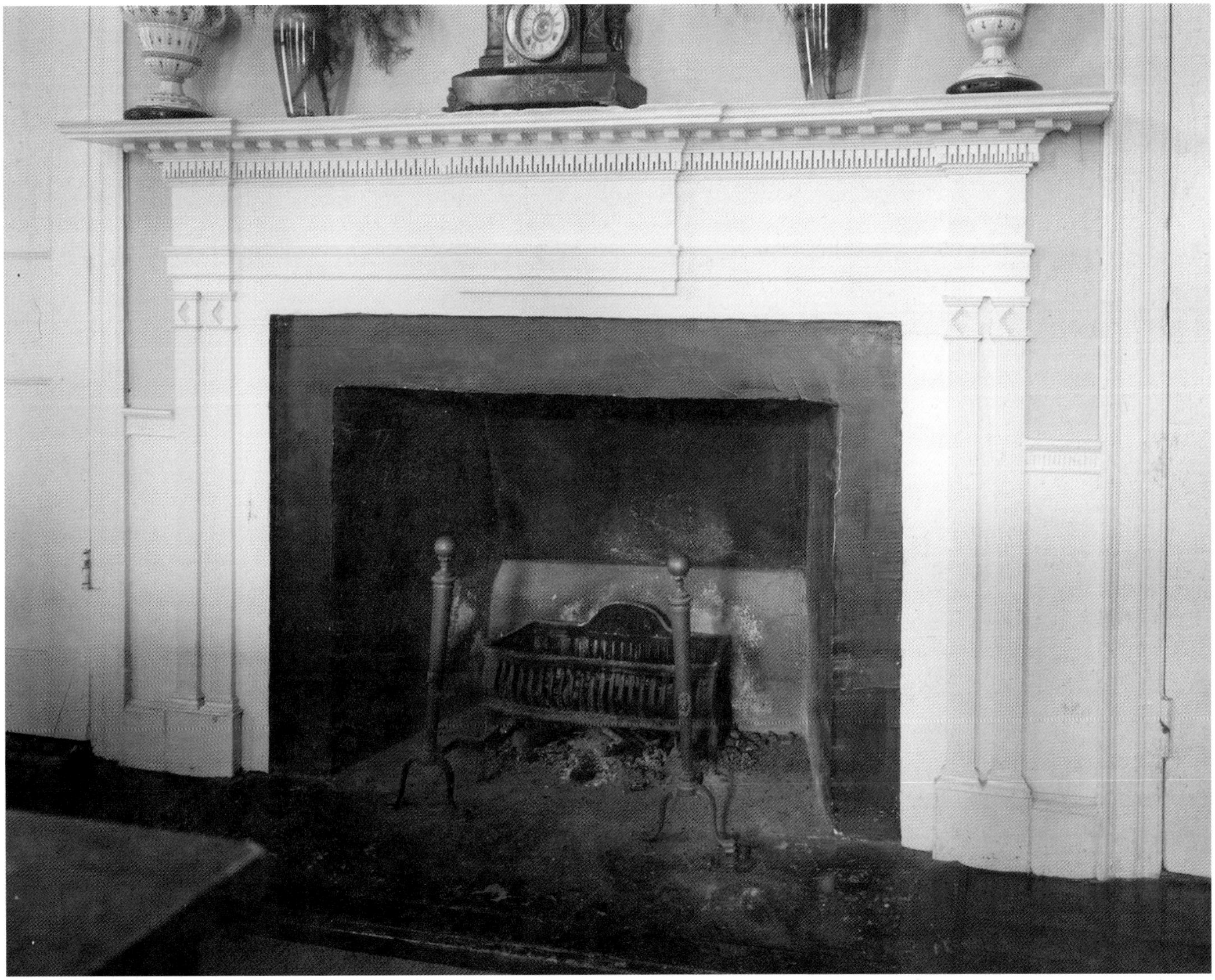

Henry Farmer House

Mantel detail.

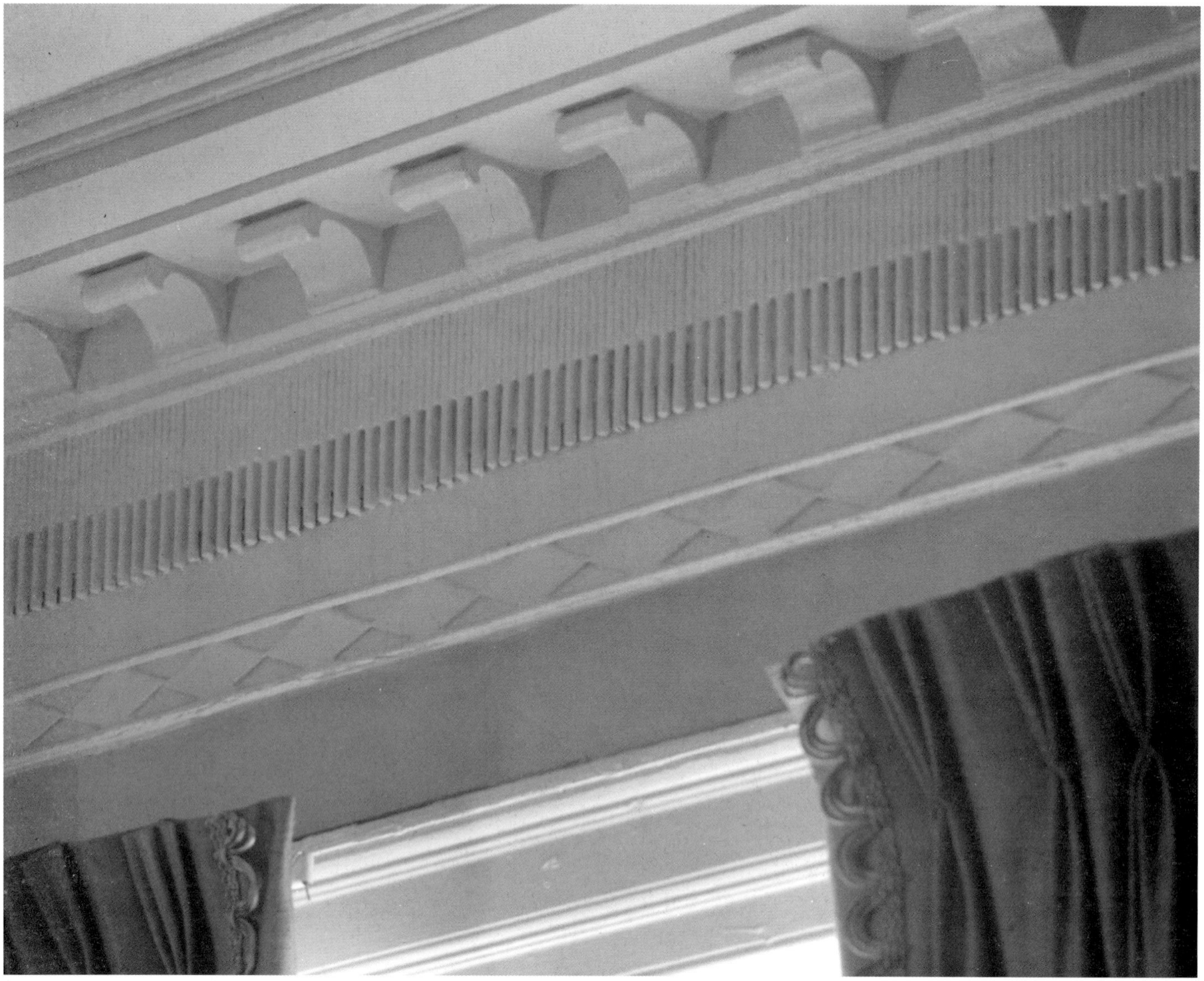

Henry Farmer House

The cornice, sedate by Beaufort standards.

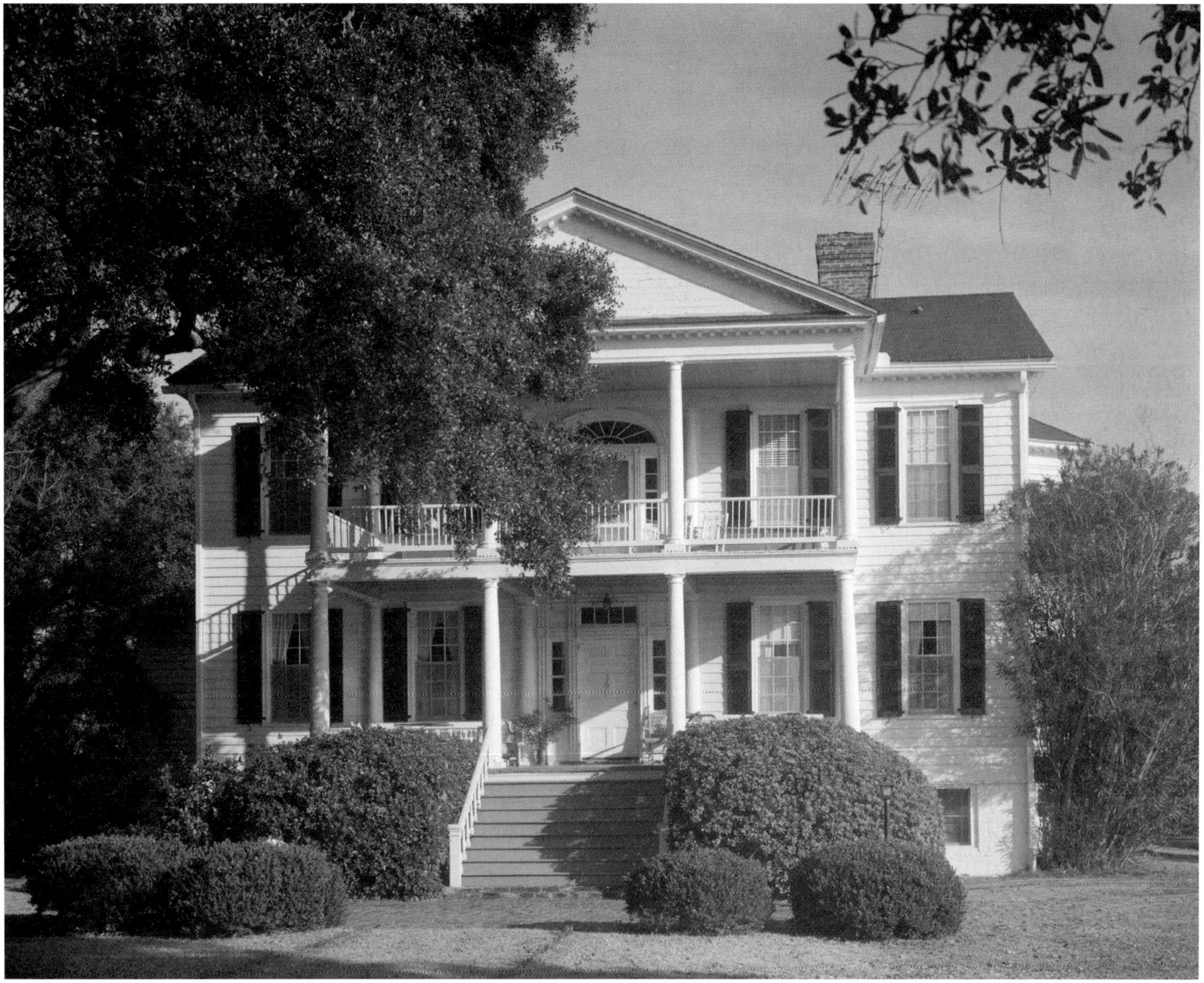

TIDEWATER — Charles N. Bayless, 1978 (photo series)

Noted St. Helena Island planter "Good Billy" Fripp built this house in 1830. The broadening portico suggests a transition toward full piazzas across the front.

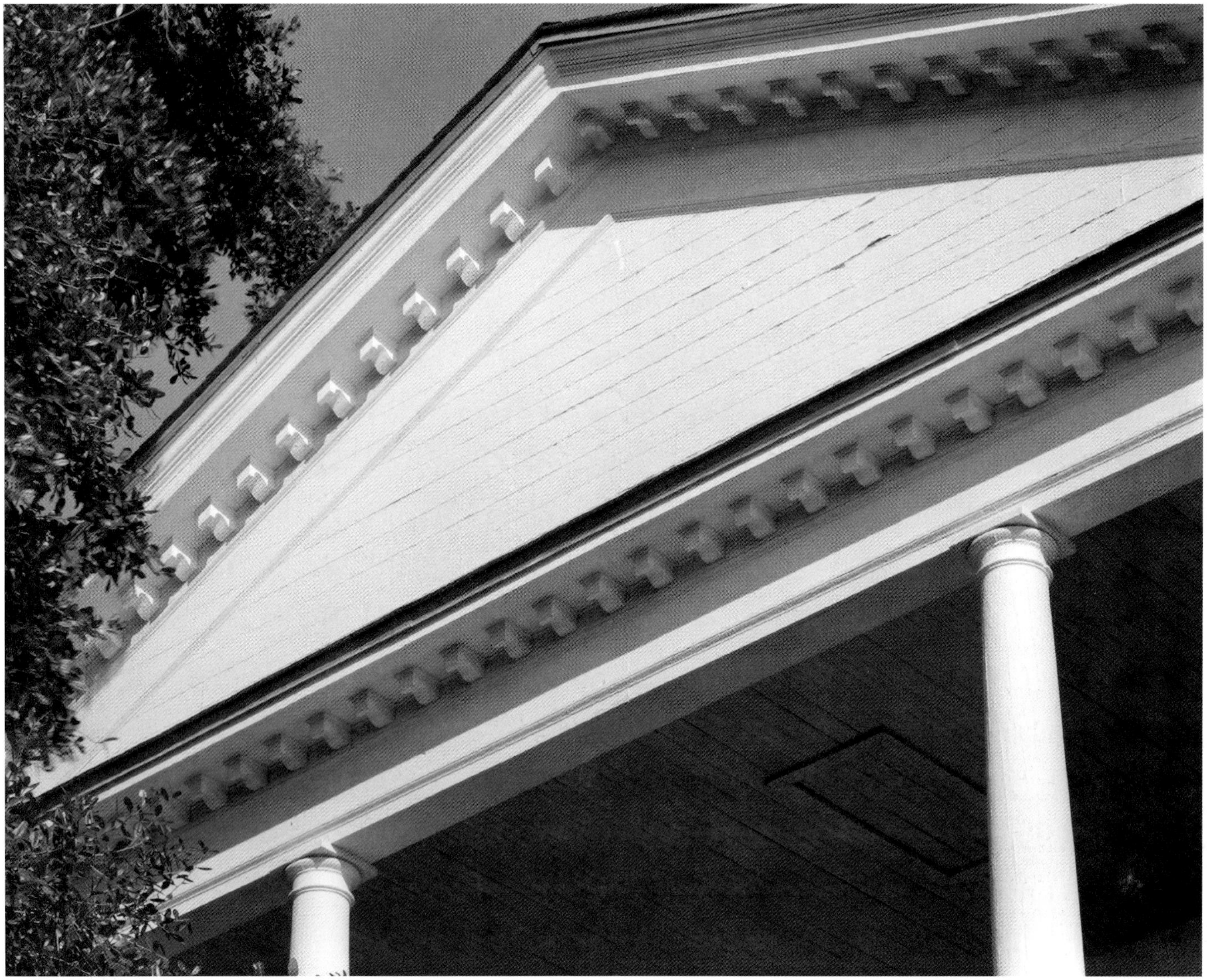

Tidewater

Simple dentil molding. “Denticulate cornice” is how that’s said.

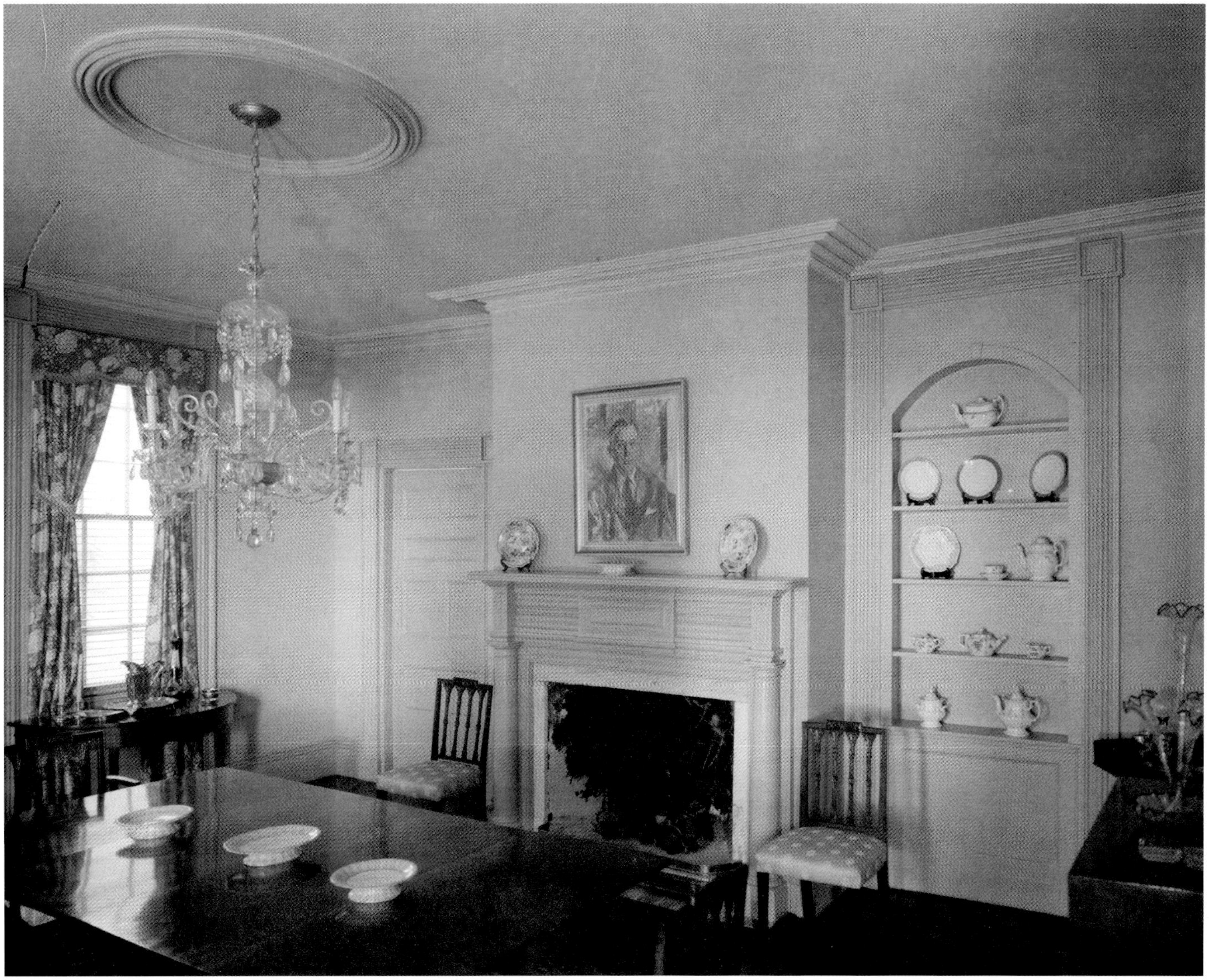

TIDEWATER

A comfortable room.

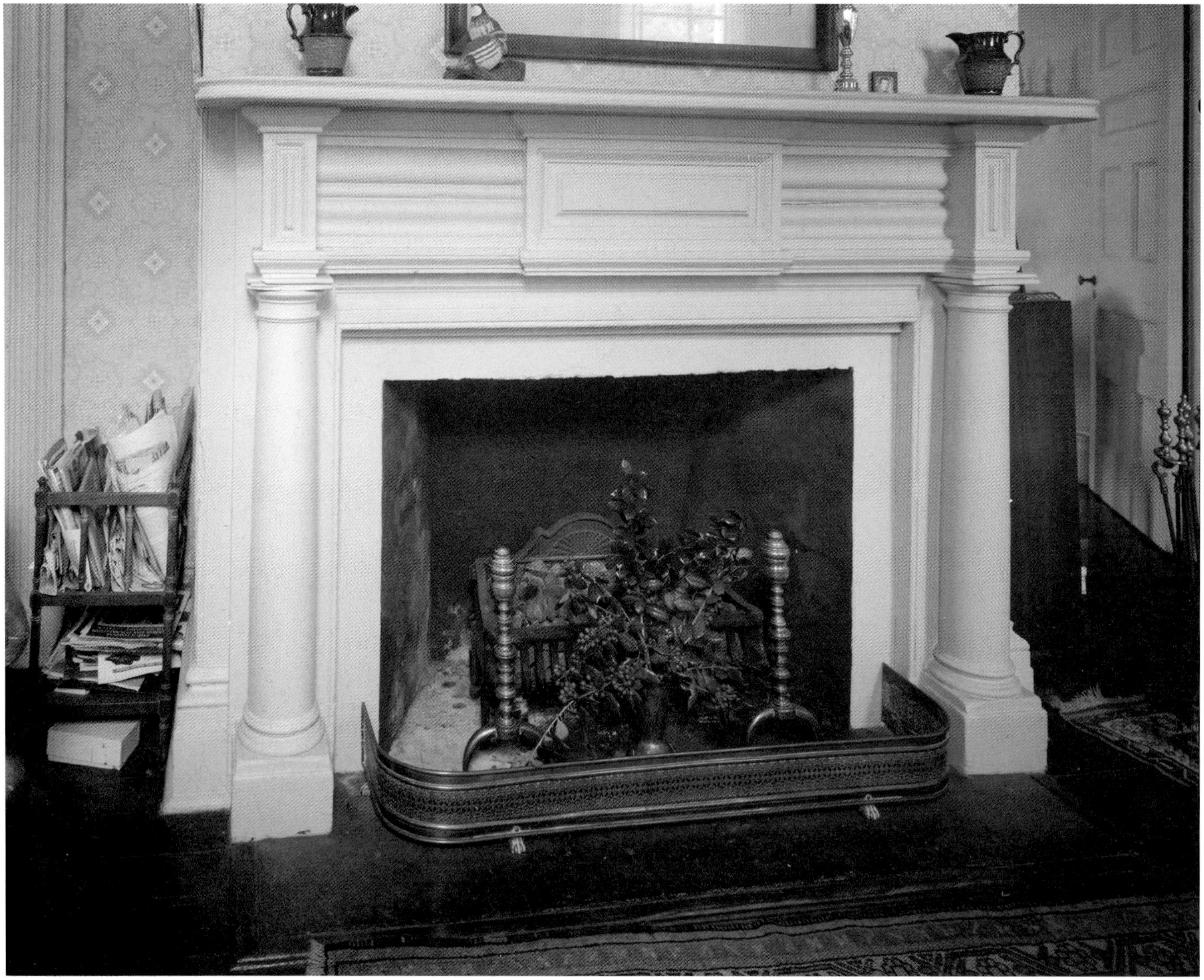

Tidewater

Mantel detail.

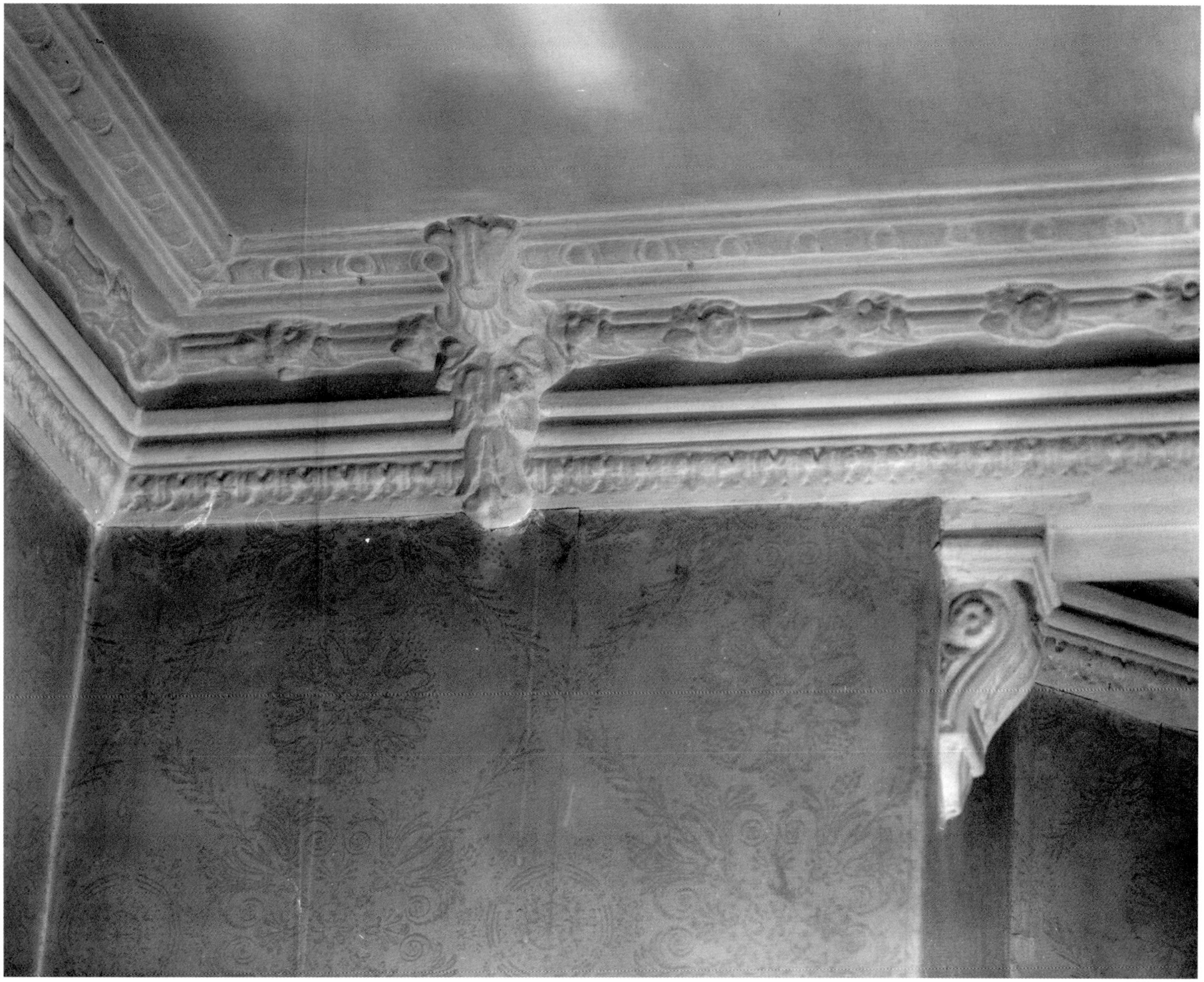

James Rhett House — Charles N. Bayless, 1978 (photo series)

An intricate cornice from the Victorian era. Built to impress the young woman he wished to marry. So goes the story.

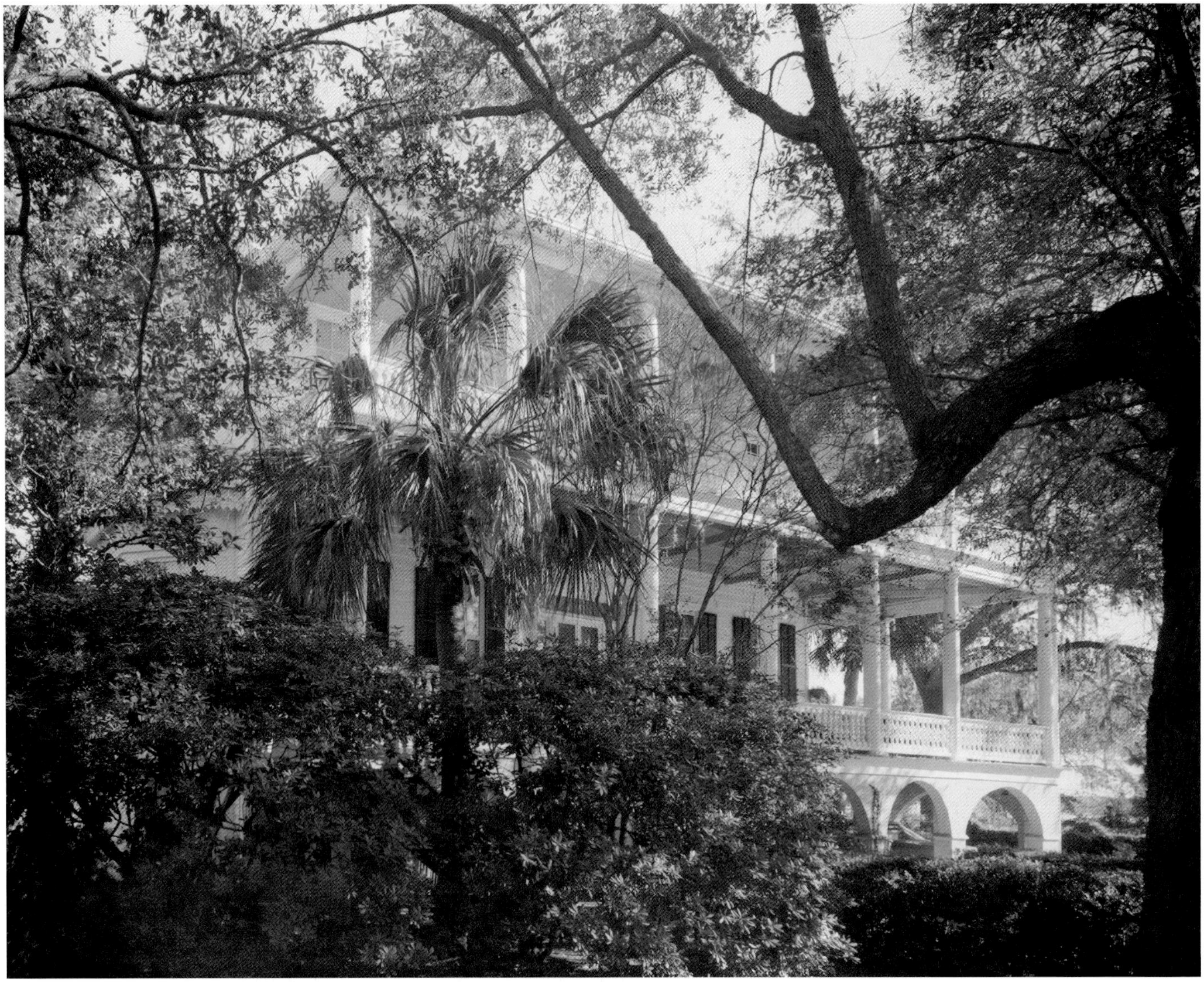

James Rhett House

In 1884, twenty-three-year-old James Rhett began construction of this typical Beaufort-style house to impress his bride-to-be. The money ran out, though, and he built the house one room deep instead of two.

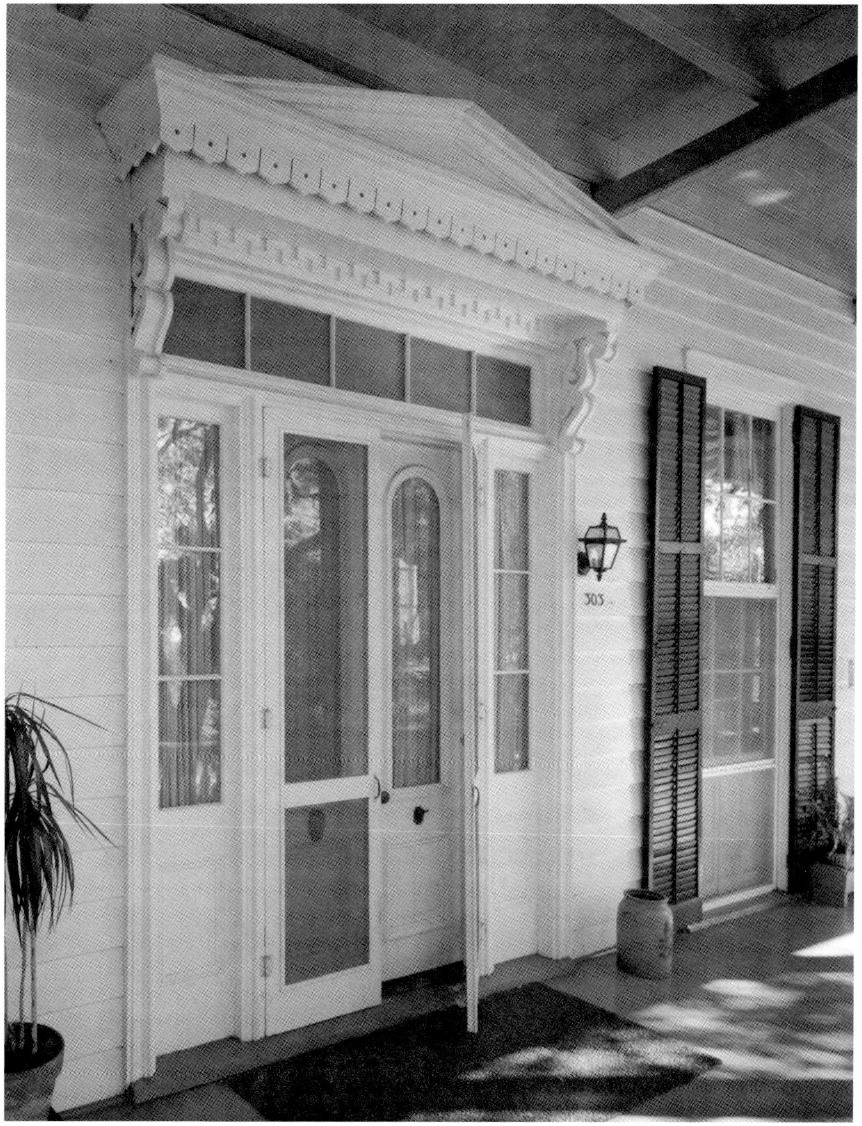

James Rhett House

The main entry. Note the Victorian-age double doors. The house is called "Rhett's folly." A reference to grand architectural plans and perhaps love, as well.

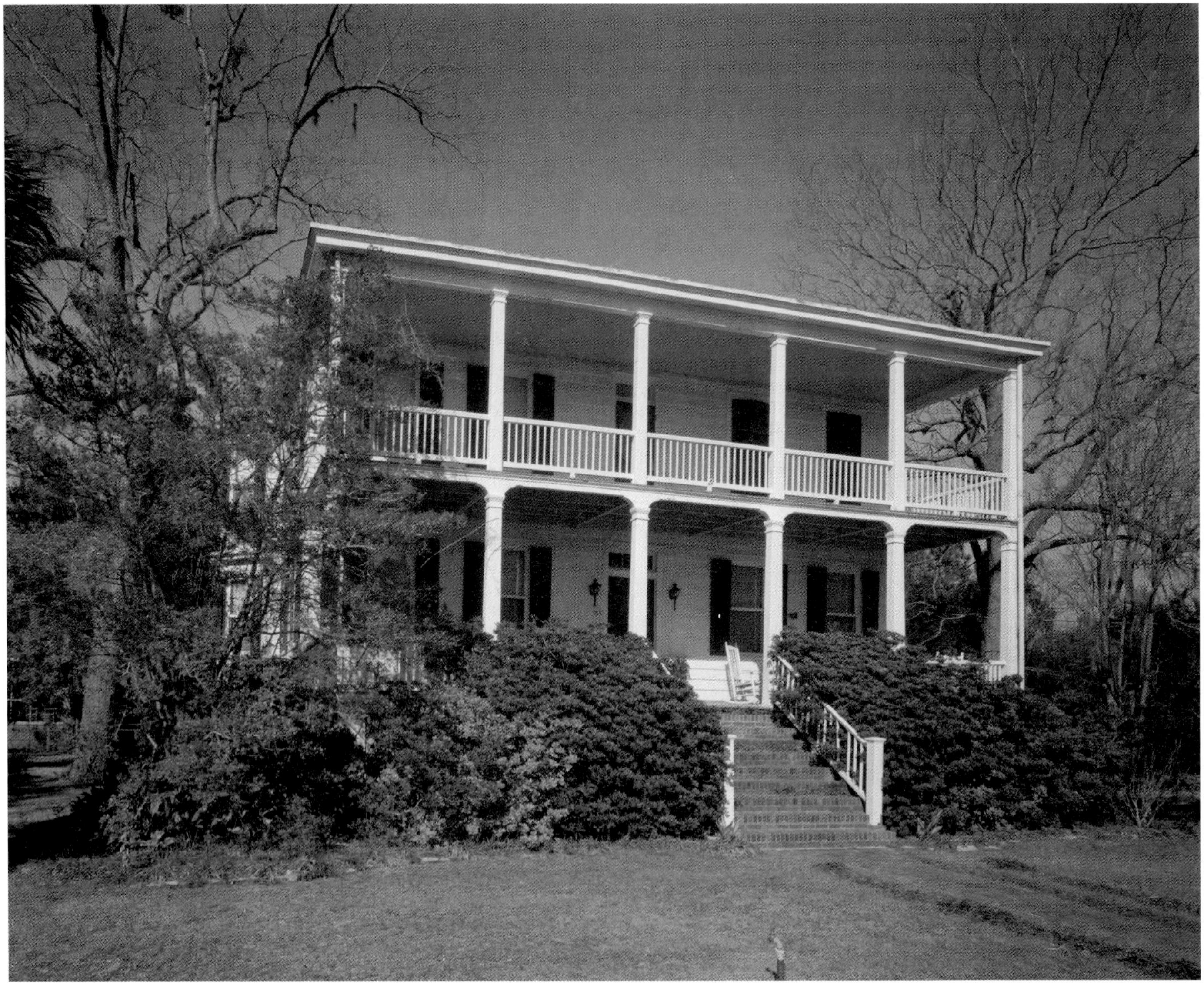

CASSENA

Charles N. Bayless, 1978 (photo series)

Built in the early 1800s by John Blythewood, the house was purchased in 1863 by a former slave of the family, Mary Belle. Again the Beaufort-style piazzas were a late addition.

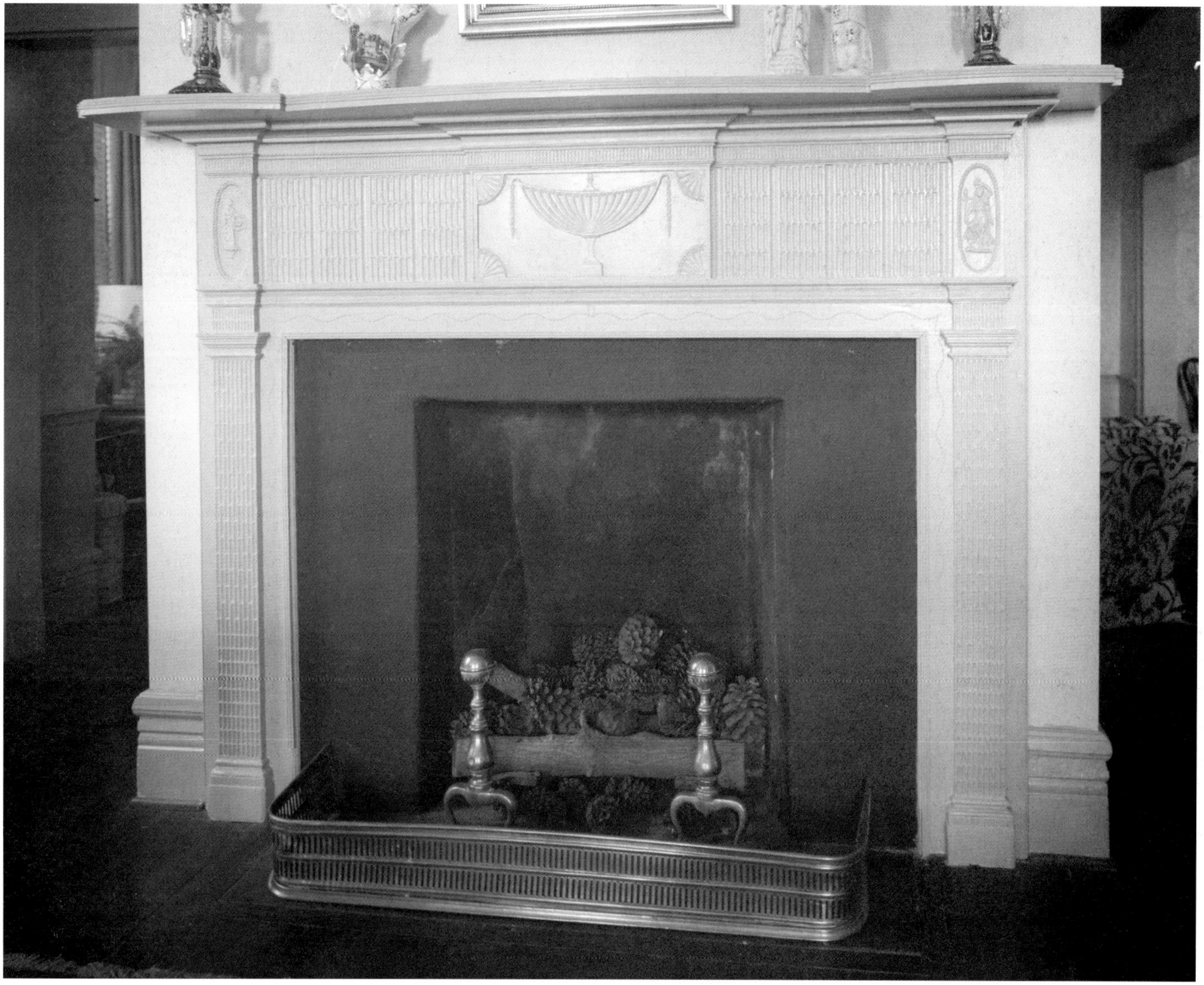

Cassena

The hurricane of 1893 severely damaged the house; this formal mantel is probably from the twentieth century.

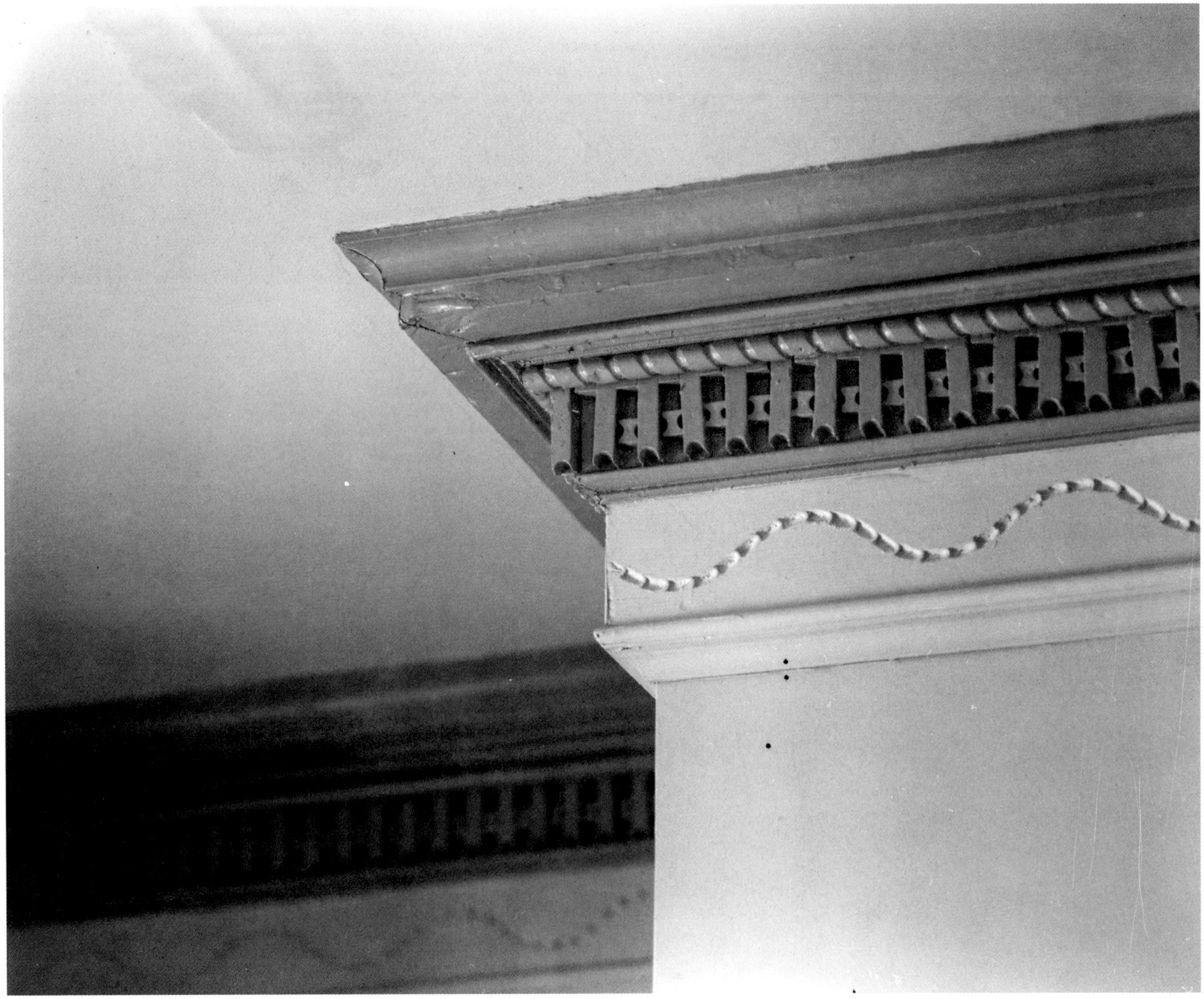

Cassena

A simple but elegant cornice.

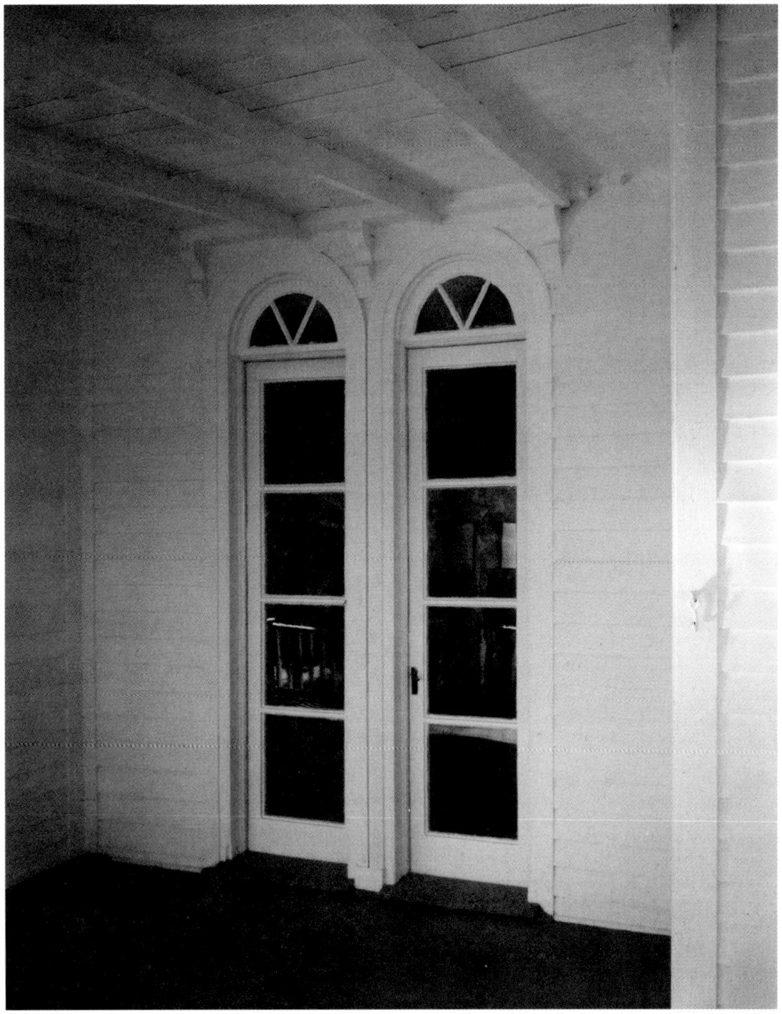

TIDALHOLM Charles N. Bayless, 1978 (photo series)

A place of transition. Porch banister reflected. Interior revealed.

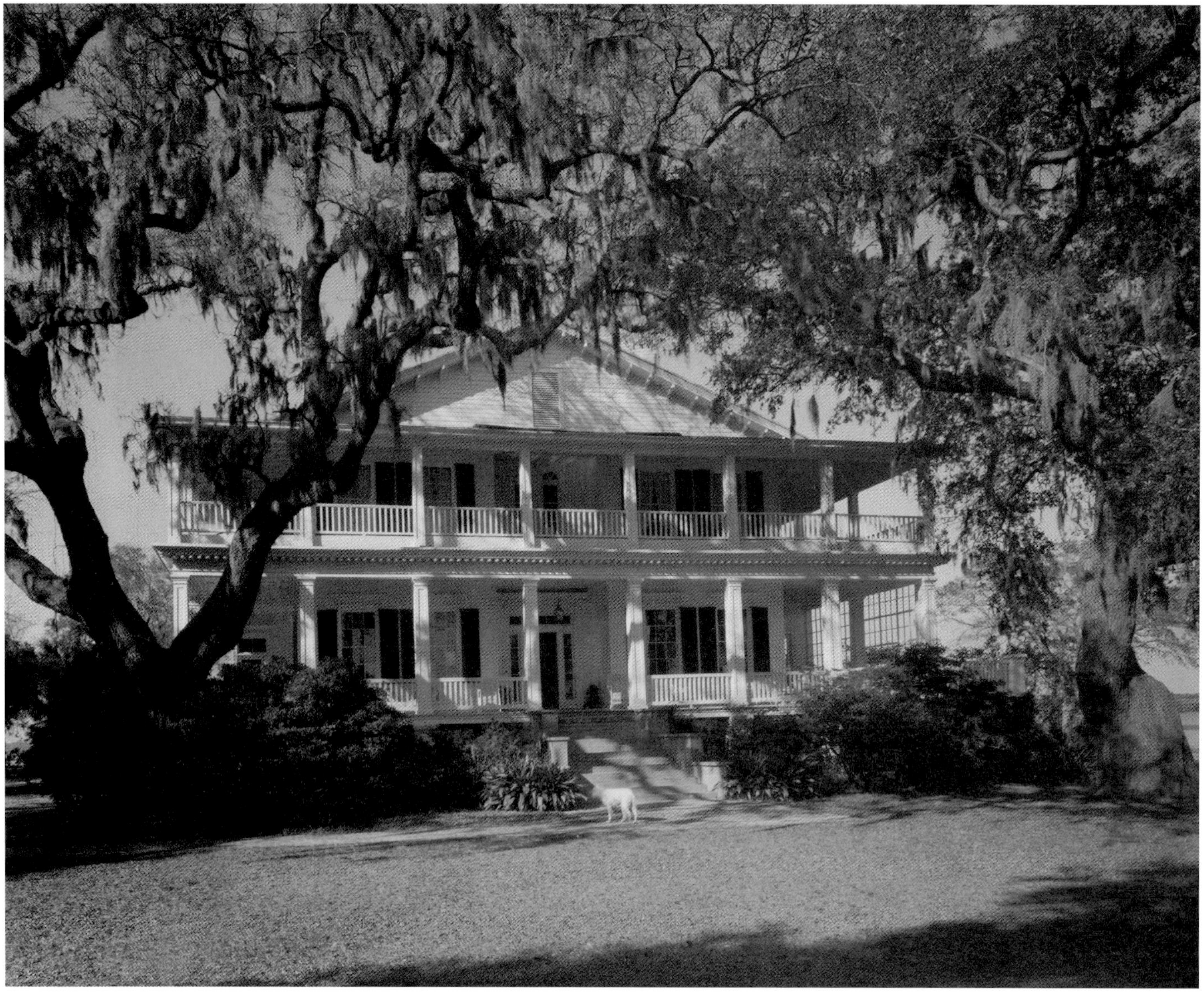

Tidalholm

Tidalholm was built in 1853 by Sea Island planter Edgar Fripp. Originally in the Italianate style popular with the Victorians.

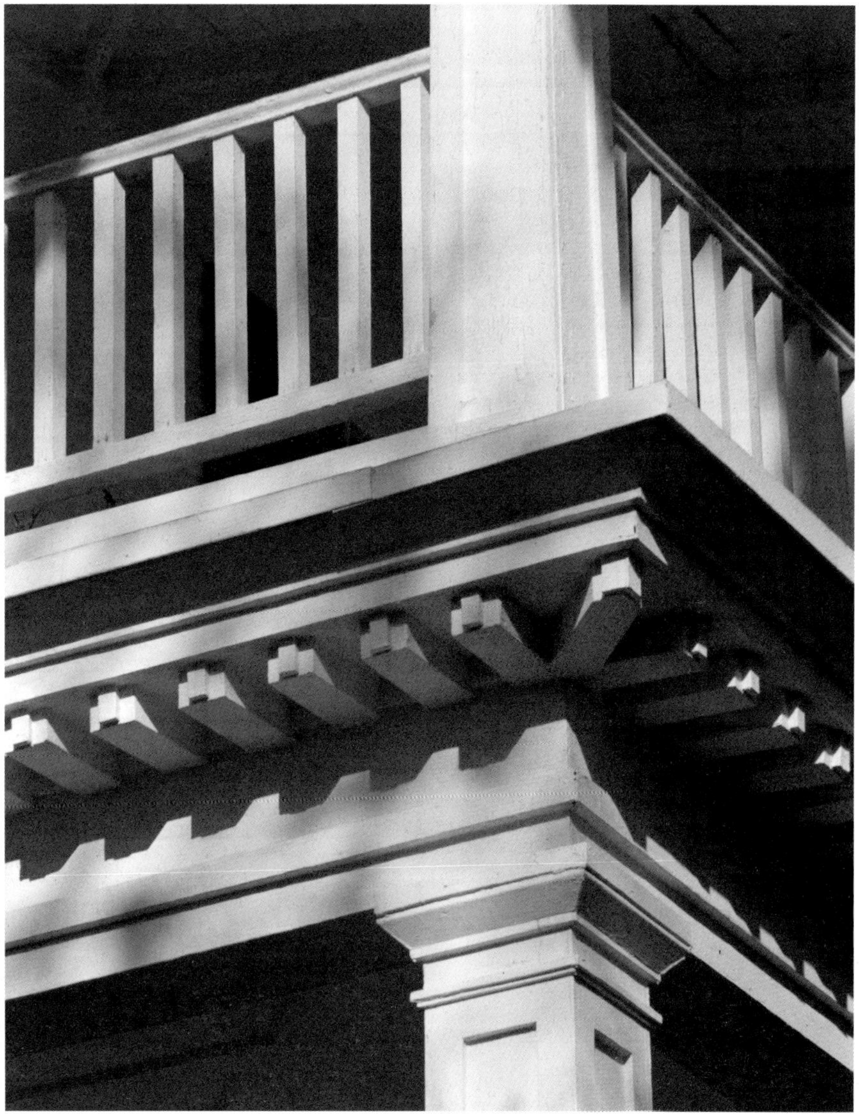

Tidalholm

The great hurricane of 1893 blew off the second-story roof, and this Beaufort-style piazza came along with the replacement.

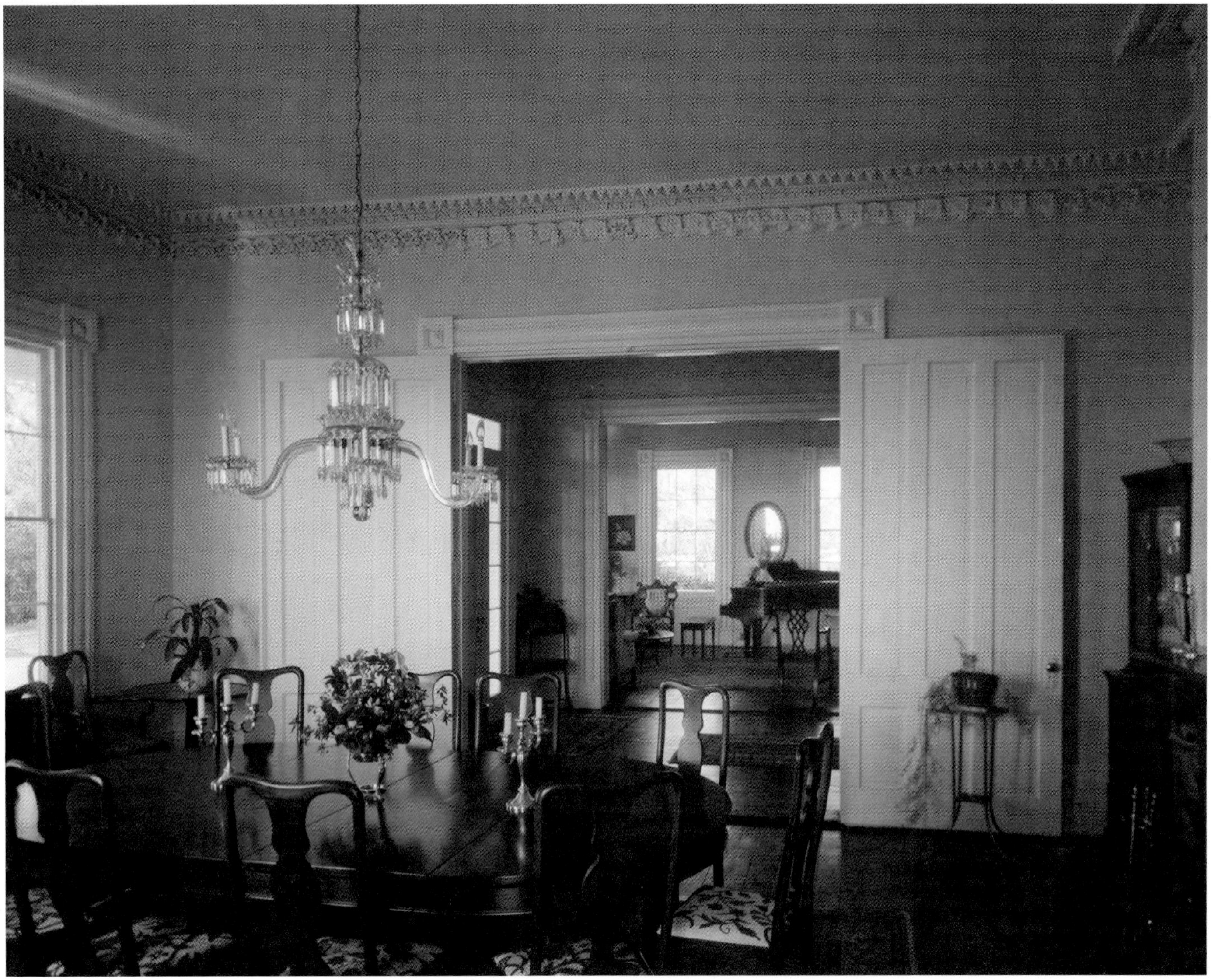

TIDALHOLM

A first-floor drawing room.

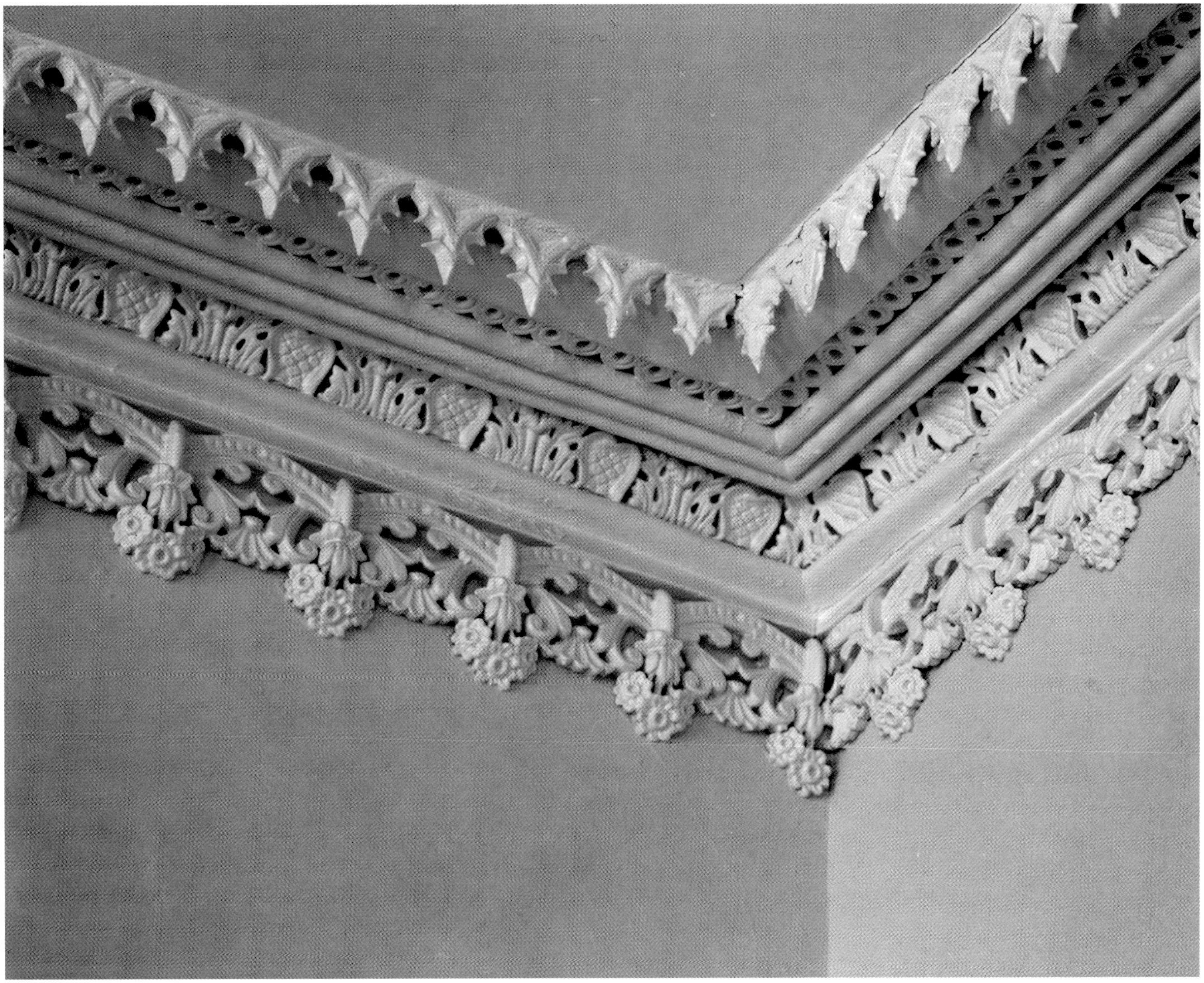

Tidalholm

A cornice of bouquets and lyres, plus a row of fencing.

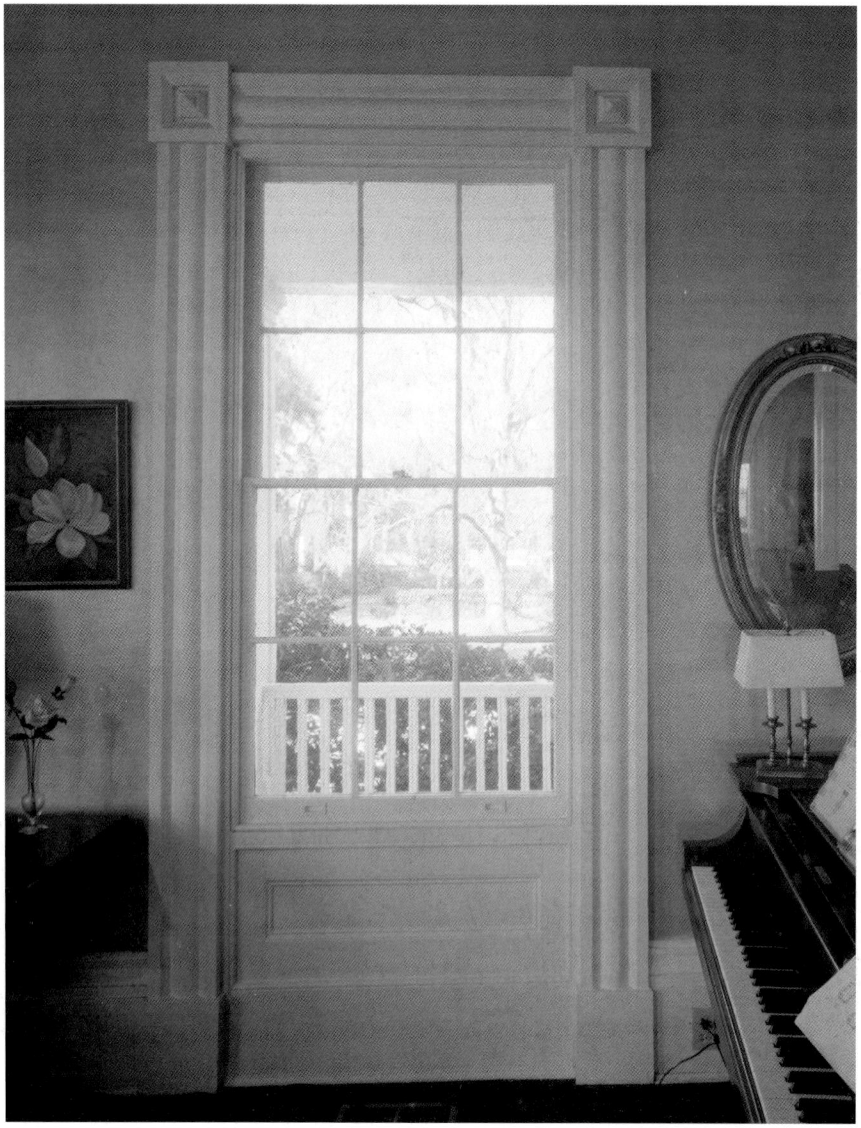

TIDALHOLM

Tidalholm was used in the filming of *The Great Santini*. But the piano suggests the entertainment of an earlier era.

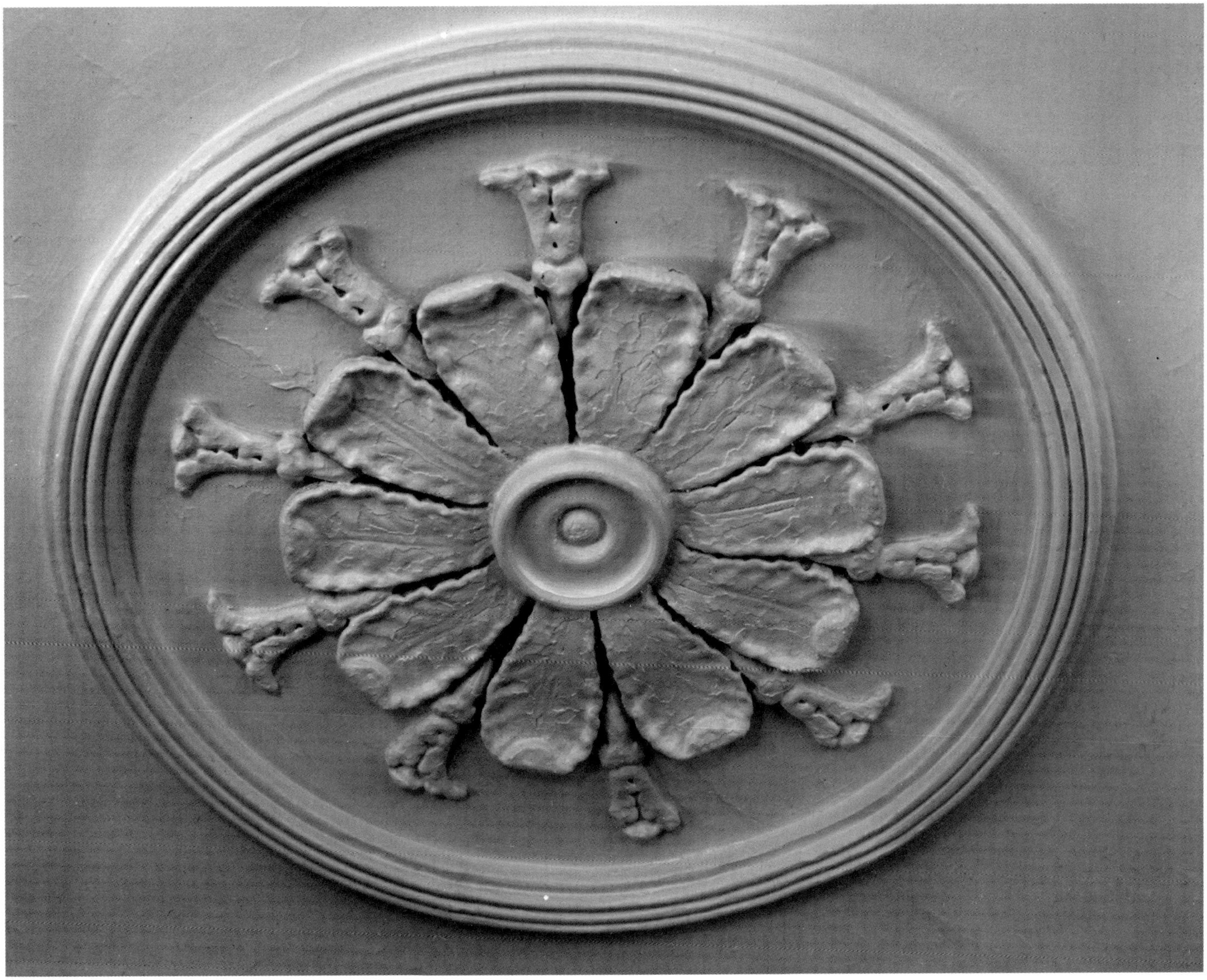

Tidalholm

Ceiling medallion.

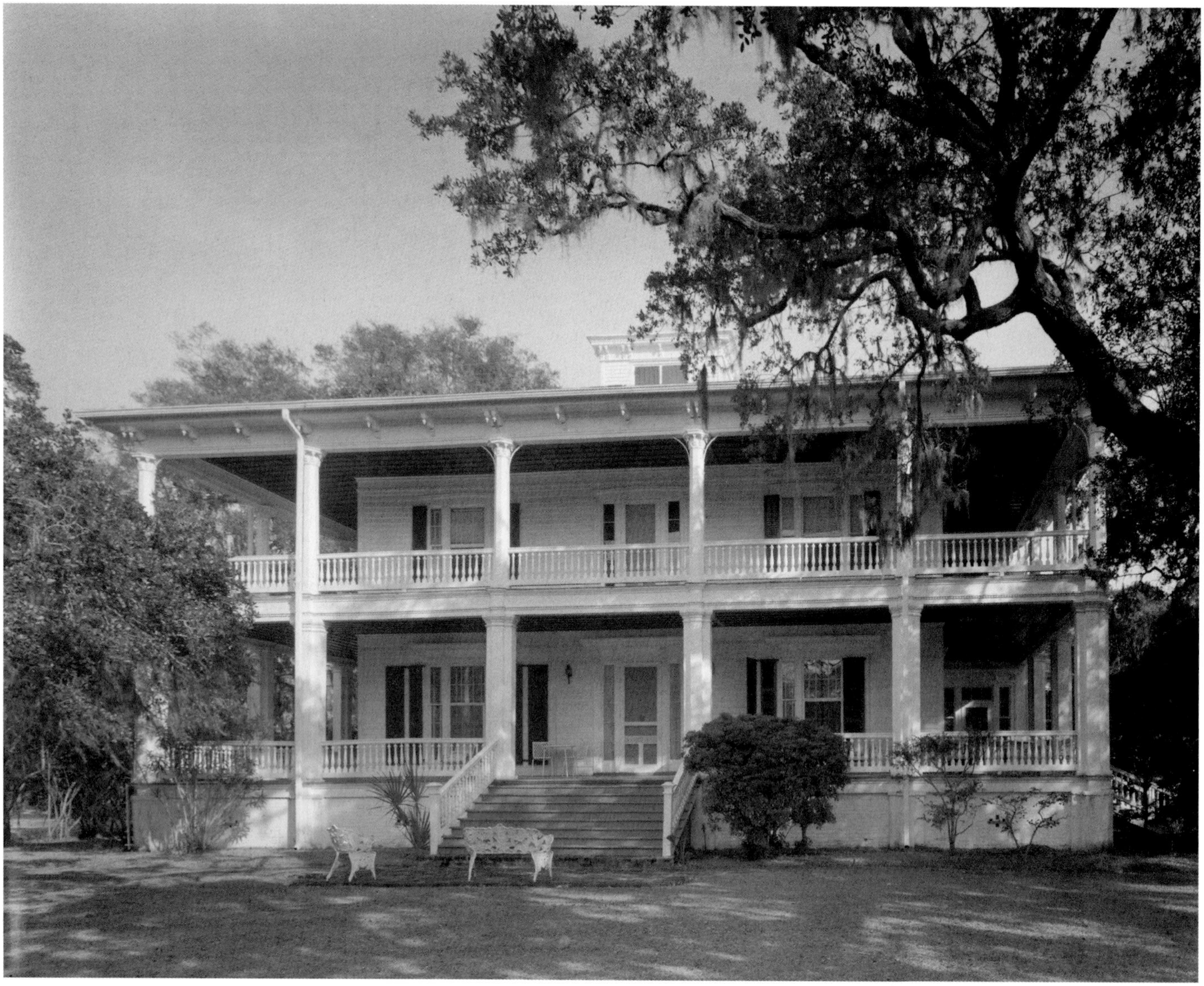

THE OAKS — Charles N. Bayless, 1978 (photo series)

Built by Paul Hamilton in 1856, the Oaks is one of those rare houses to have double piazzas at its origin. Look closely and you can see the cupola on the roof.

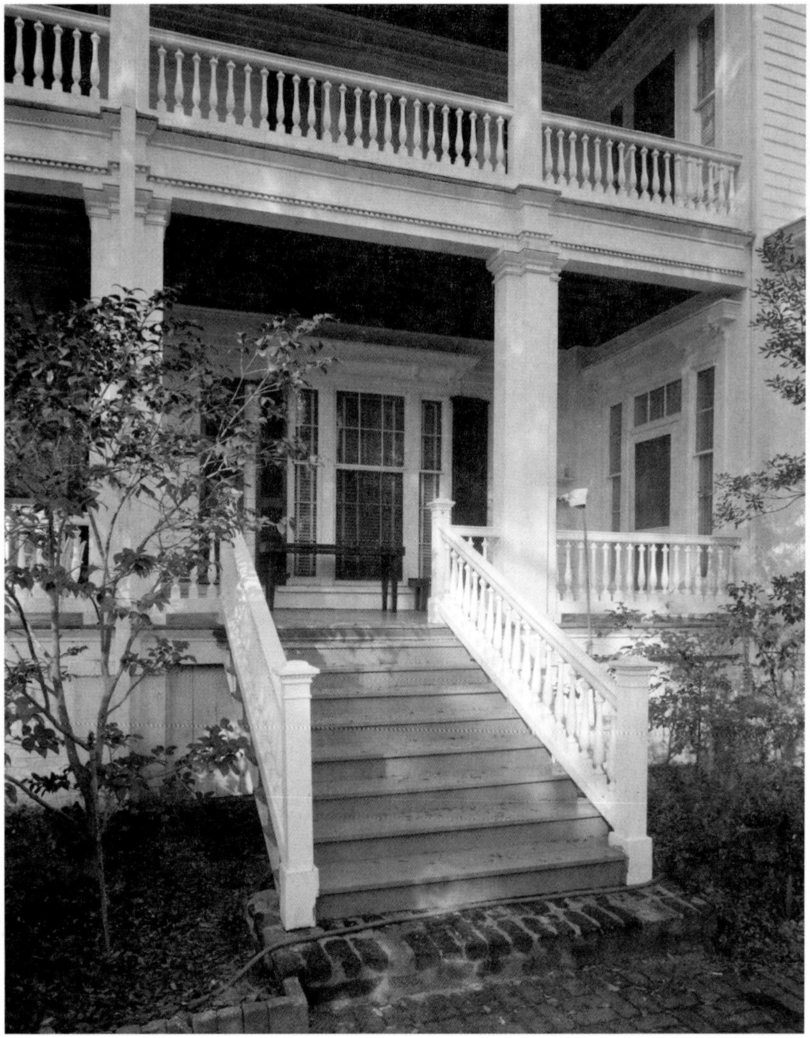

The Oaks

Like the neighboring Tidalholm, the Oaks was done in the Italianate style. Note the detailing and turned balustrade.

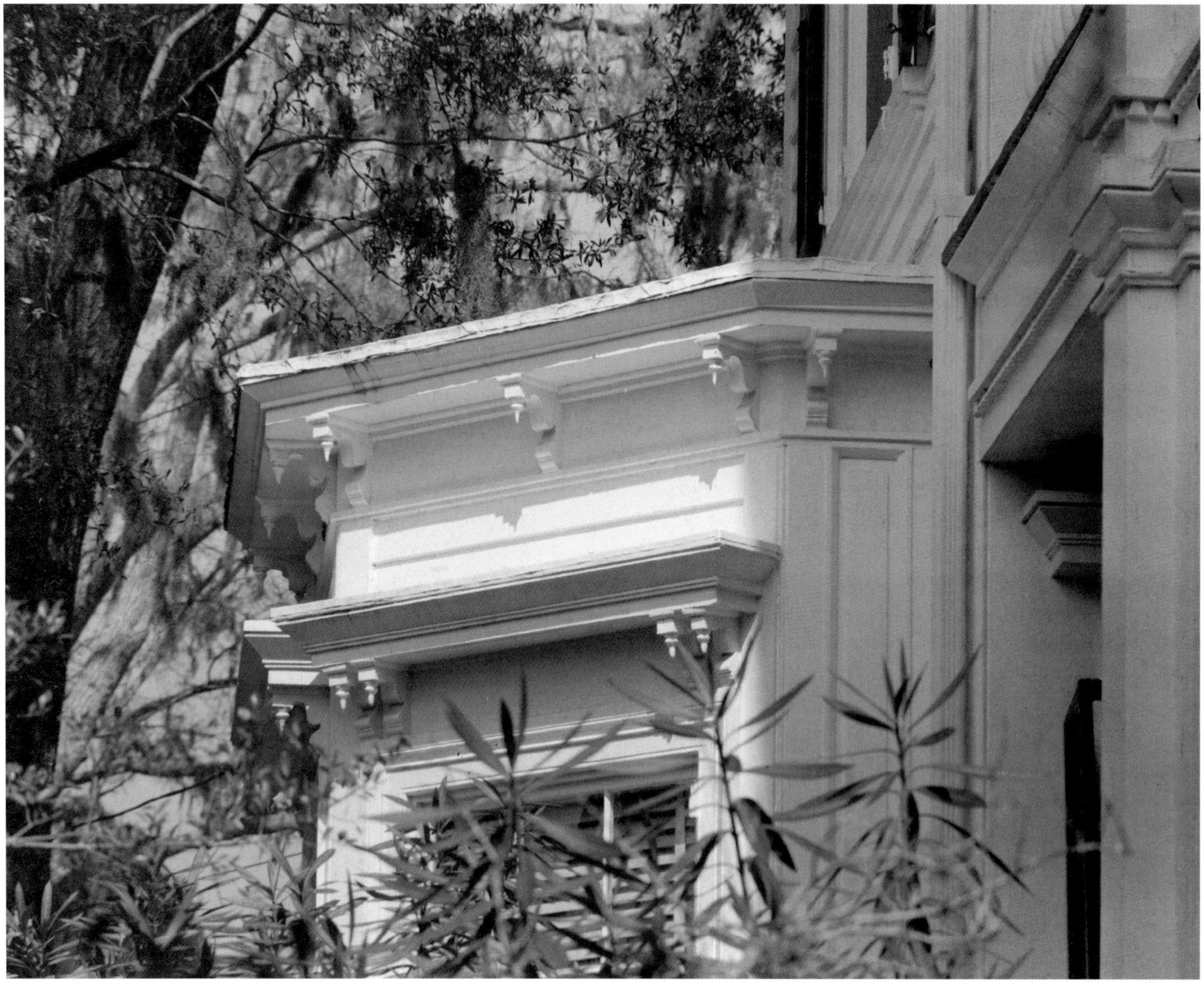

The Oaks

A purely Victorian window treatment.

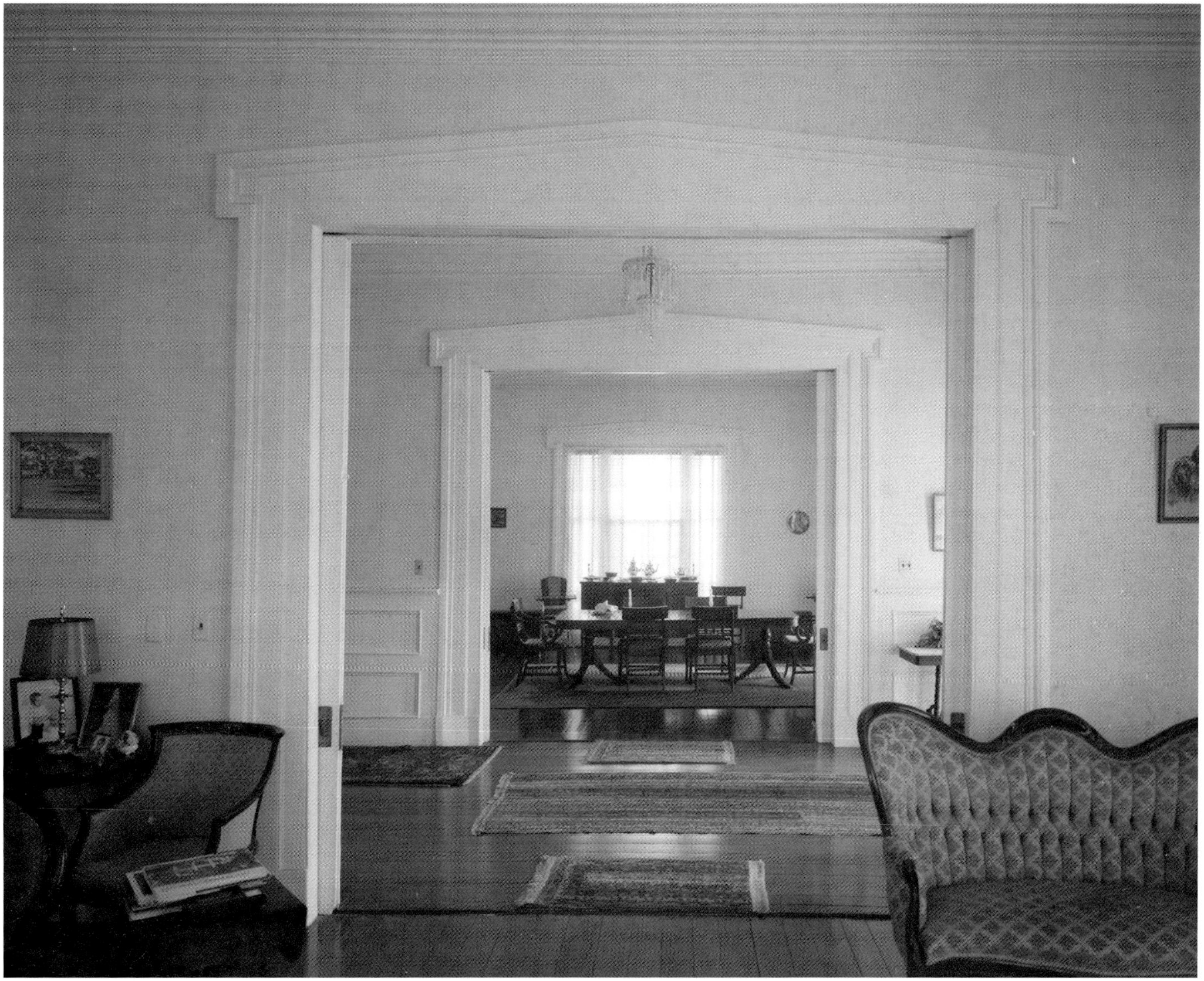

The Oaks

Drawing rooms off entry.

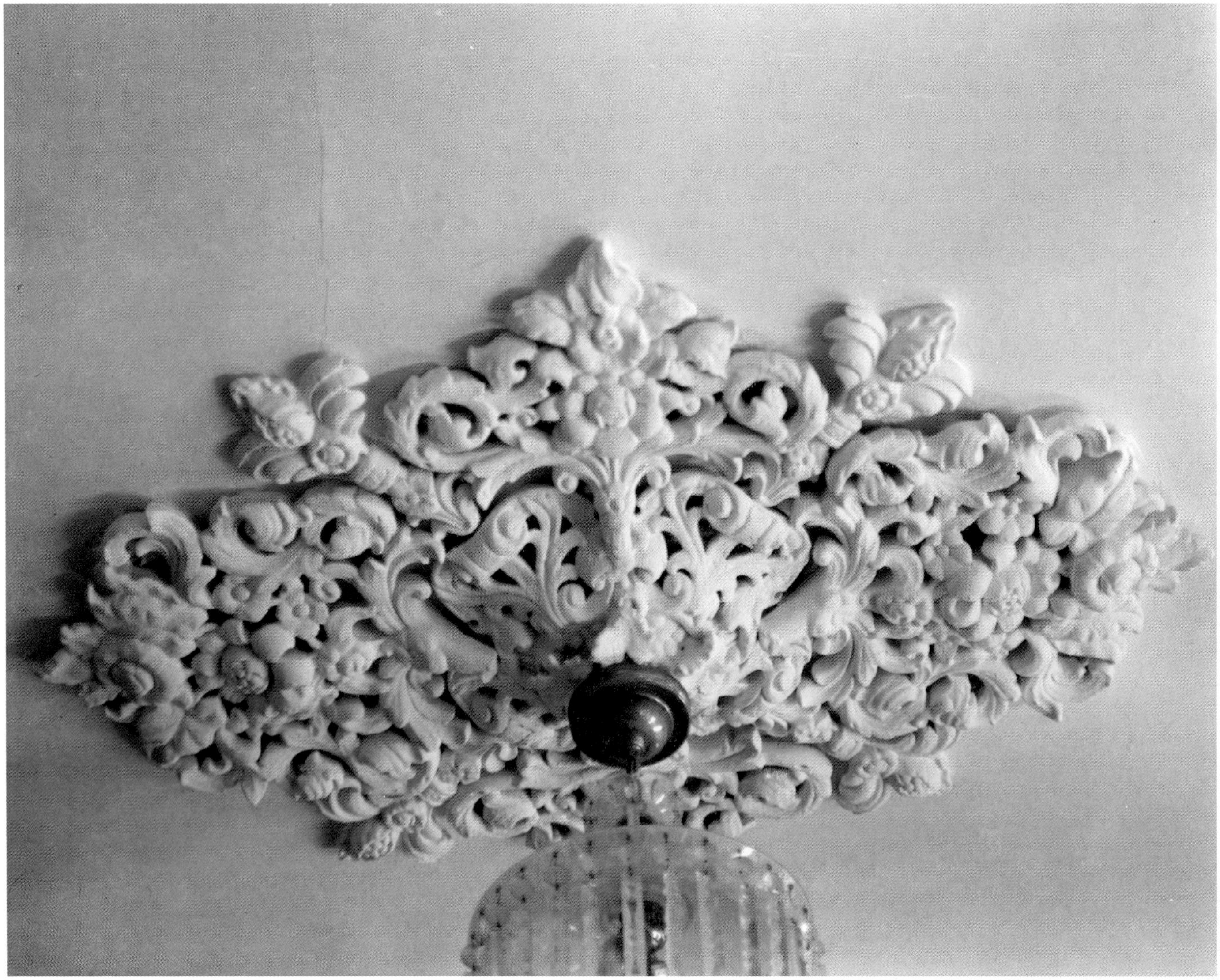

The Oaks

Sold for taxes after the Civil War, the Oaks was rescued for the Hamiltons with the help of a Northern merchant. “We had said we would never shake hands with a Yankee,” wrote Hamilton’s daughter. Here was the exception.

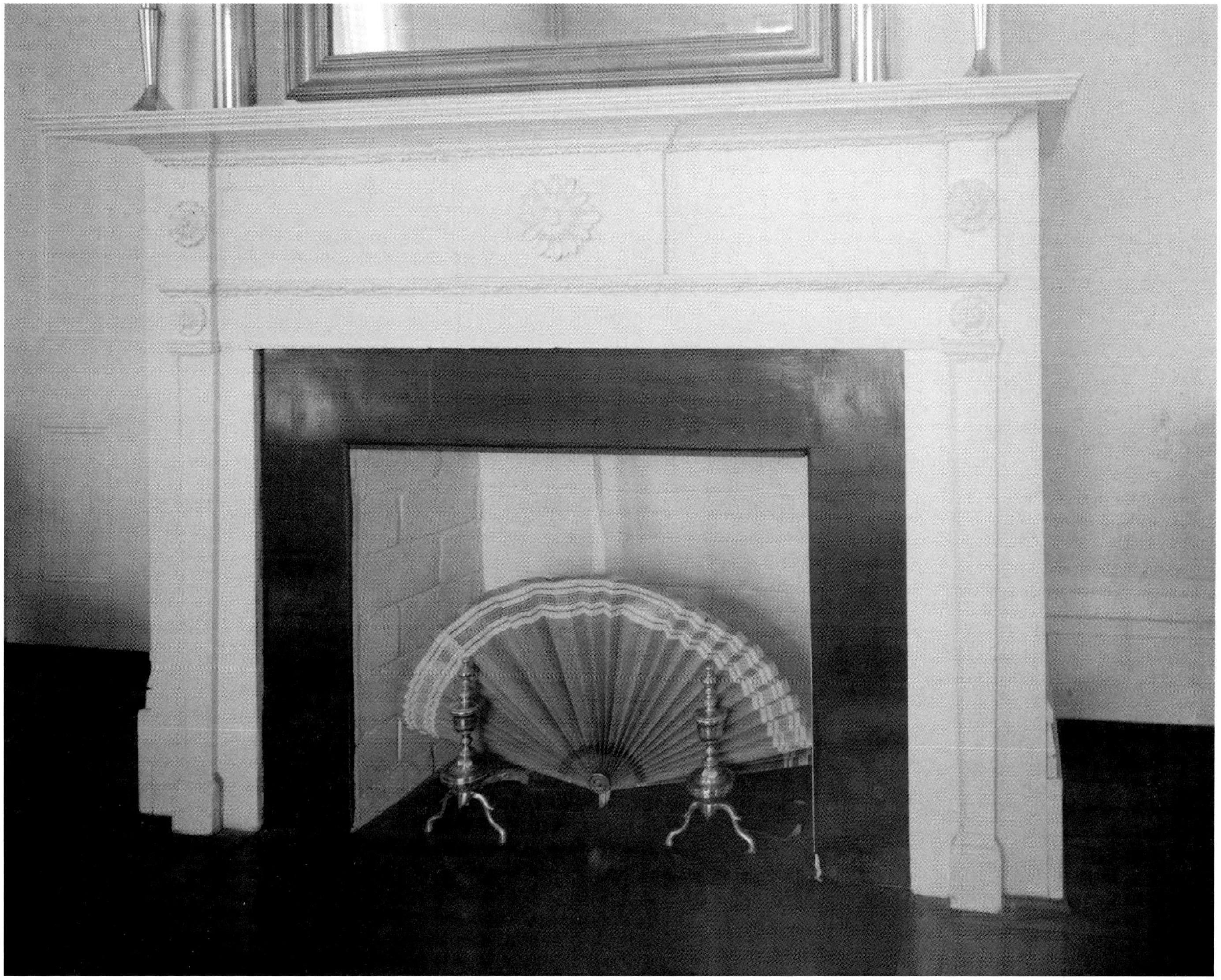

The Oaks

Typical of the mantels.

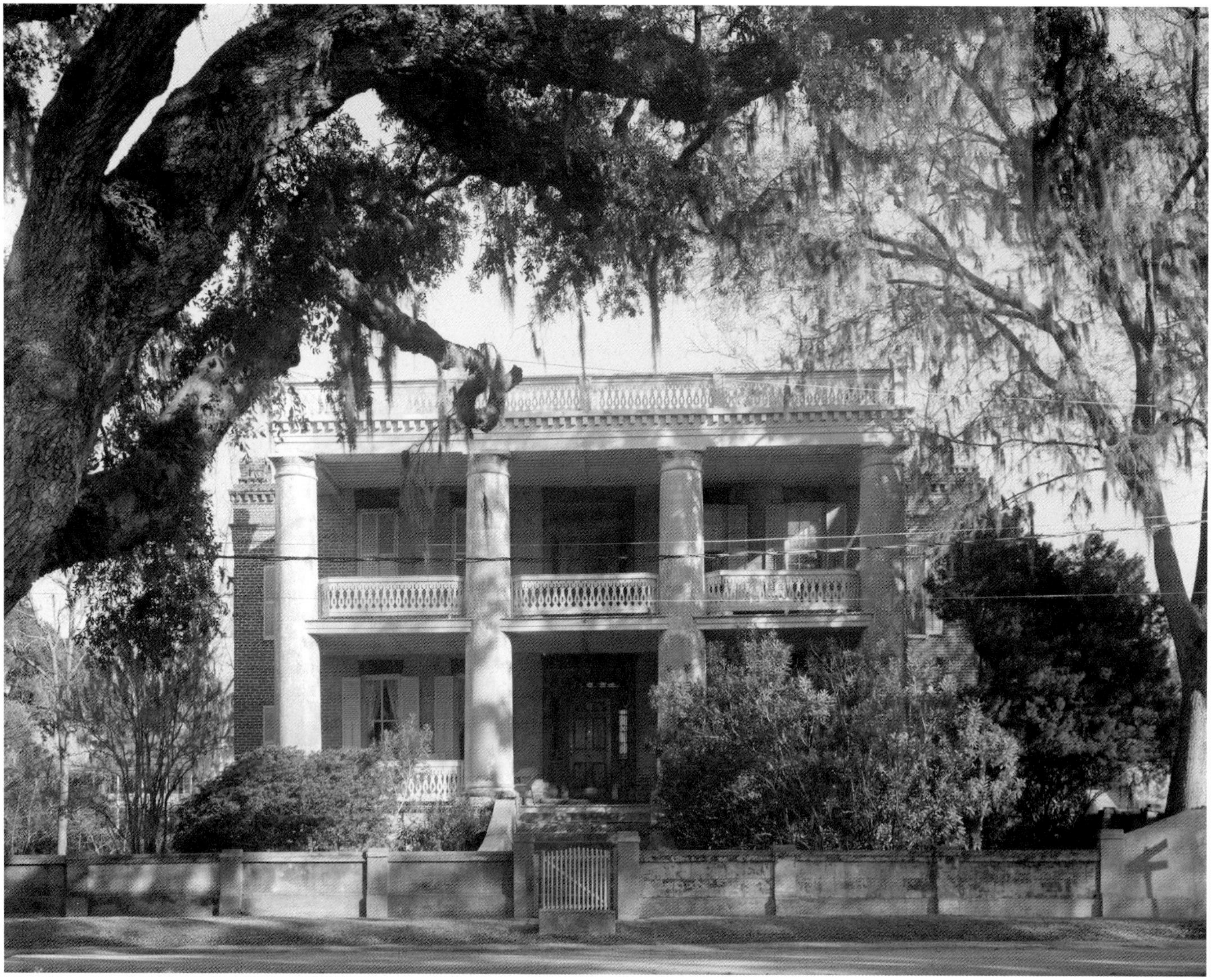

Barnwell Sams House — Charles N. Bayless, 1978 (photo series)

In 1852, the successful planter needed an impressive town house. It was from here he generously practiced medicine on his friends and relatives.

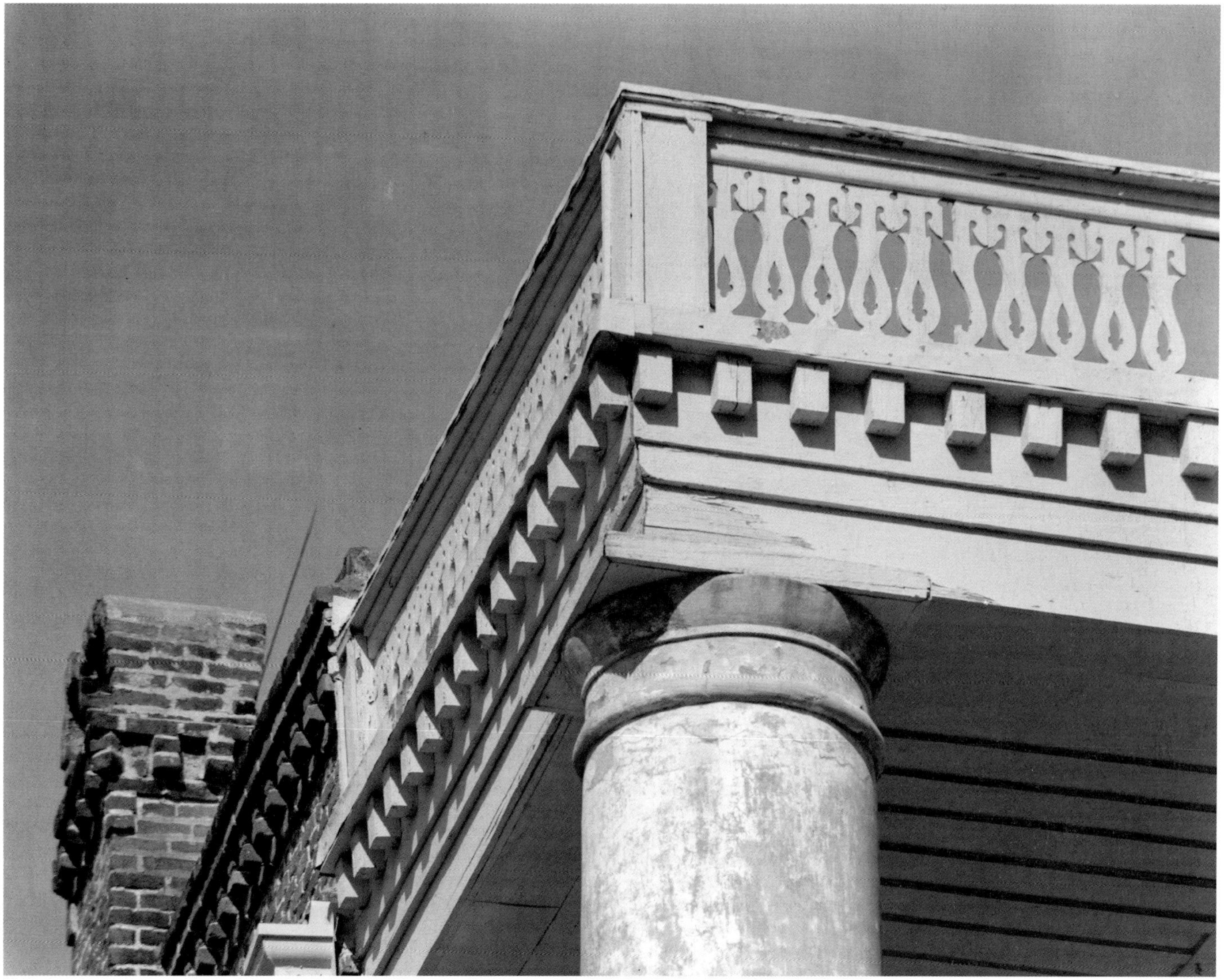

Barnwell Sams House

This great columned brick building is in the Regency style. A detail of the portico.

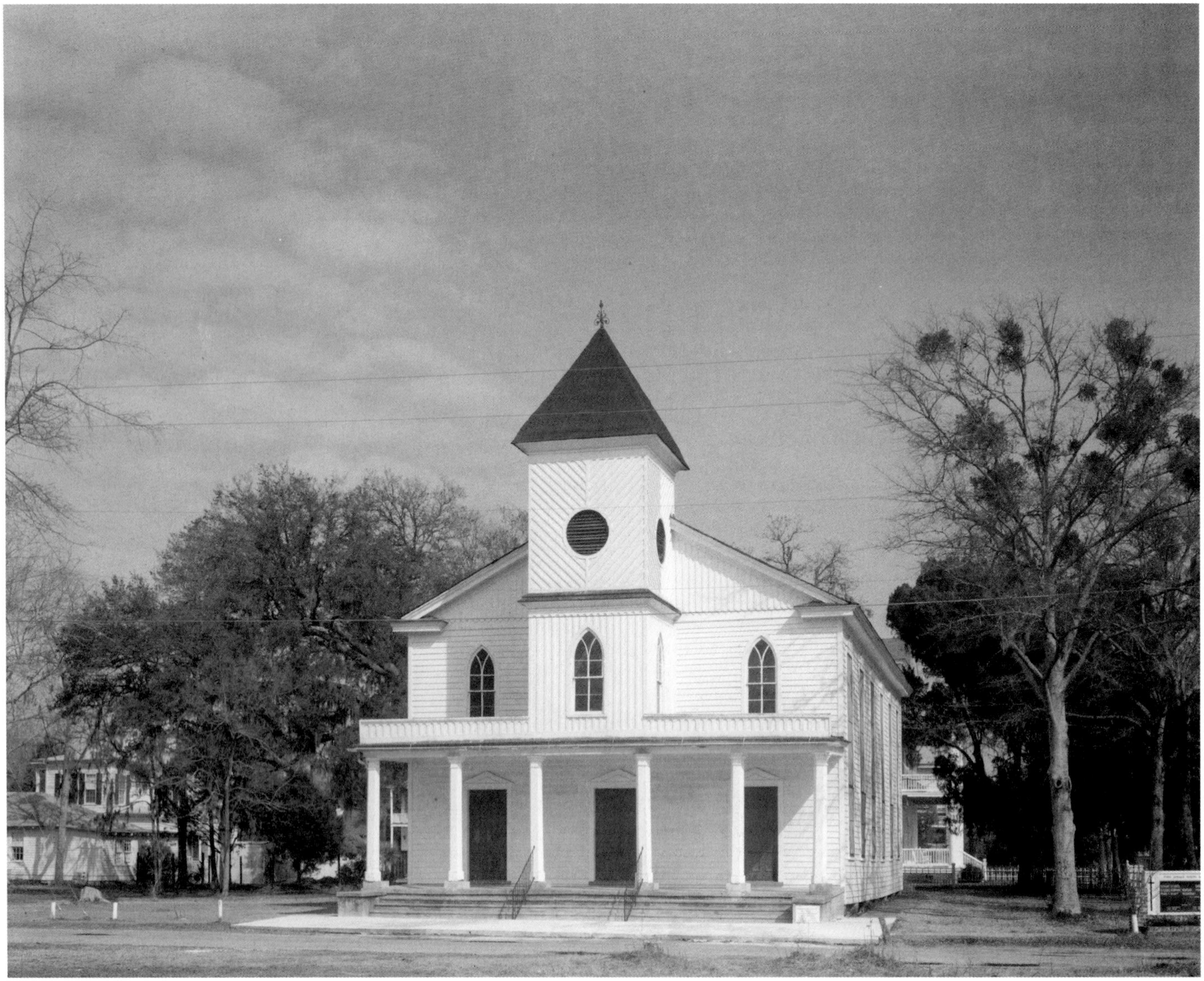

First African Baptist Church — Charles N. Bayless, 1978 (photo series)

Built by freed slaves in 1865, this was originally called "the Praise Church."

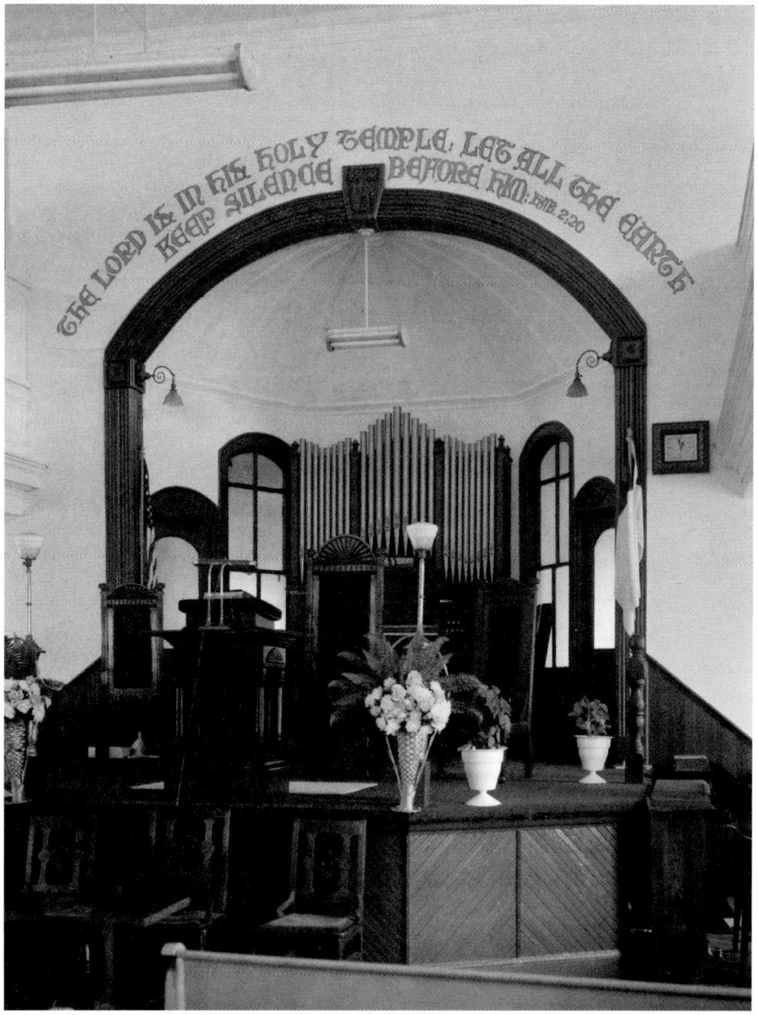

First African Baptist Church

A joyful if reverent invitation.

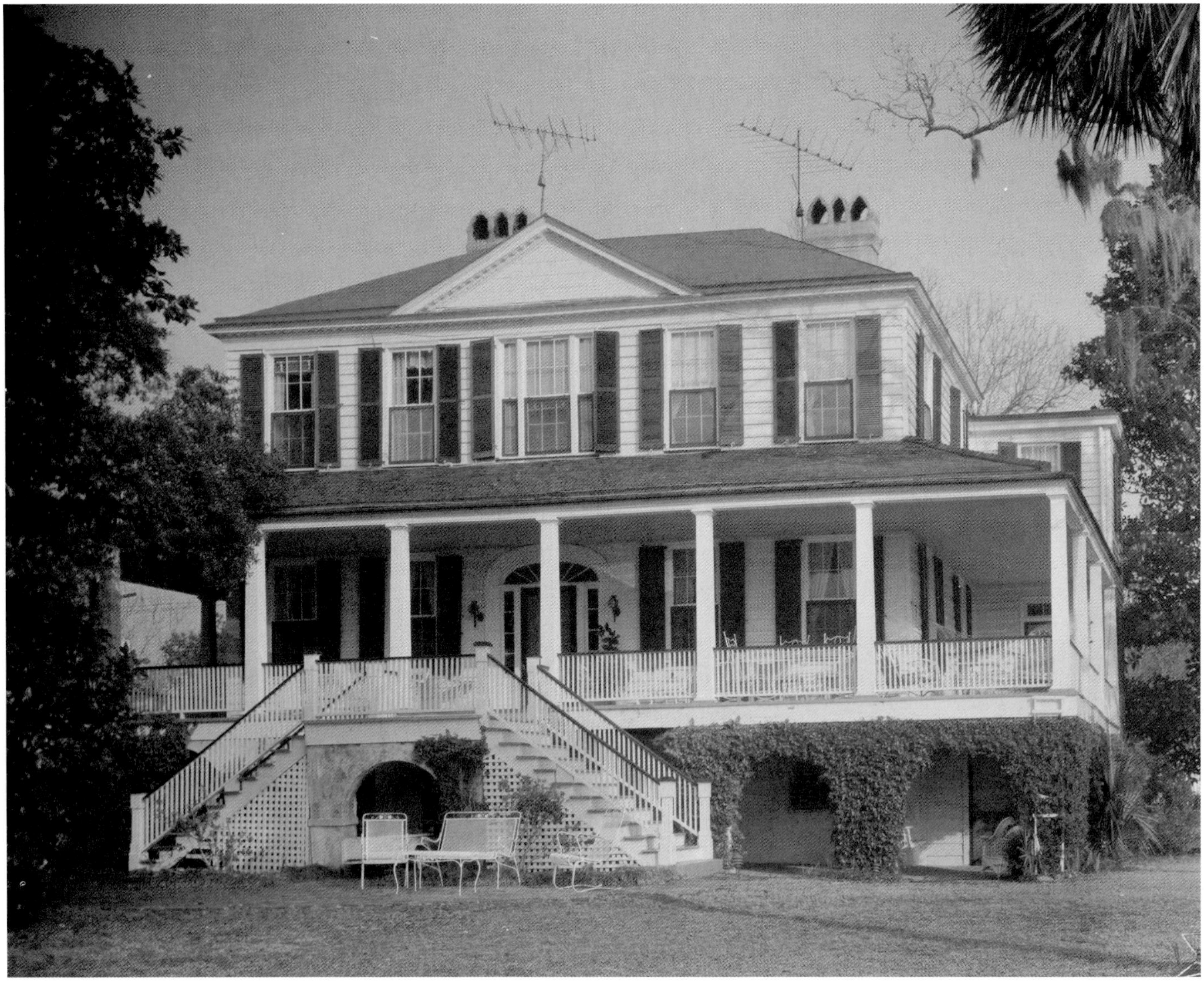

James Robert Verdier House — Charles N. Bayless, 1978 (photo series)

The encircling veranda of this 1814 house is said to show Barbadian influence.

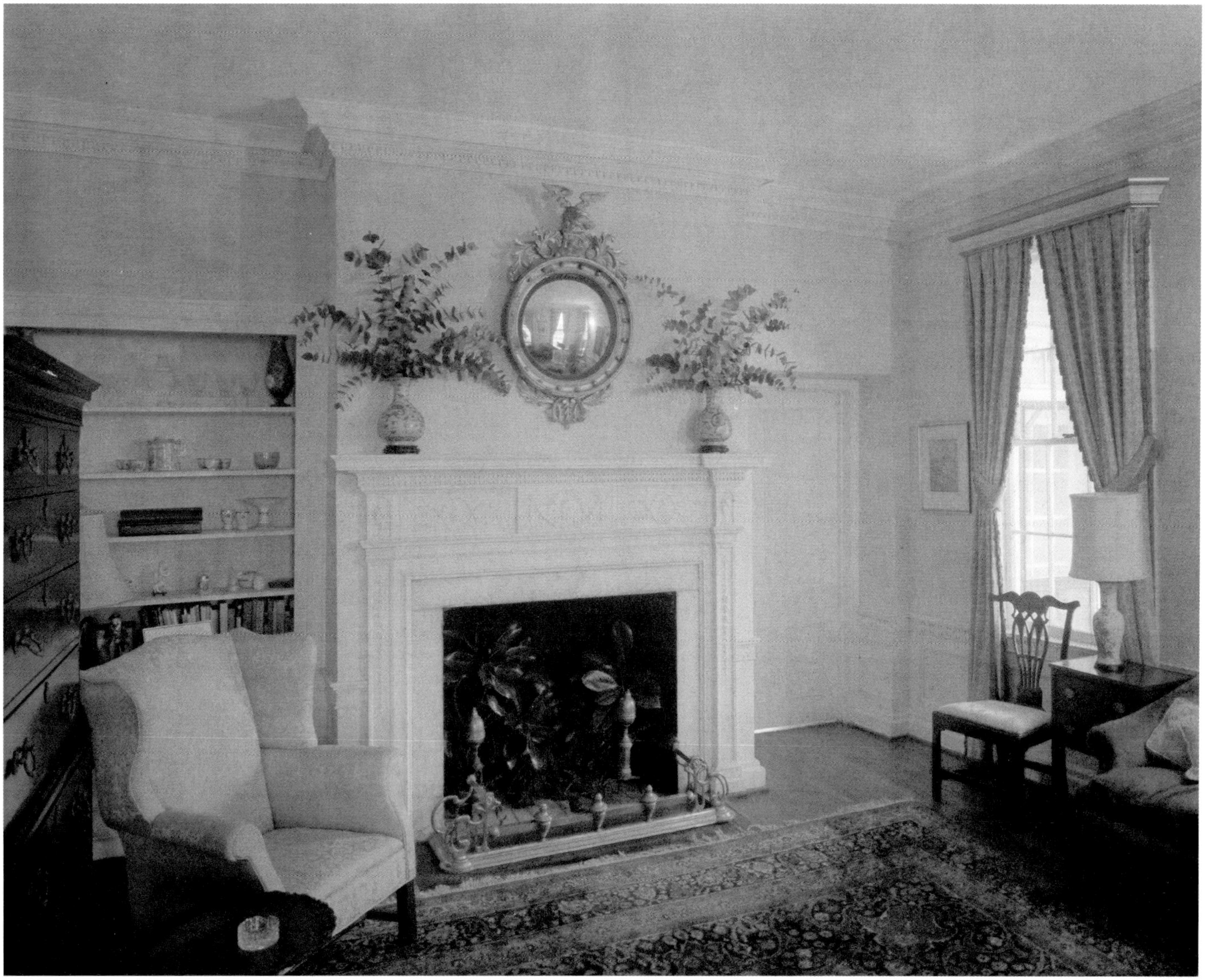

James Robert Verdier House

As with the rest of the house, the mantel and trim are in the Federalist tradition. This is the setting for Griswold's mammoth *A Sea Island Lady*.

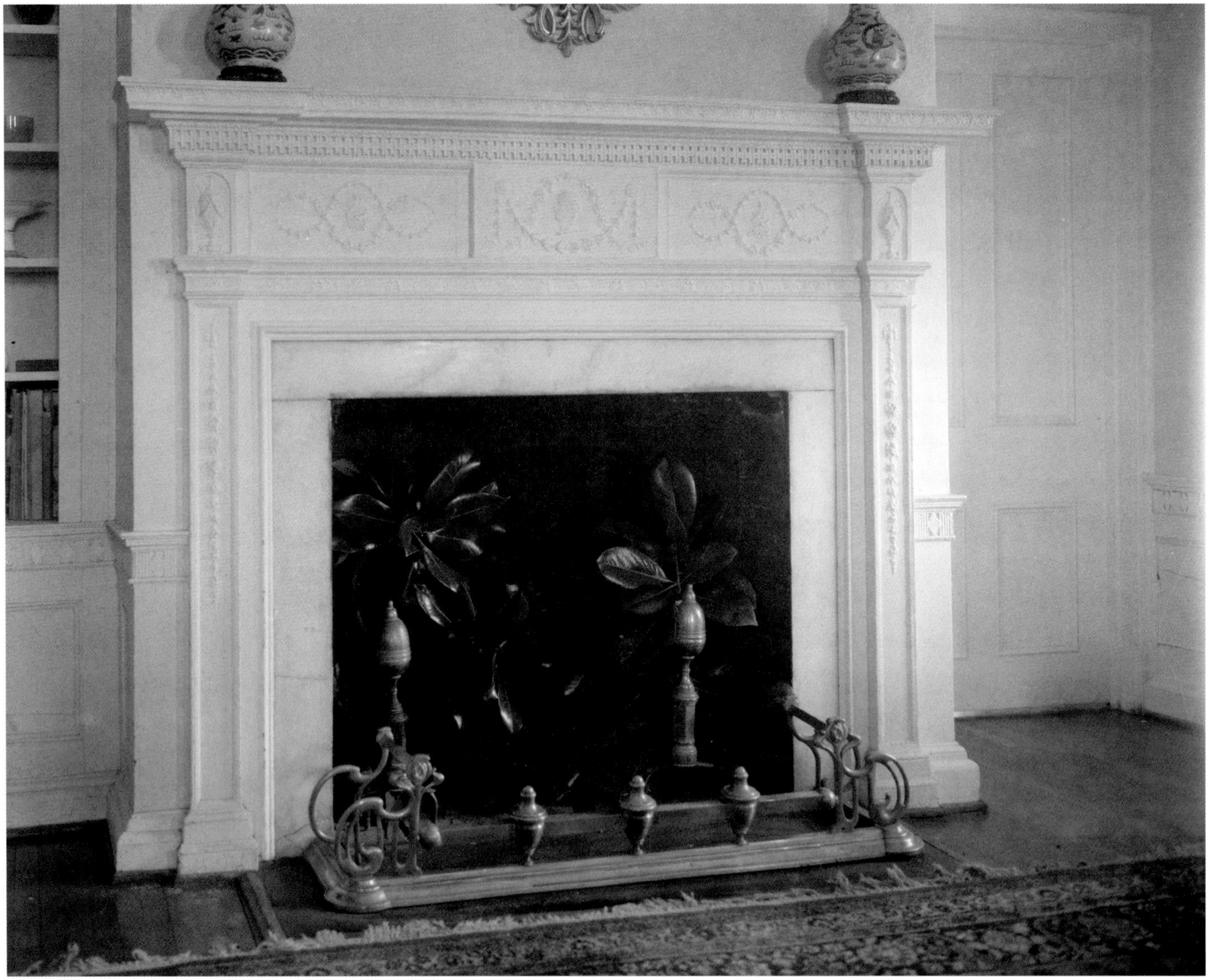

James Robert Verdier House

A detail of the mantel.

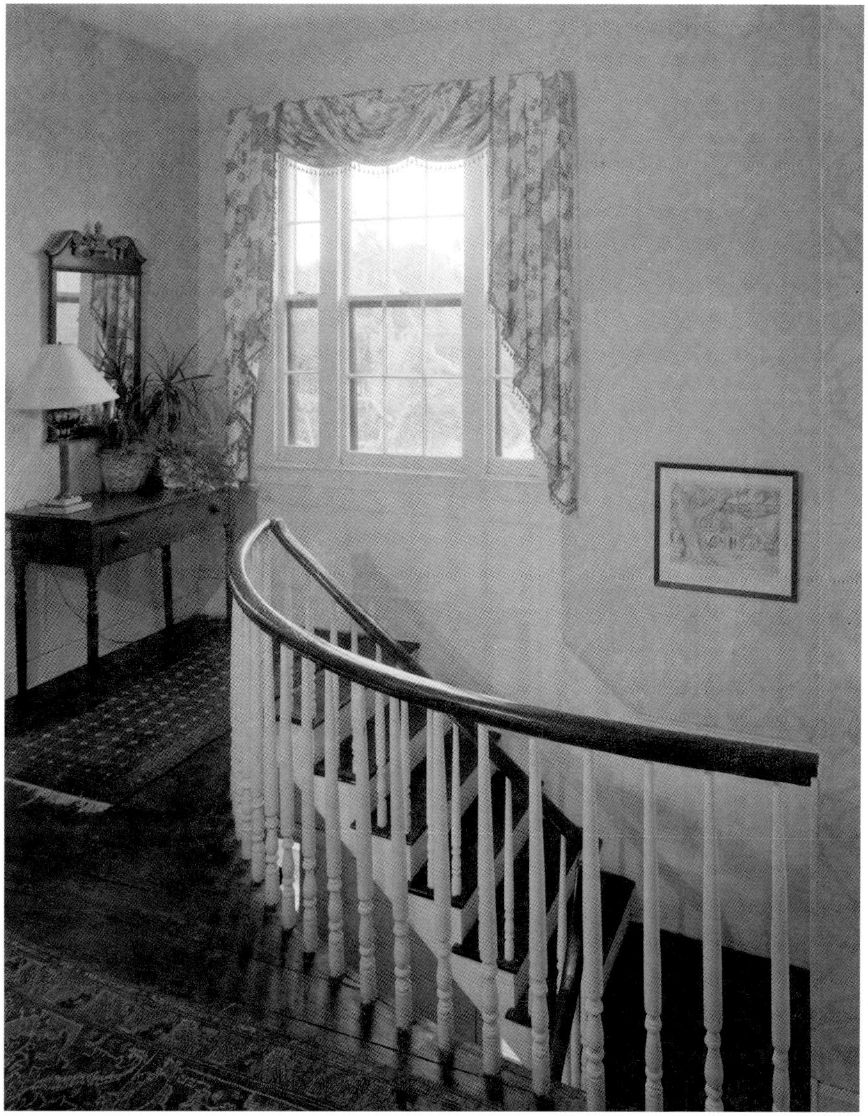

James Robert Verdier House

Dr. Verdier was most noted for his brave work with yellow fever patients.

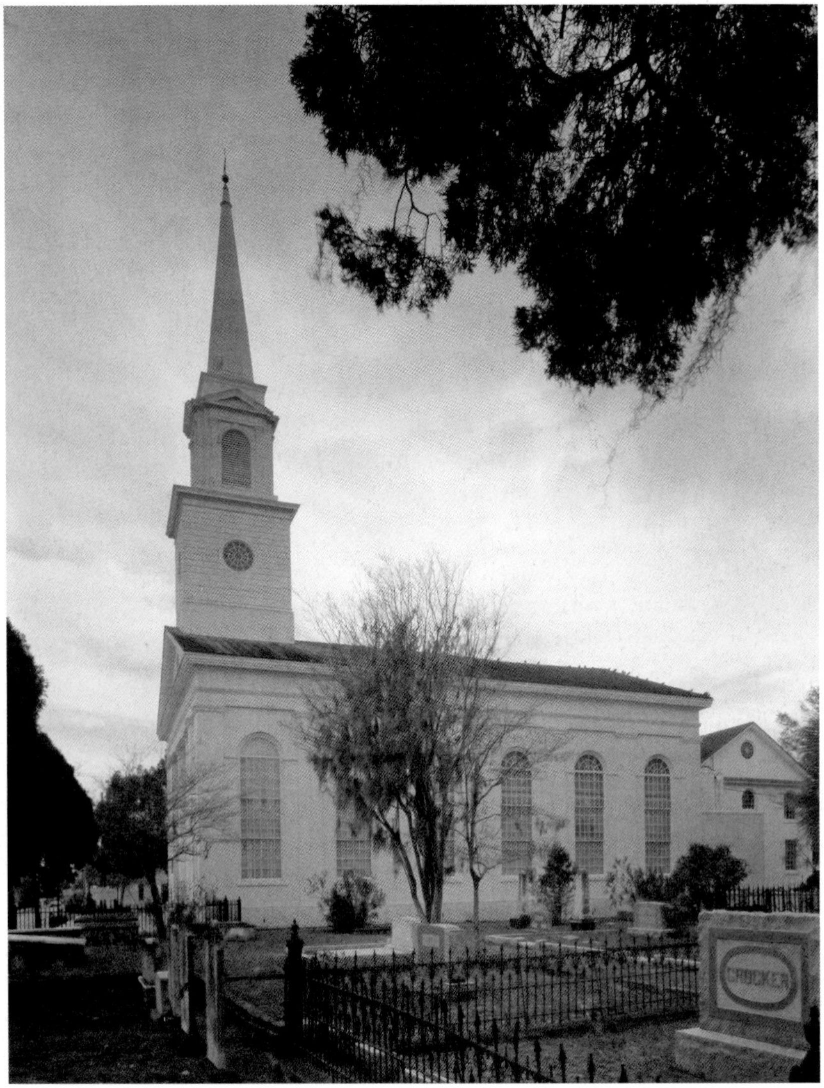

Baptist Church of Beaufort — Charles N. Bayless, 1978 (photo series)

In Beaufort, Sunday was once a day of "boat racing, foot racing, drinking and fighting." But in 1832 a great religious revival swept through. This church was one result.

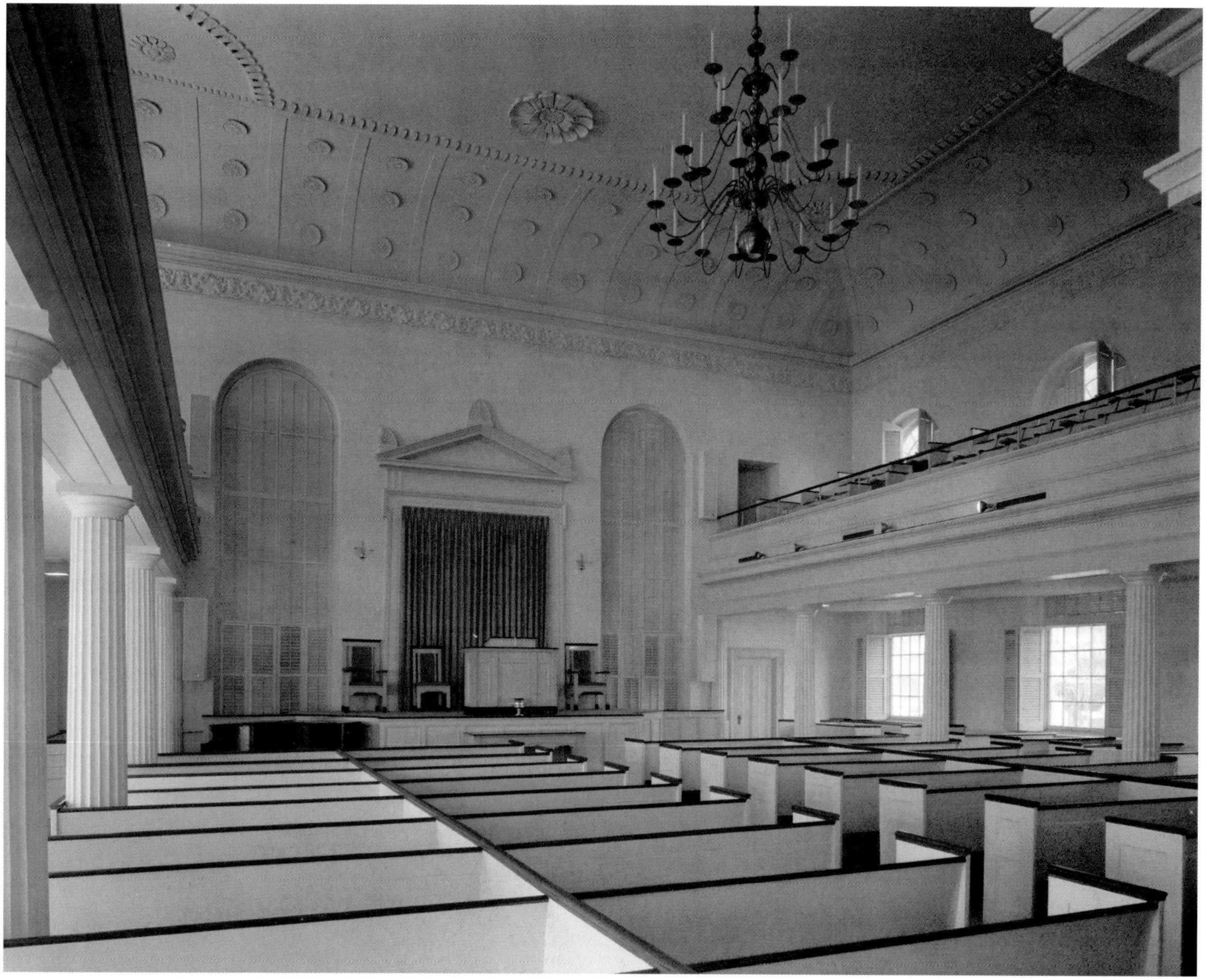

Baptist Church of Beaufort

An early opposition to slavery made for a slow Baptist beginning, but by the time of this 1844 construction, Baptists were in the majority. The church is considered one of the most beautiful in America.

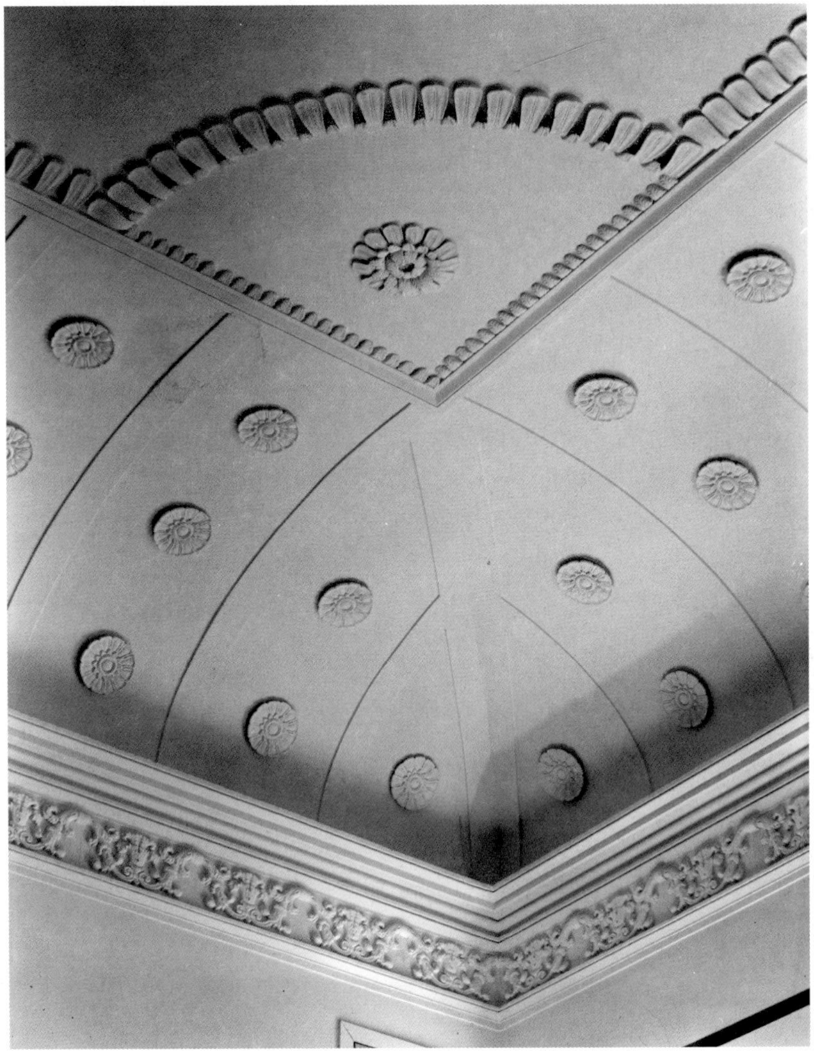

Baptist Church of Beaufort

Cornice and ceiling medallions.

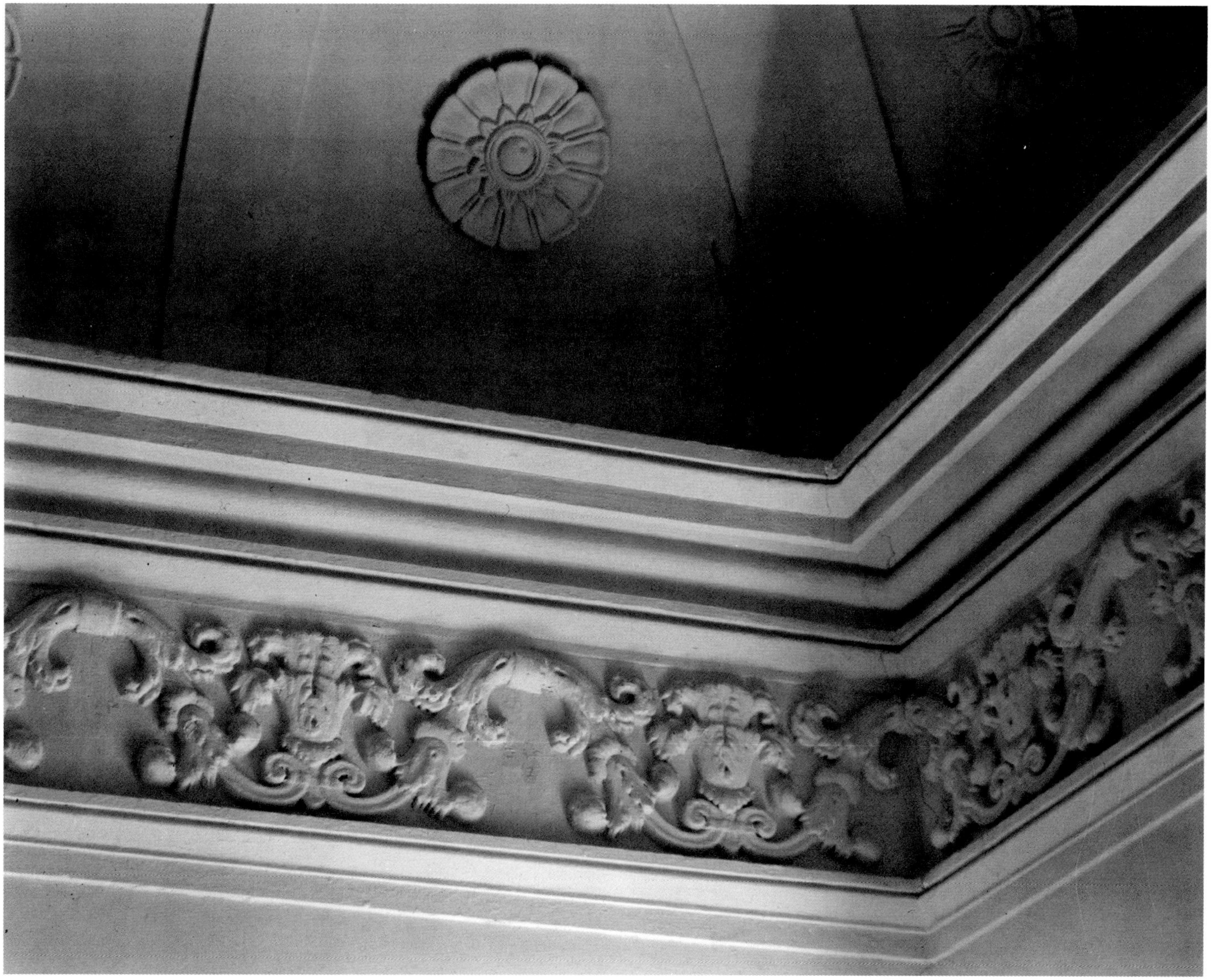

Baptist Church of Beaufort

Detail of the cornice.

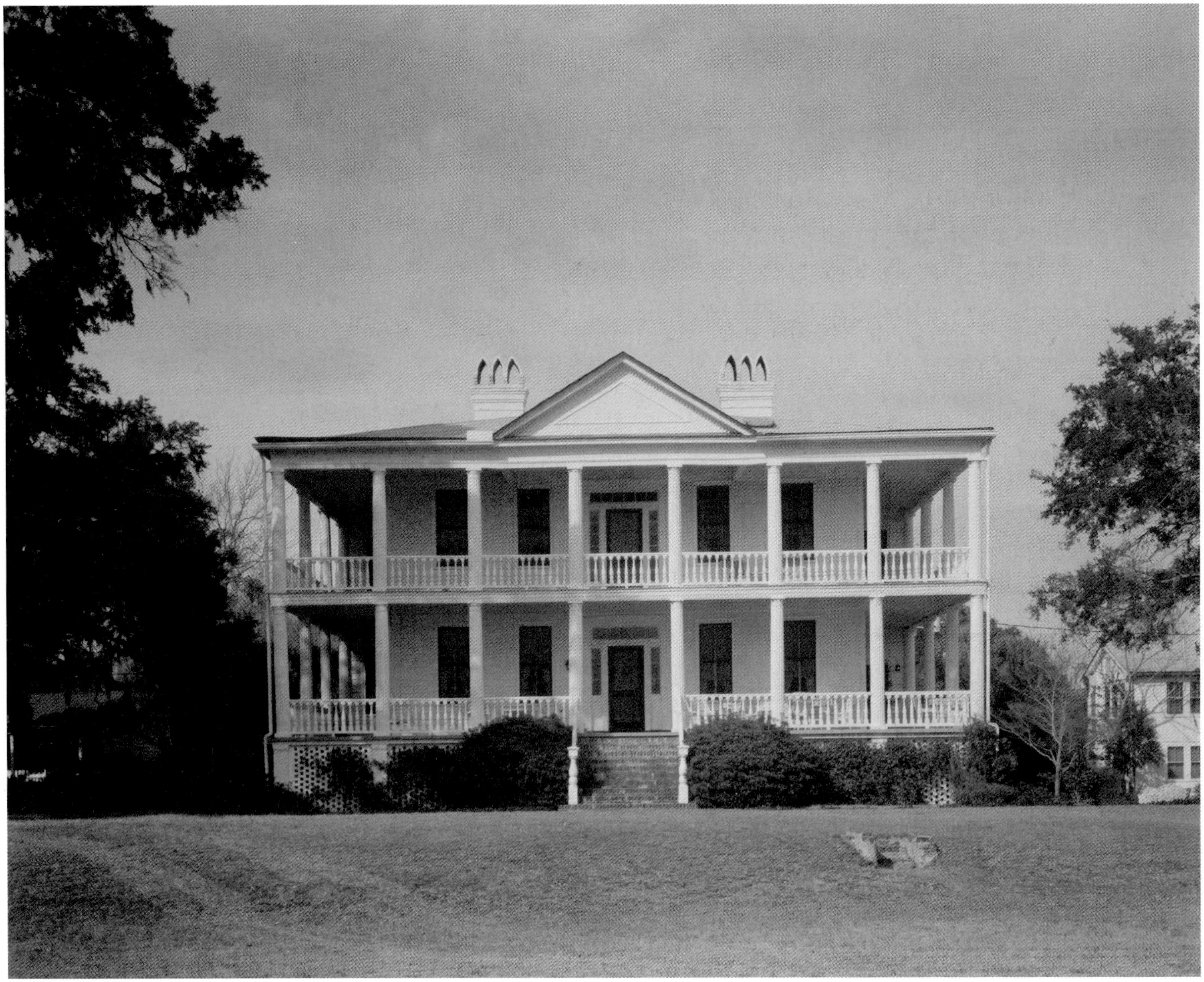

Mosse Stoney House Charles N. Bayless, 1978 (photo series)

Built in 1825, this house with its surrounding piazzas offers a perfect view of the river.

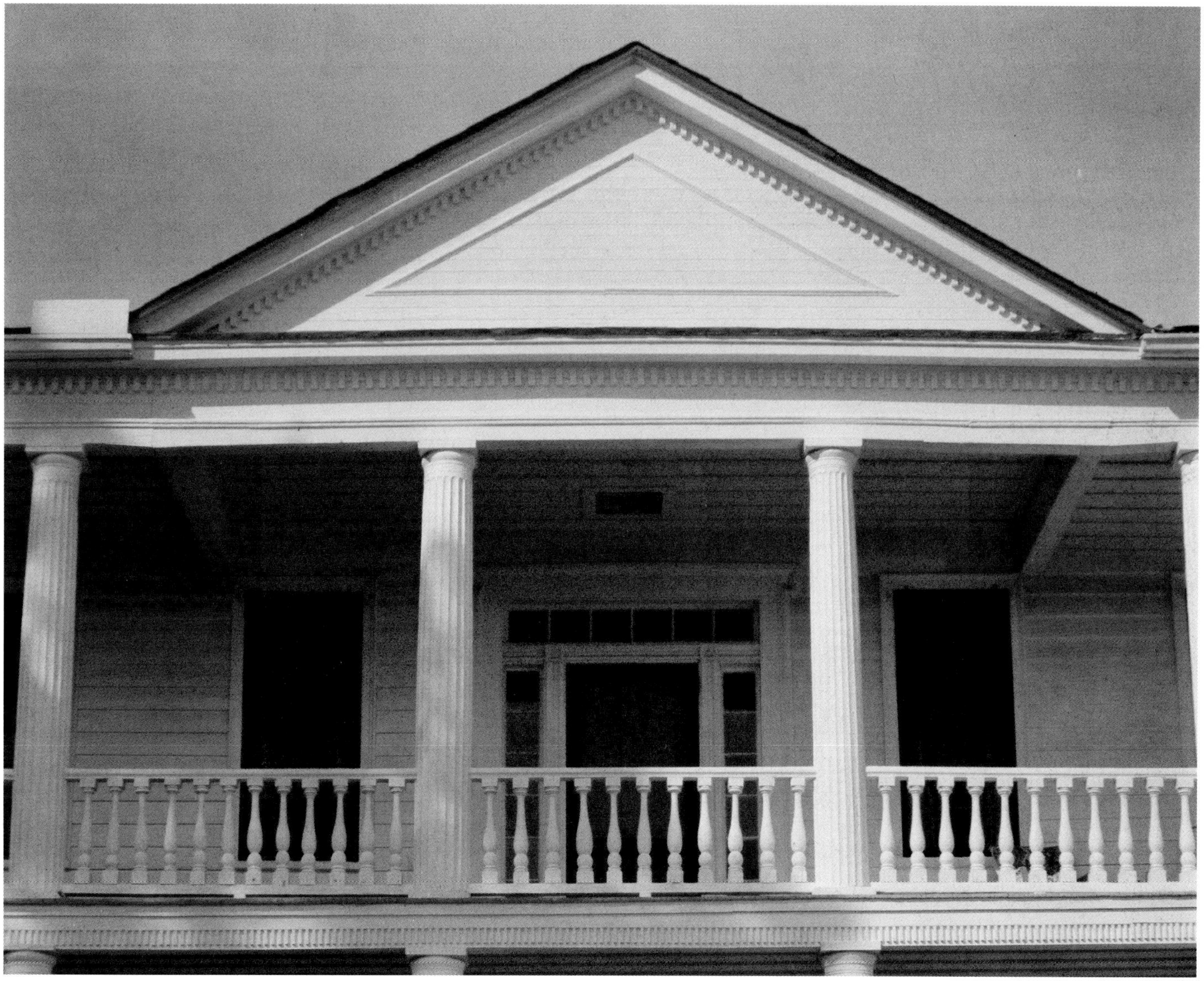

Mosse Stoney House

Portico detail: Doric order columns and turned balustrades.

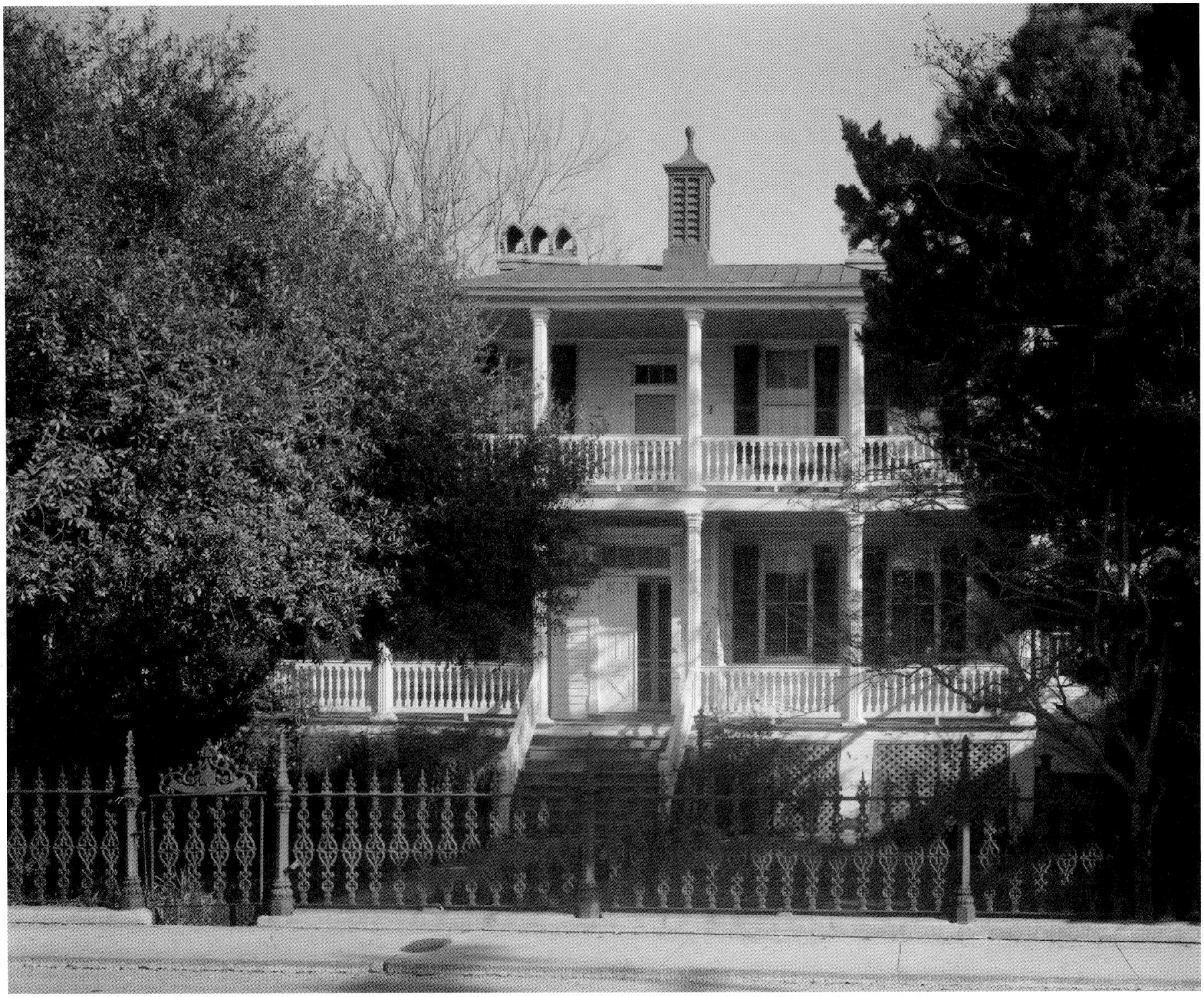

Lucius Cuthbert House — Charles N. Bayless, 1978 (photo series)

Cuthbert was here in 1820, but in a much smaller version of the house. The second-story veranda and cupola were added in 1876, along with the wrought-iron fence.

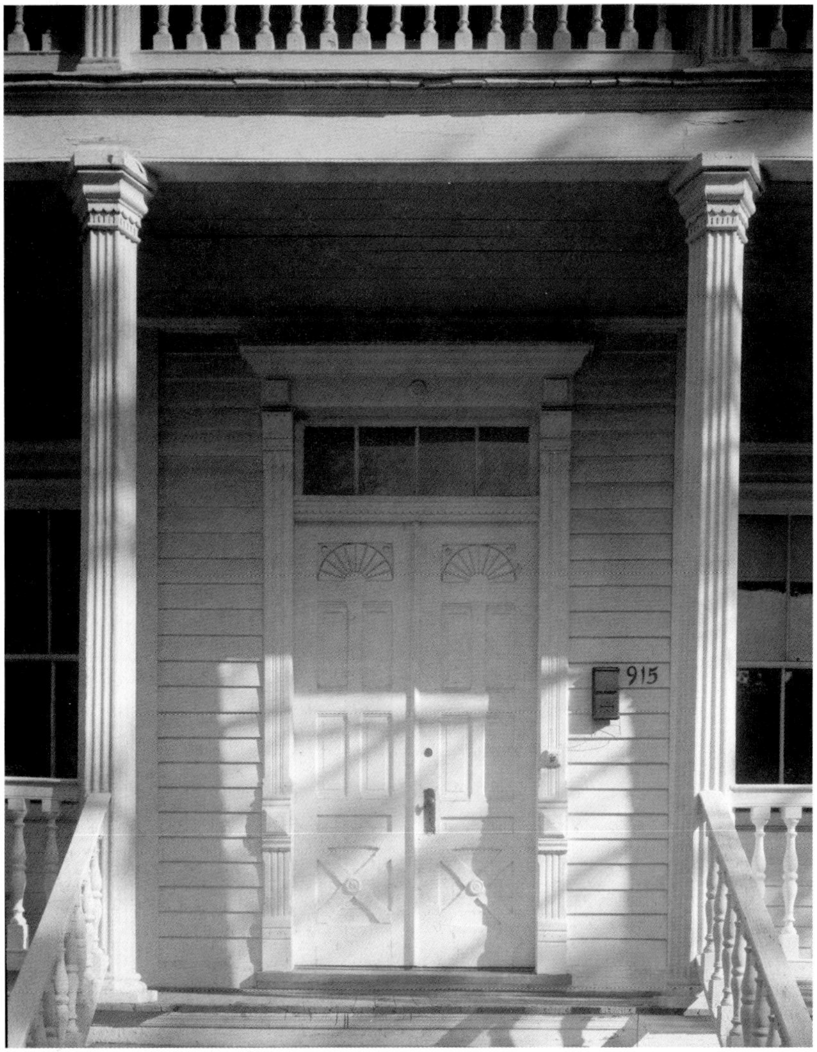

Lucius Cuthbert House

This handsome entry was also the product of renovation.

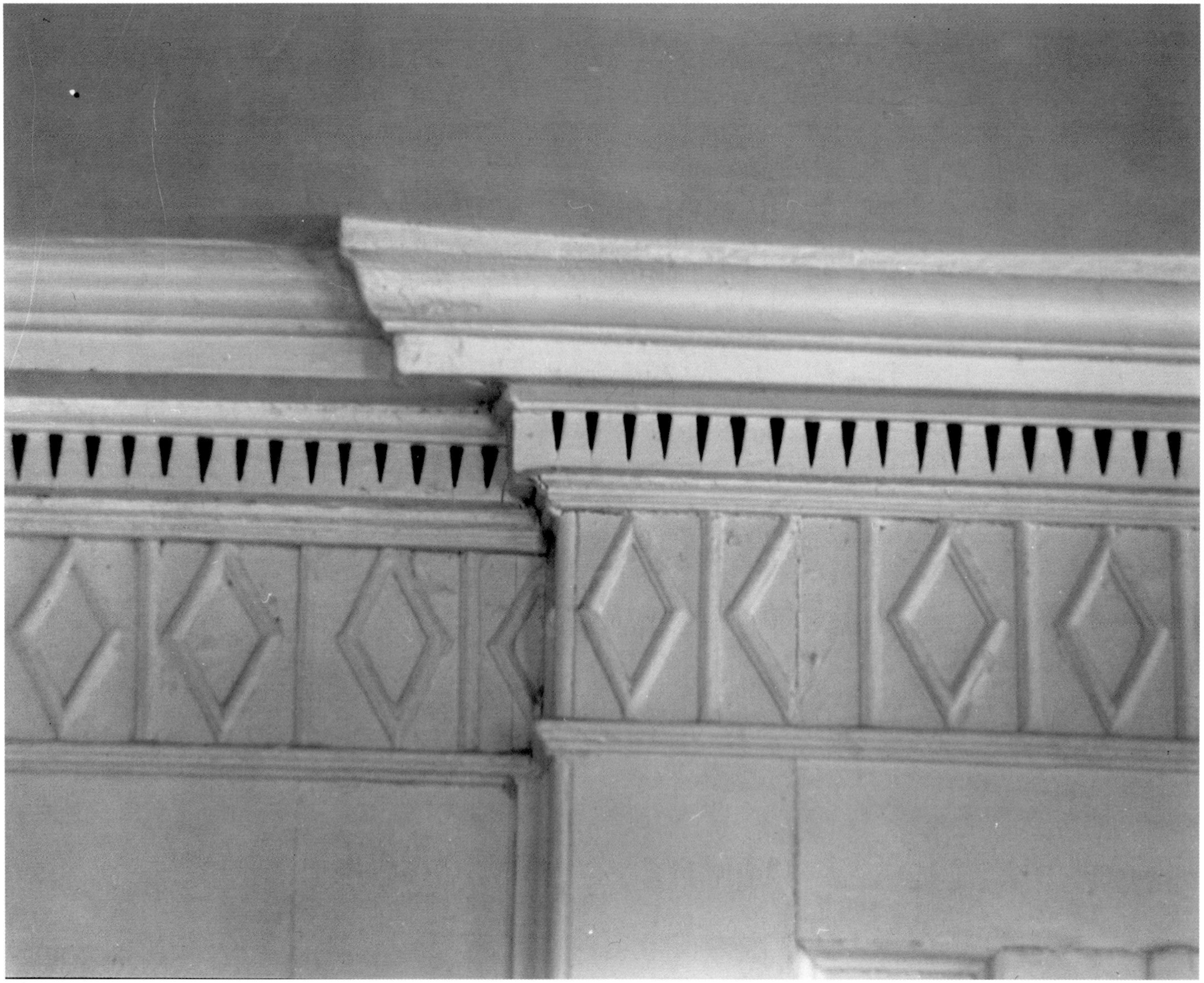

Lucius Cuthbert House

Interior detailing.

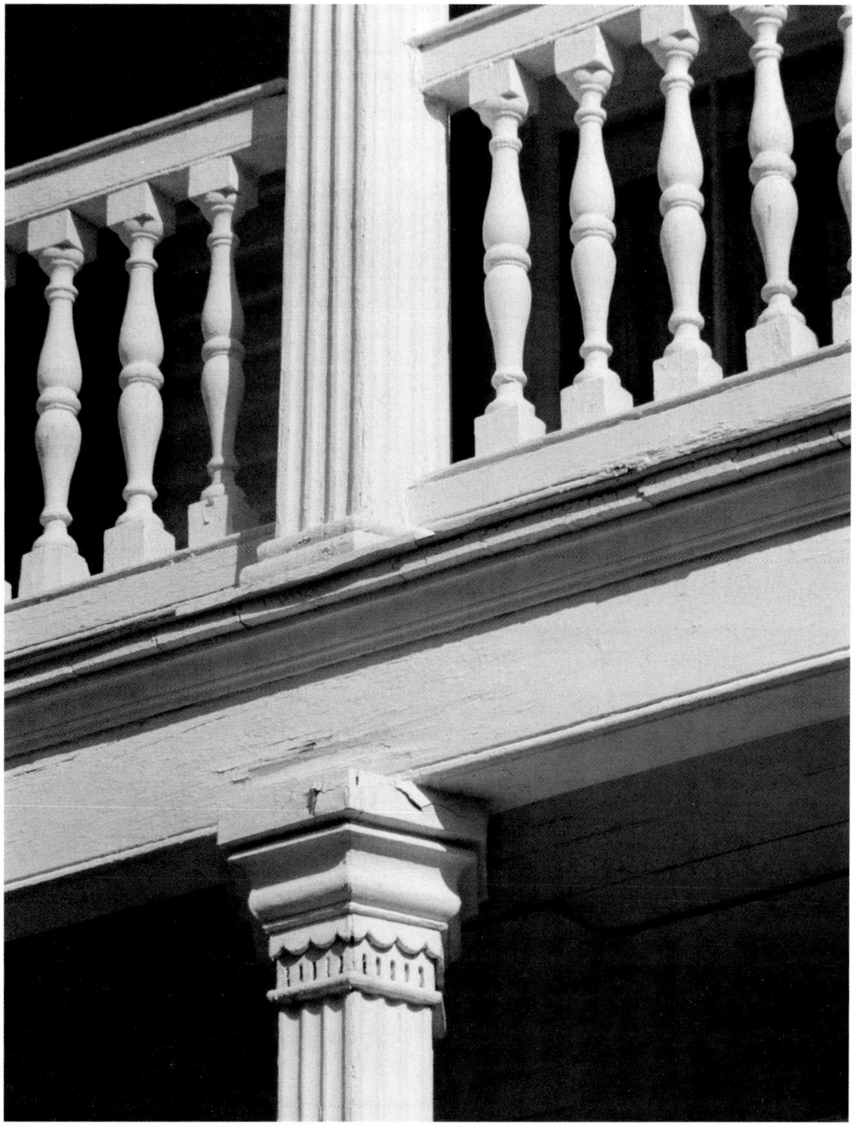

Lucius Cuthbert House

Exterior detailing.

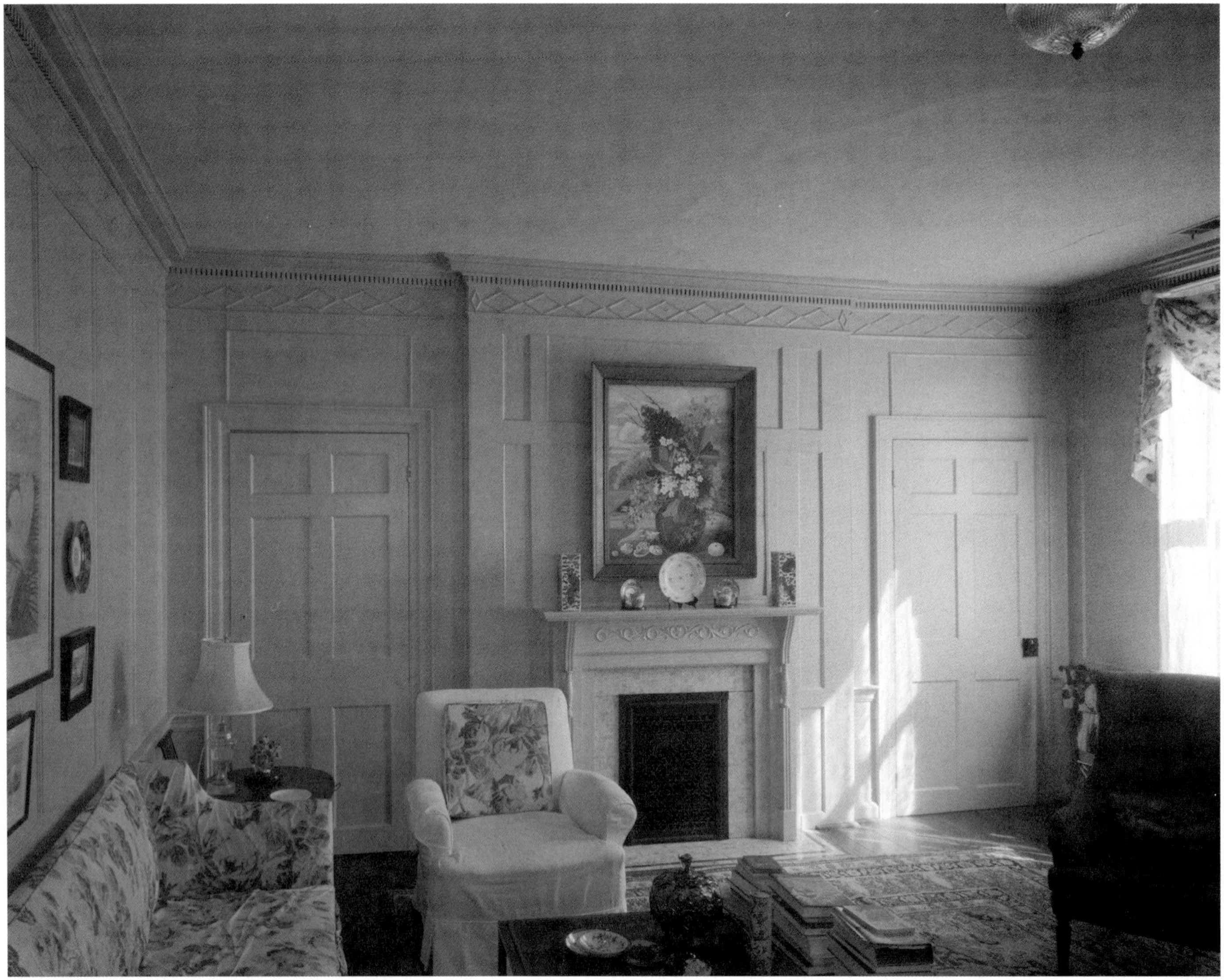

Lucius Cuthbert House

The Federal forces used the house for a bakery. I sense the ghosts of flour-dusted fresh bread. Yankee cinnamon buns.

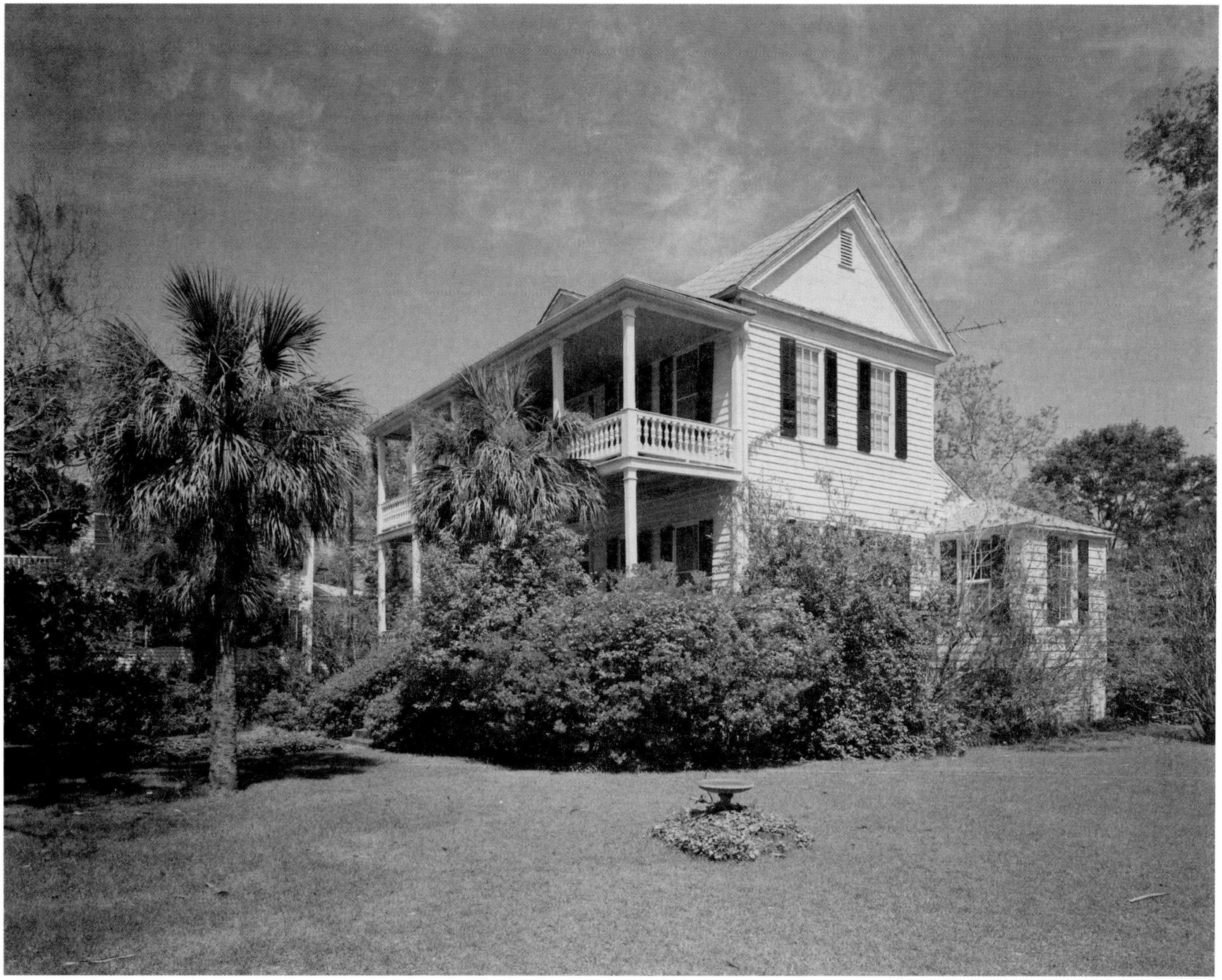

McKee Smalls House — Charles N. Bayless, 1978 (photo series)

Built in 1834 by Henry McKee, this Federalist-style house enjoys larger-than-life Greek Revival proportions. Renowned slave pilot Robert Smalls was born in a cabin on the property and owned the main house following the war.

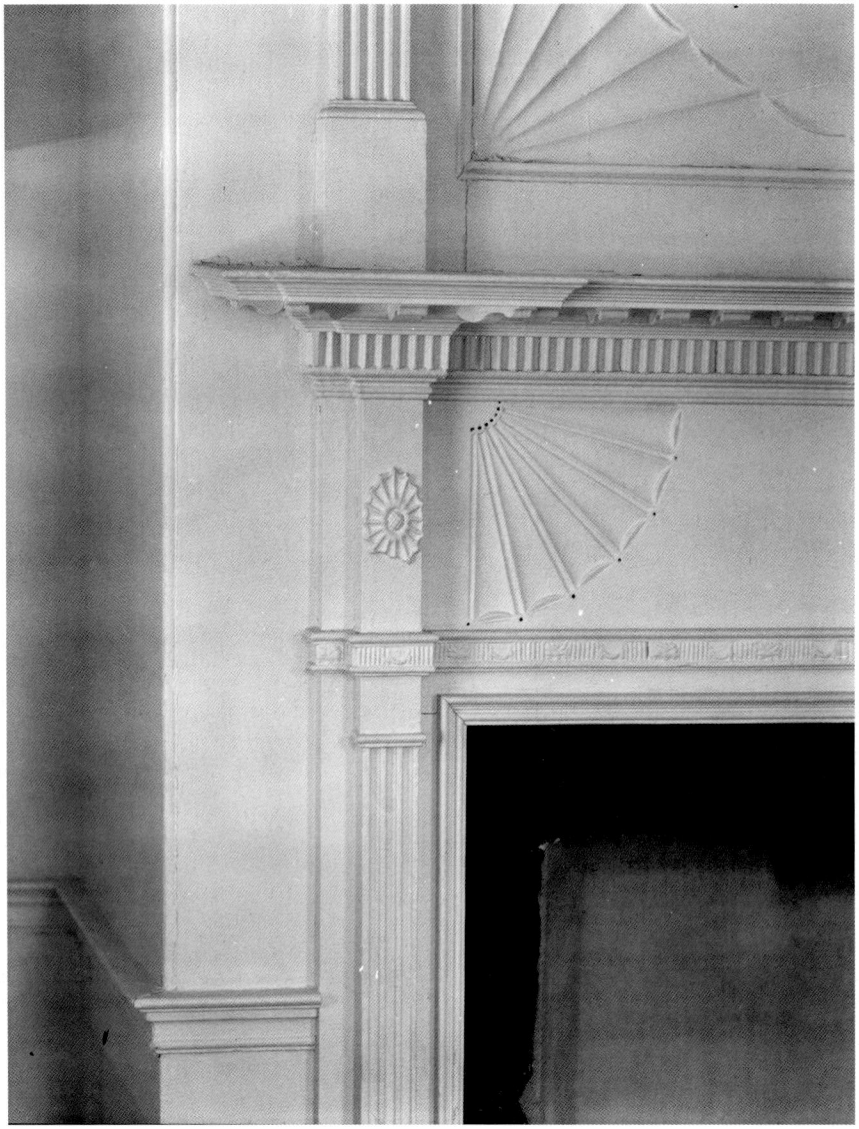

McKee Smalls House

Detail of the mantel. A graceful blend of eighteenth- and nineteenth-century decoration.

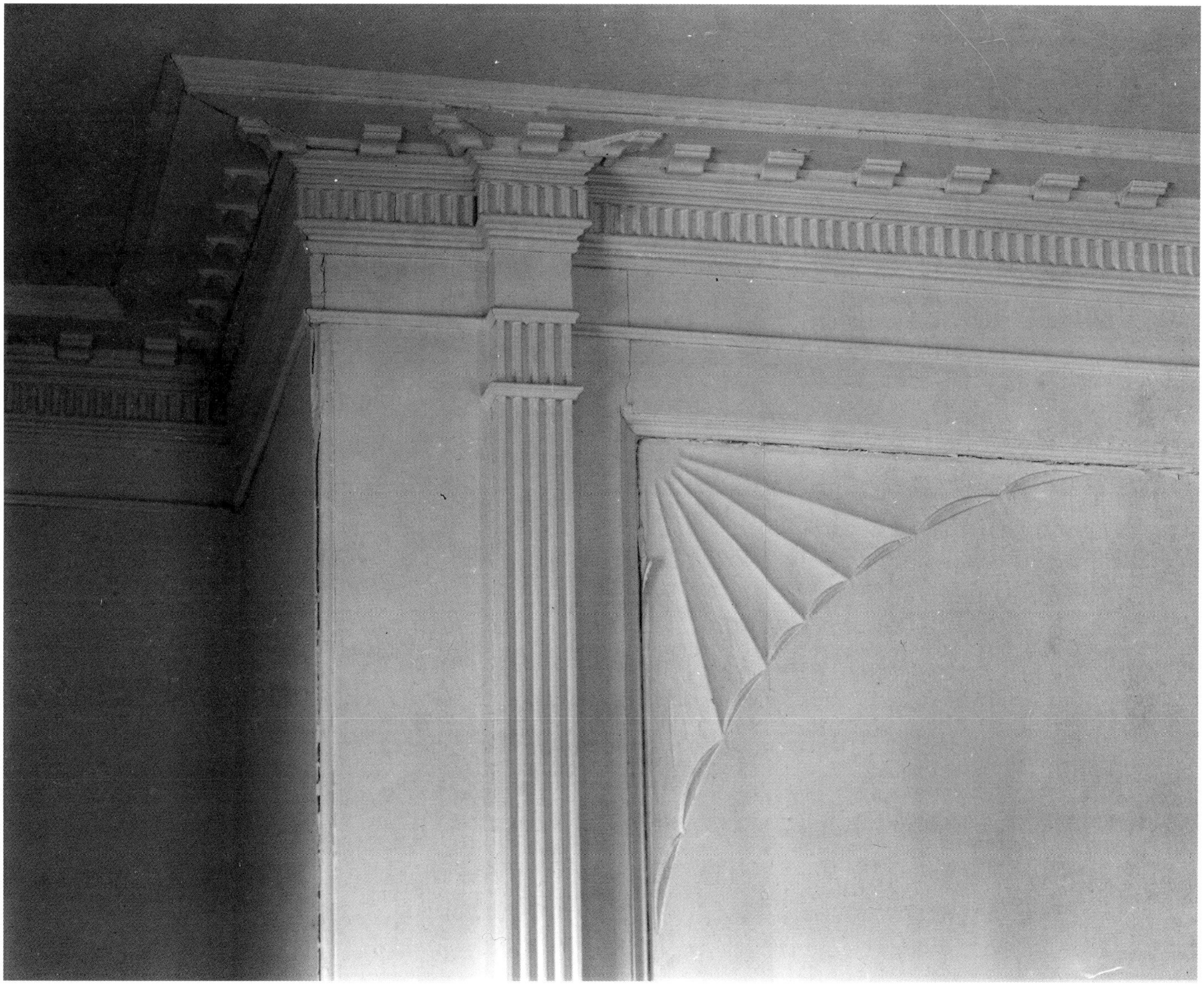

McKee Smalls House

Closer detail.

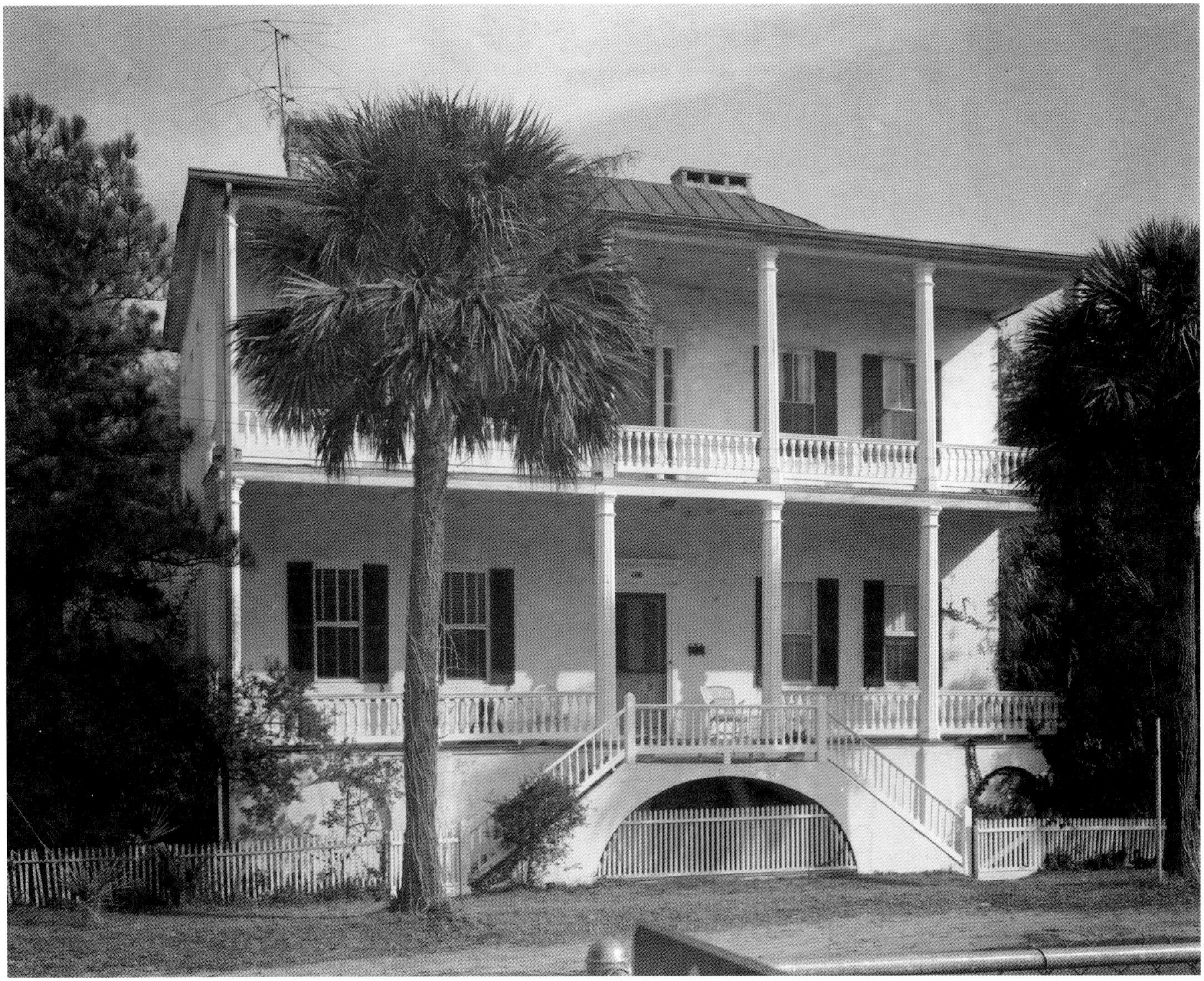

Fraser House Charles N. Bayless, 1978 (photo series)

Graceful lines.

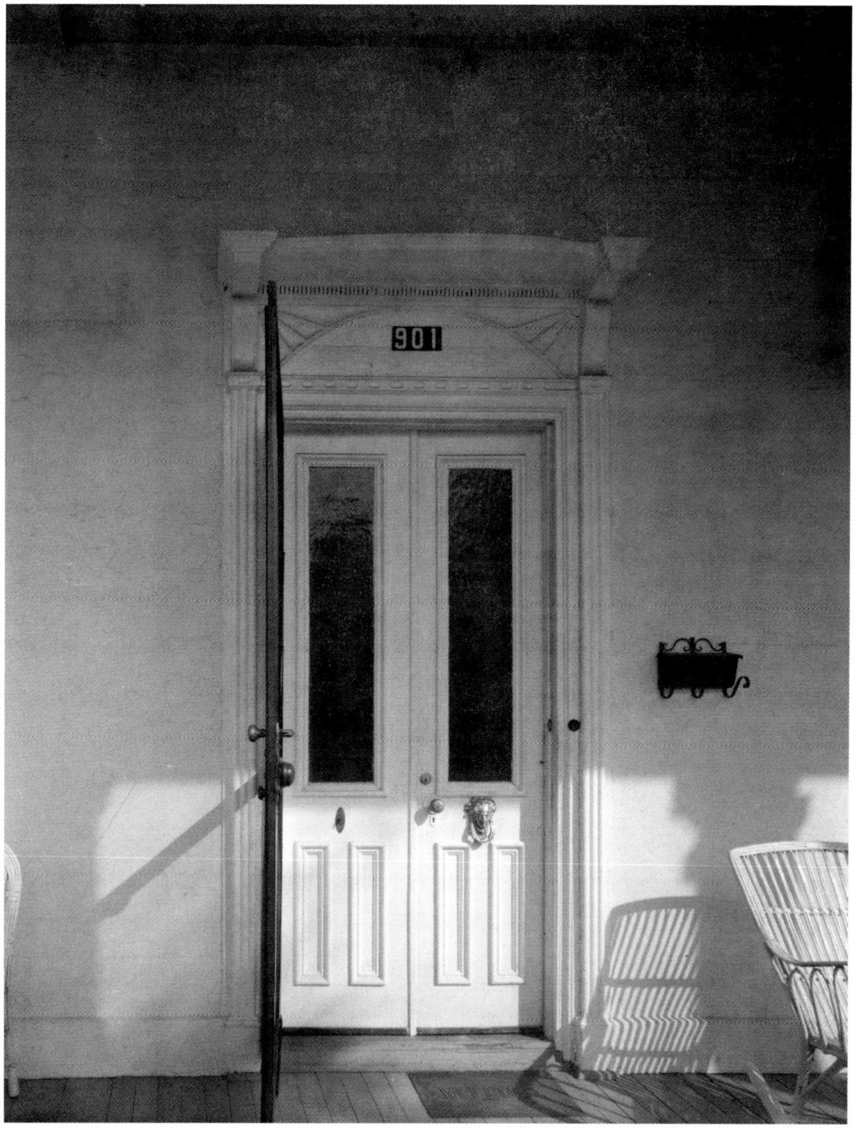

Fraser House

A simple entry.

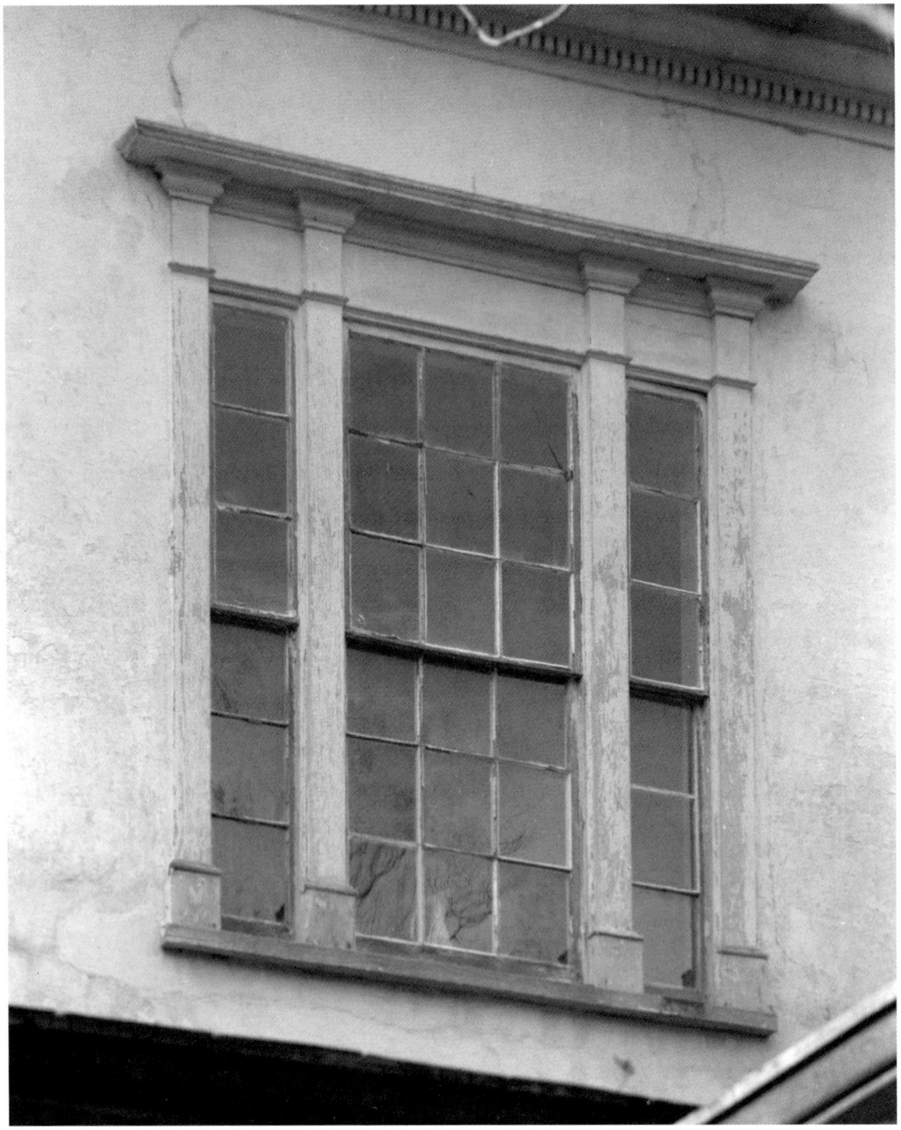

Fraser House

A typical triple window.

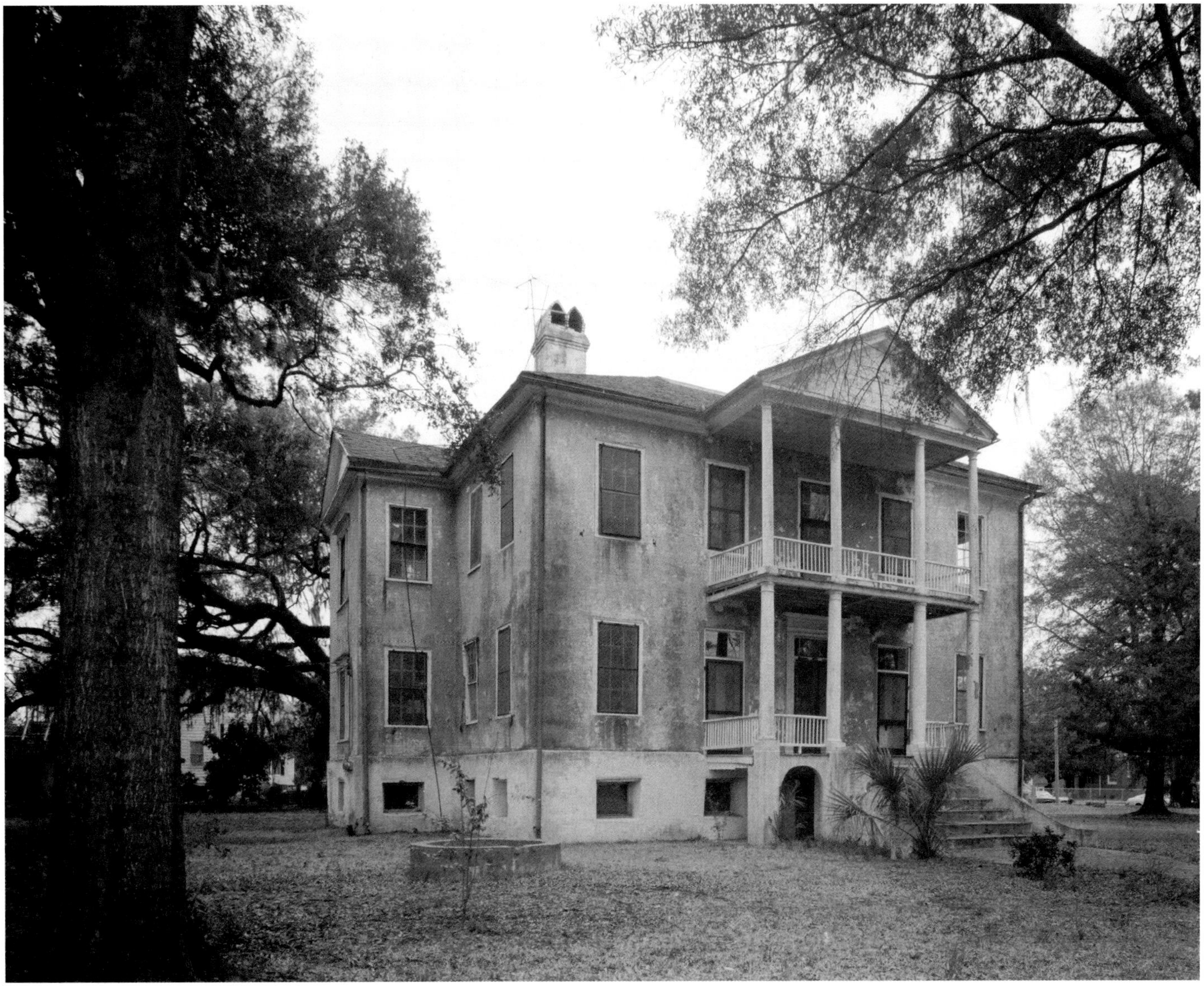

BARNWELL-GOUGH HOUSE — Charles N. Bayless, 1978 (photo series)

Built in the 1780s. Not the first house to be built of tabby, but the first in Beaufort to use the T shape. Note the projections to the rear.

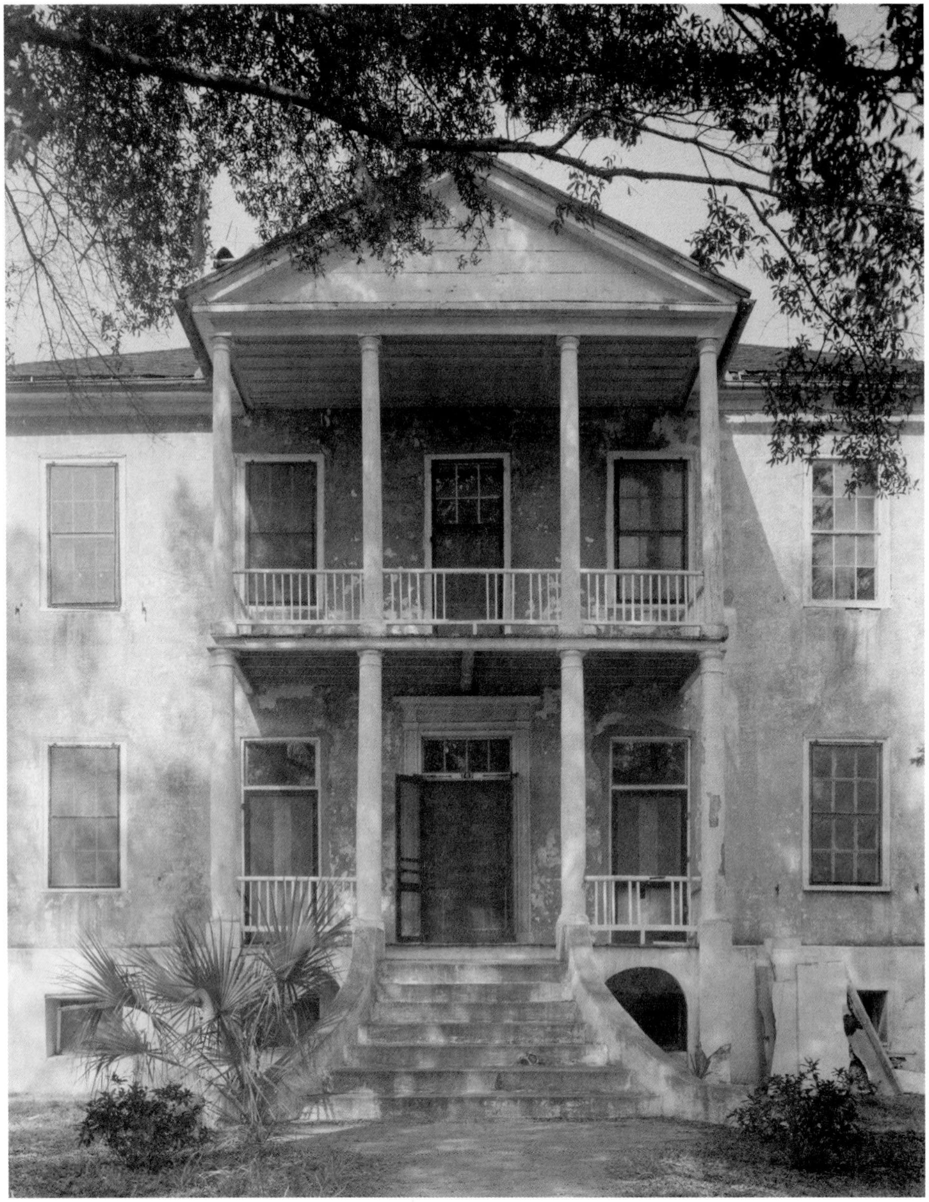

Barnwell-Gough House

"A temple like entry portico," says the HABS.

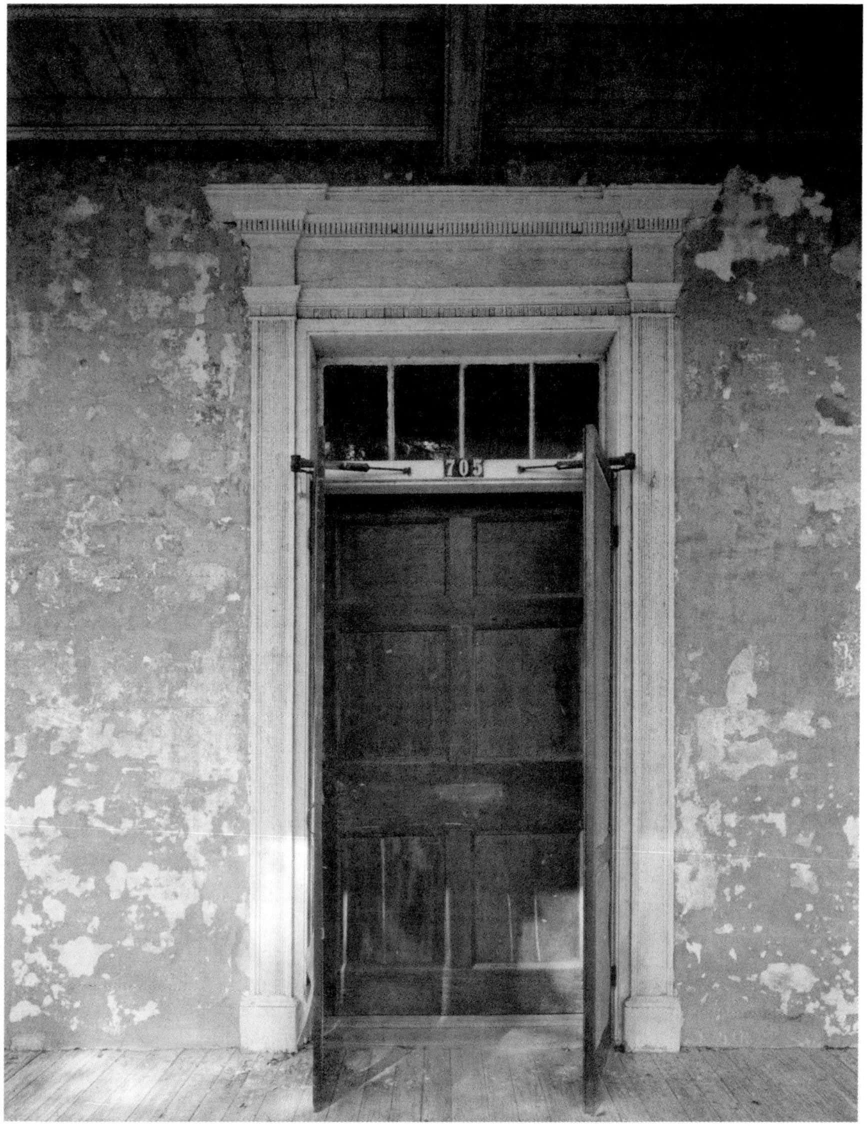

BARNWELL-GOUGH HOUSE

Elizabeth Barnwell married Mr. Gough while in London, but the relationship was a stormy one. Her father built this house for her and made certain the husband wouldn't inherit the *Barnwell* house.

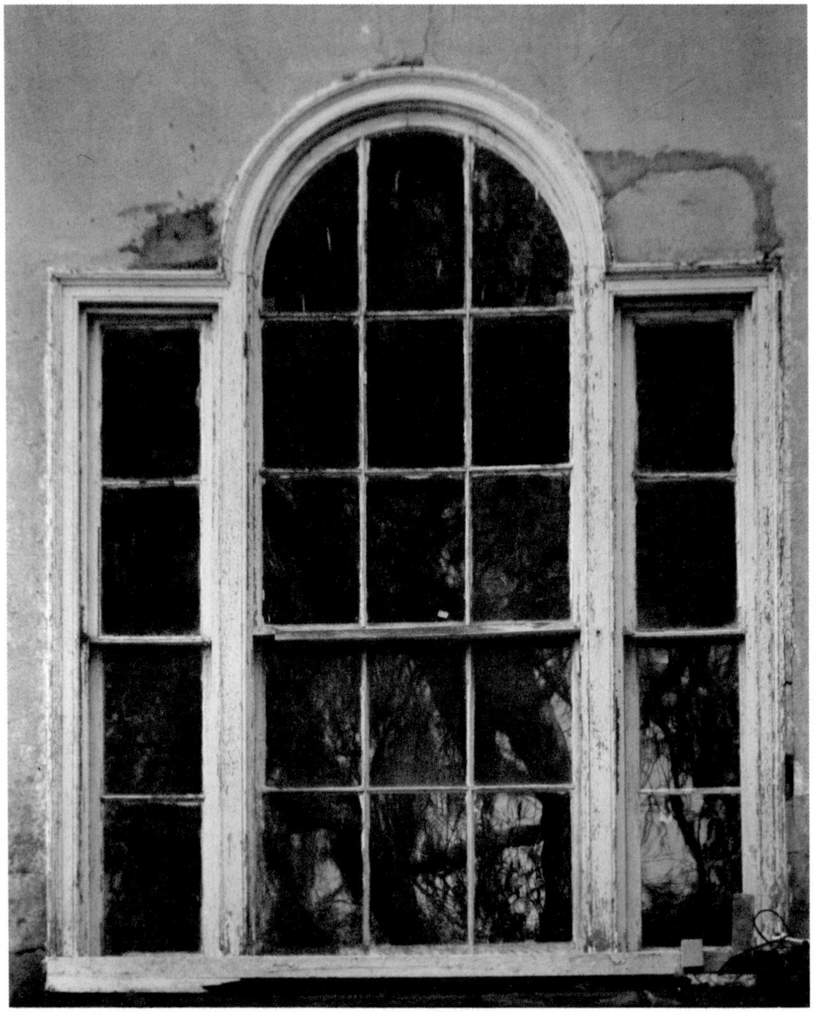

Barnwell-Gough House

Georgia photographer Elizabeth Turk and I used this image in an earlier HABS book. She said, "Tannic…the reflection is like that on dark swamp water and the waves of the old glass add to that perception. Disorienting. What's up? What's down? In? Out?"

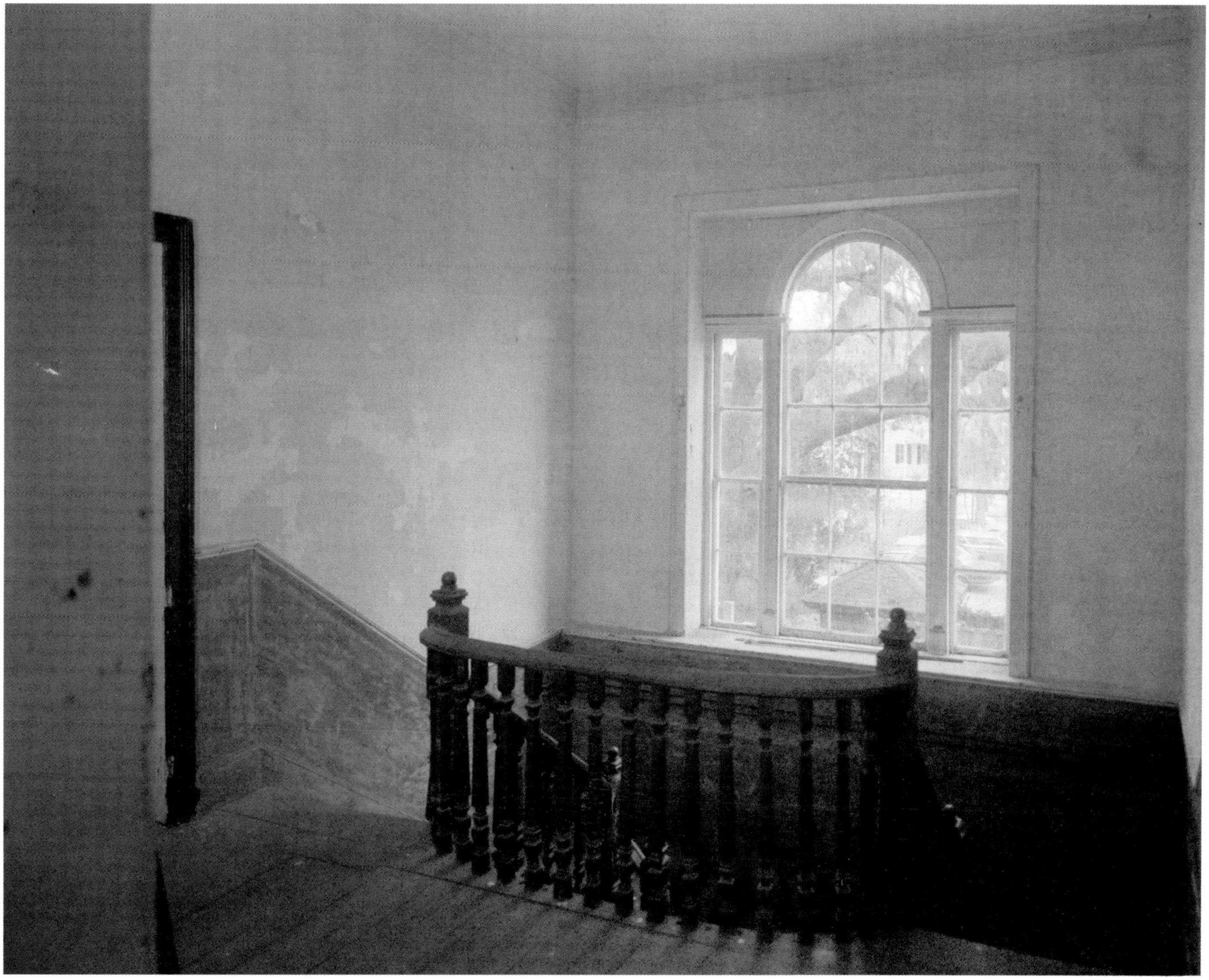

Barnwell-Gough House

The original mahogany rails "disappeared" during Union occupation. This is a Victorian replacement.

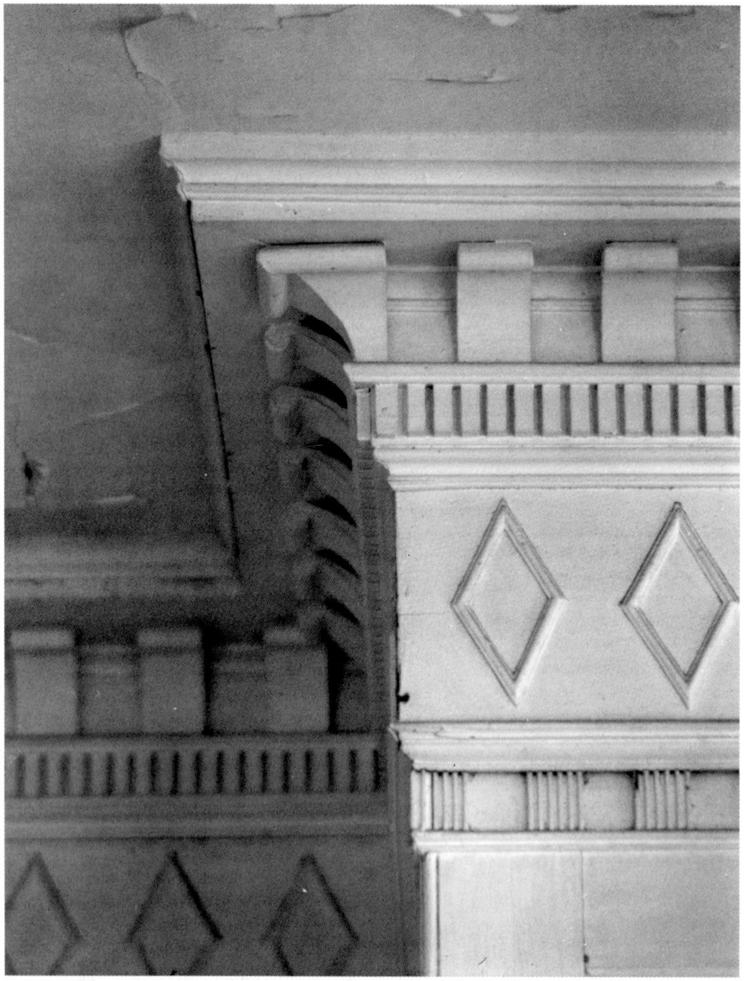

Barnwell-Gough House

Elizabeth Barnwell's father employed the best of craftsmen, but was satisfied with a relatively sedate trim.

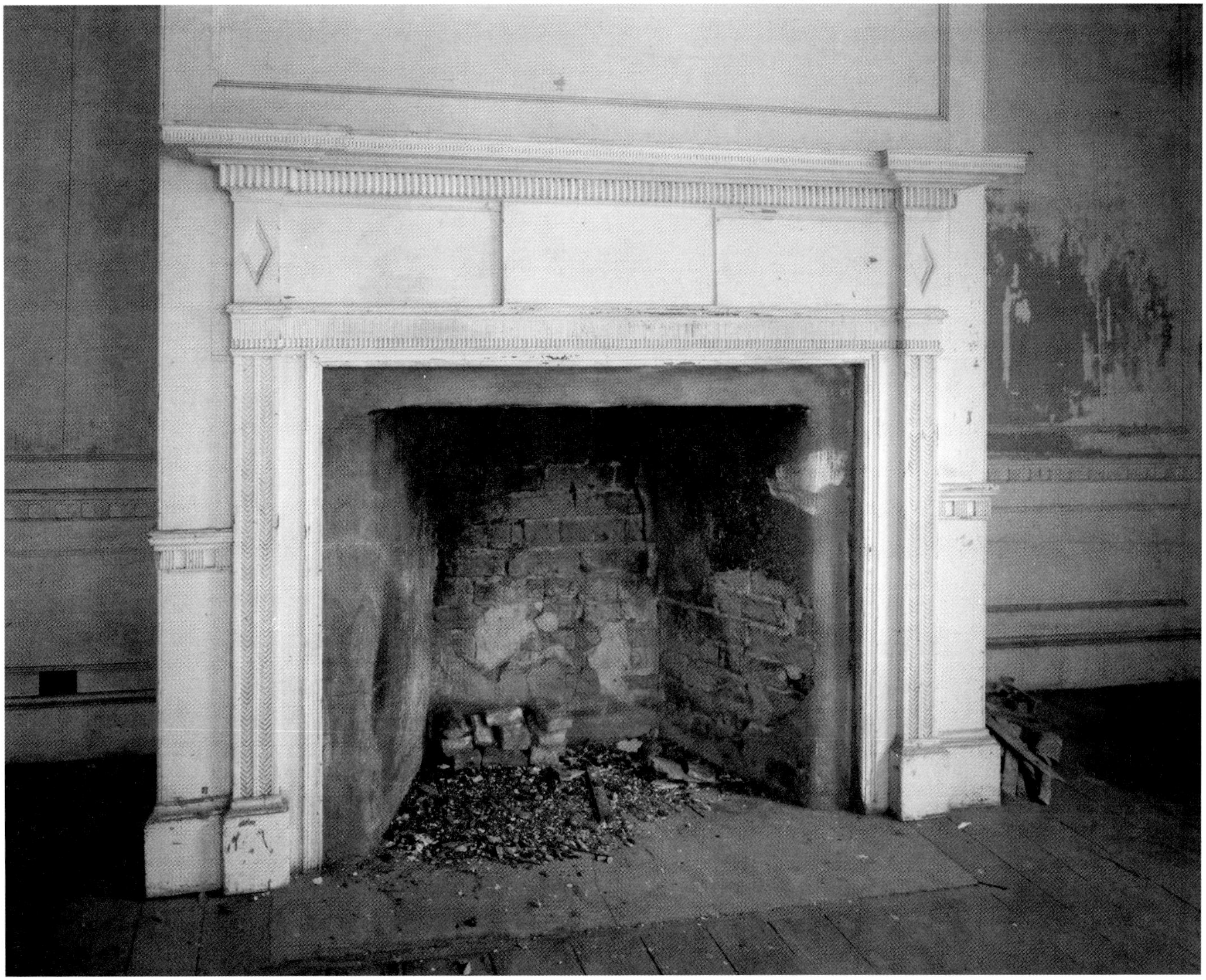

Barnwell-Gough House

Mantel detail.

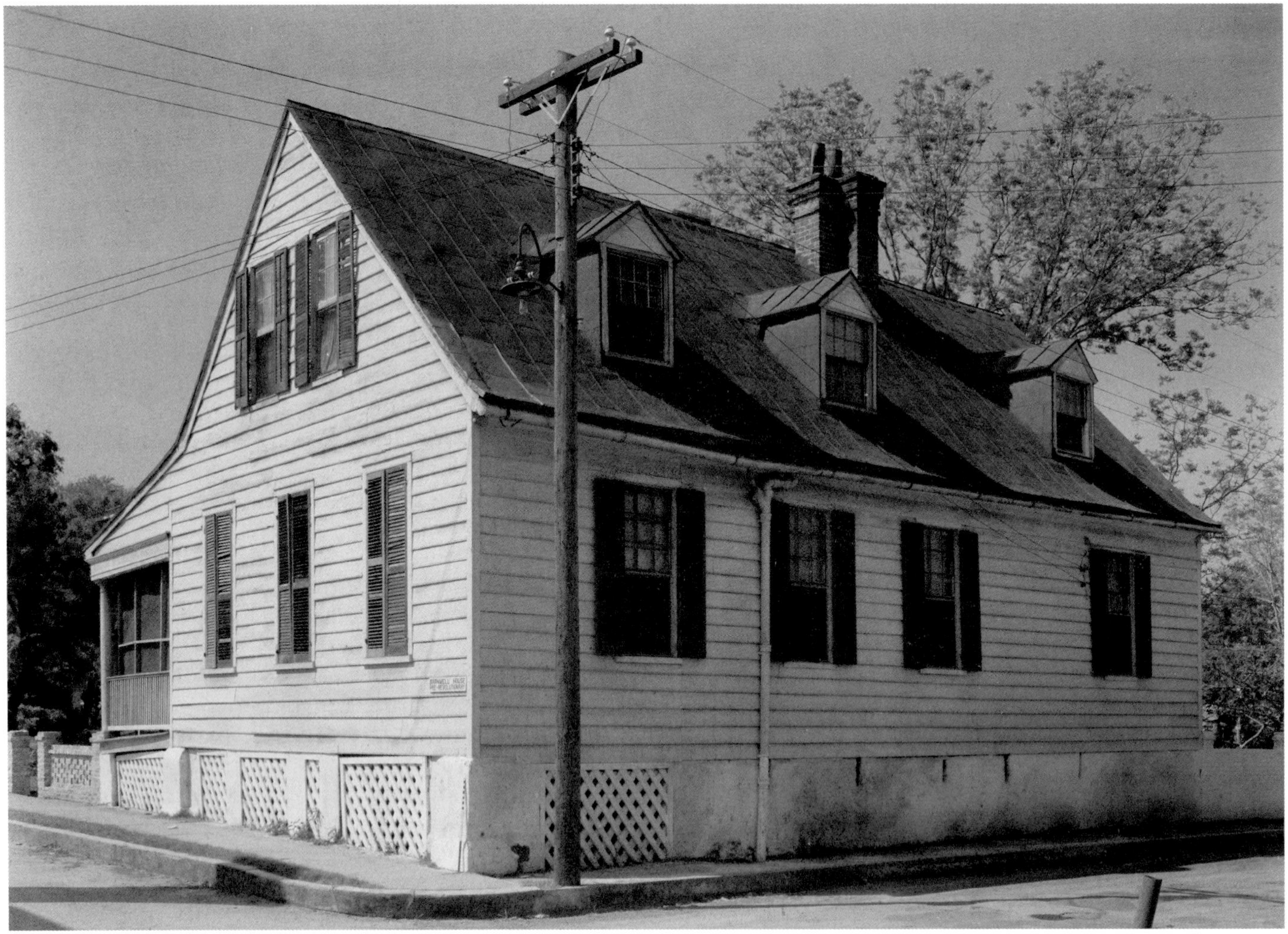

HEPWORTH HOUSE — C.O. Greene, 1940 (photo series)

Built in 1717, it's the oldest house in town. There are slits in the foundation that were probably meant for gun ports.

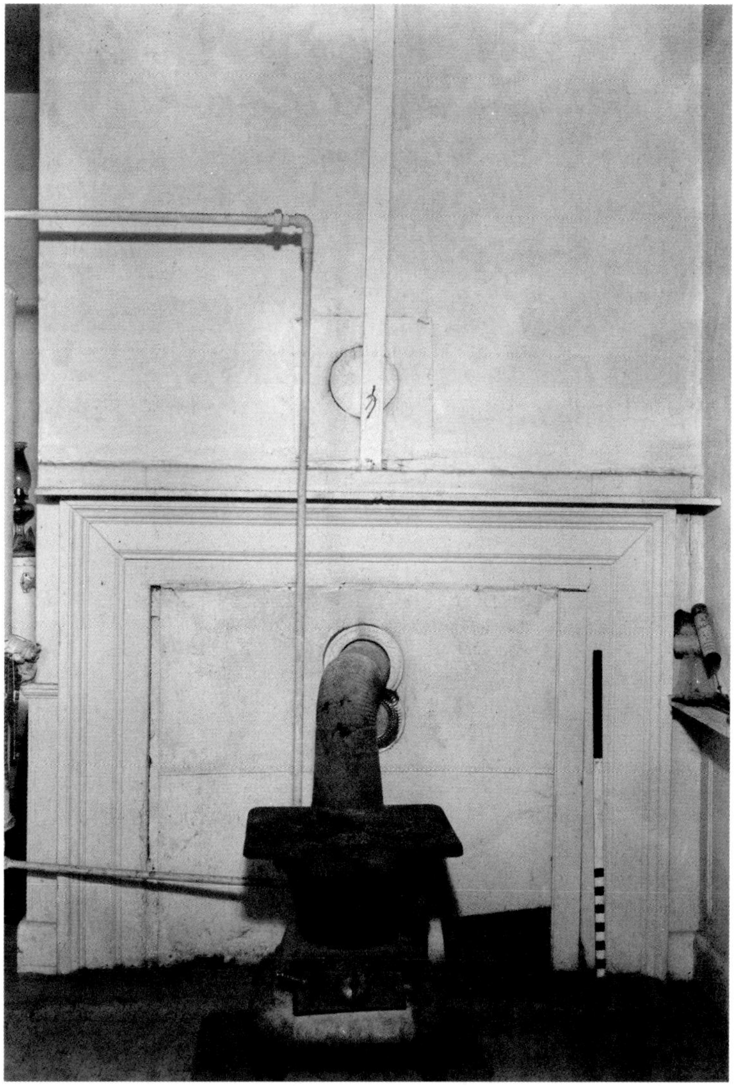

HEPWORTH HOUSE

Piping connects the woodstove to the hot water heater. The house was once called the "Temple of the Sun," for the Masons conducted their rites here. There are some Greek Revival neighbors but this is the only true temple.

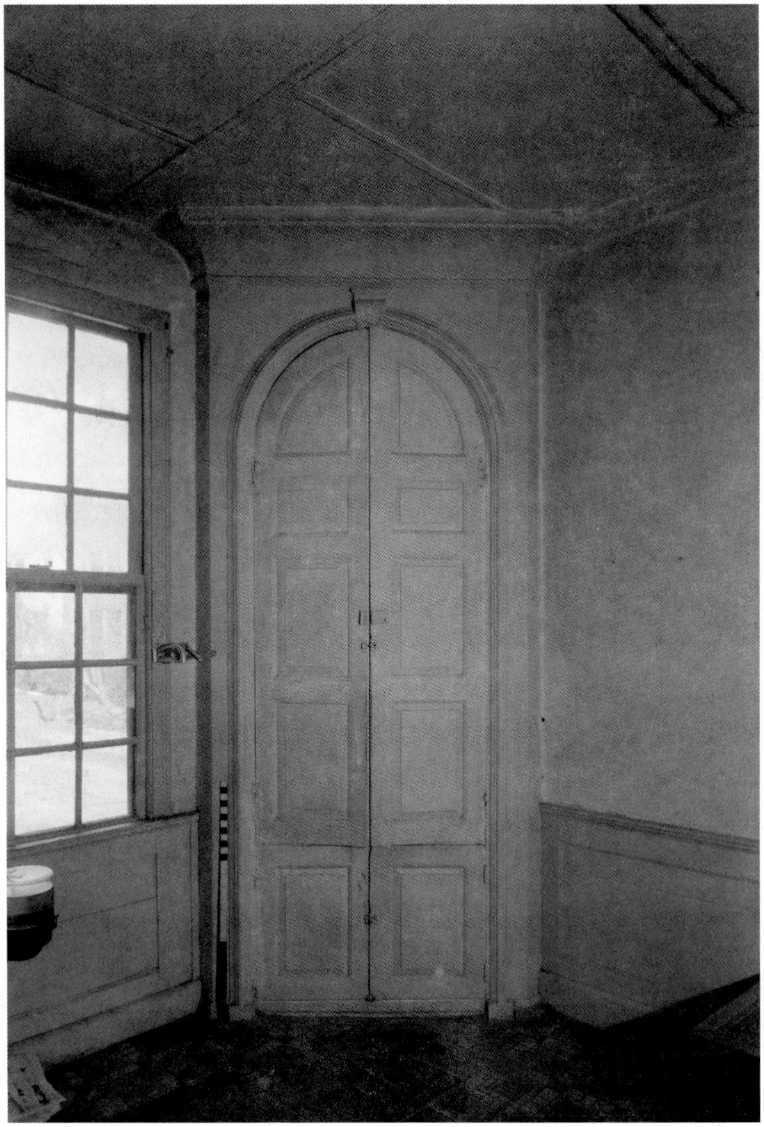

Hepworth House

A corner cupboard; it probably doesn't date from construction, but is ancient enough.

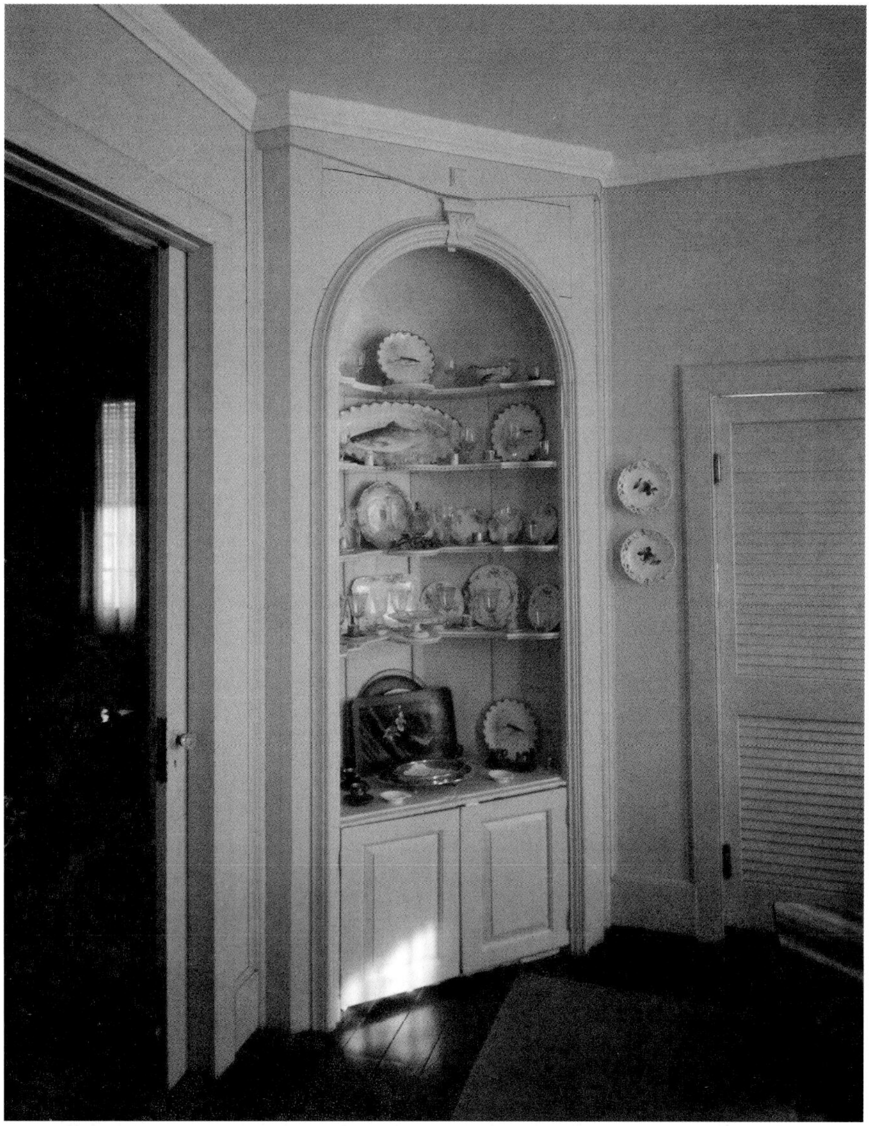

Hepworth House

Transition.

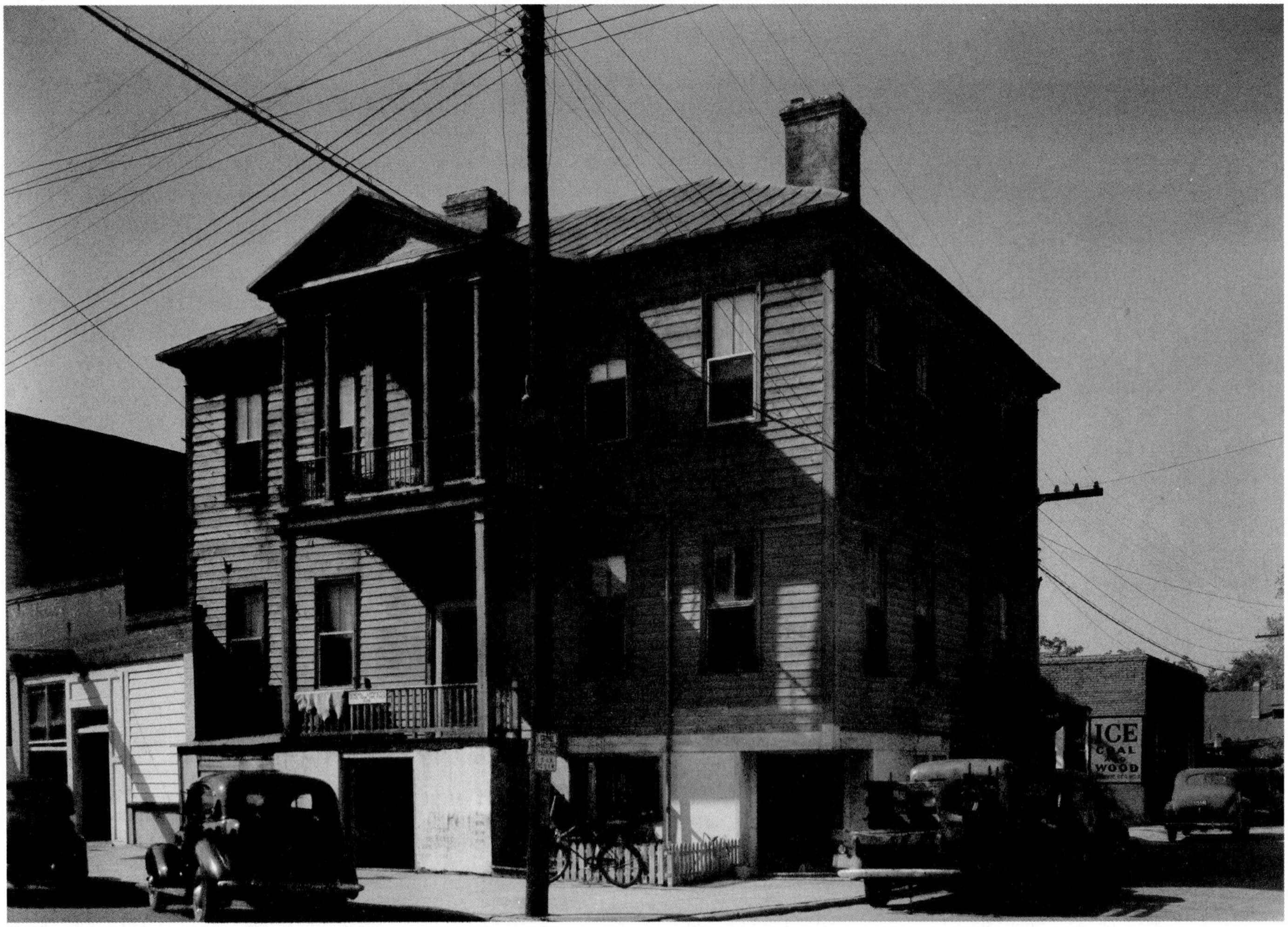

JOHN MARK VERDIER HOUSE — C.O. Greene, 1940

The Verdier house before restoration. Photographer Greene took this Depression-era photograph just a year after the more famous Walker Evans did his well-known closeup of the Lafayette House signs.

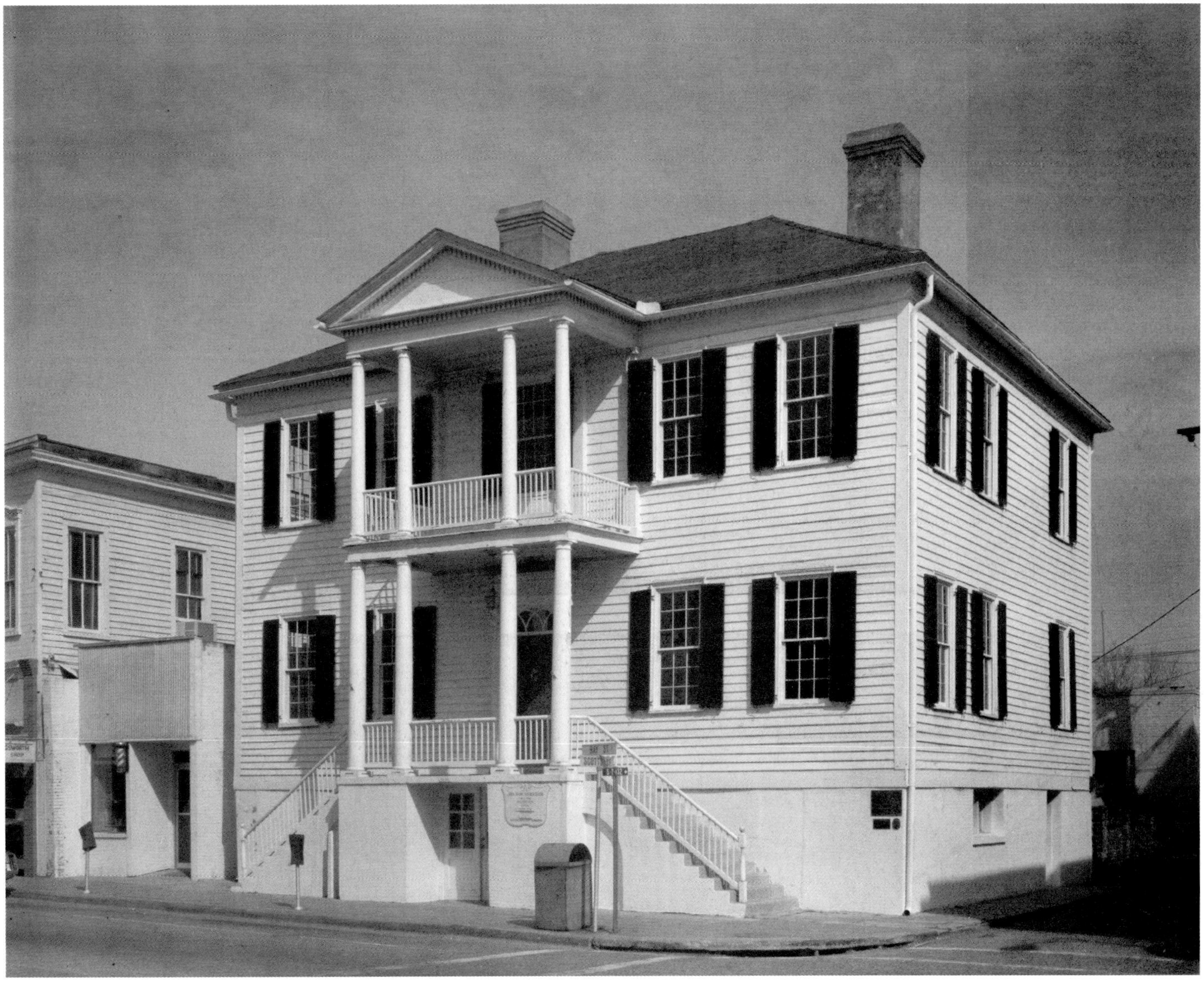

JOHN MARK VERDIER HOUSE — Charles N. Bayless, 1978 (photo series)

The Verdier house after restoration. Built by twenty-six-year-old merchant Verdier in 1790, the Adamesque house was probably the town's finest. Lafayette spoke to the citizens of Beaufort from these steps in 1825.

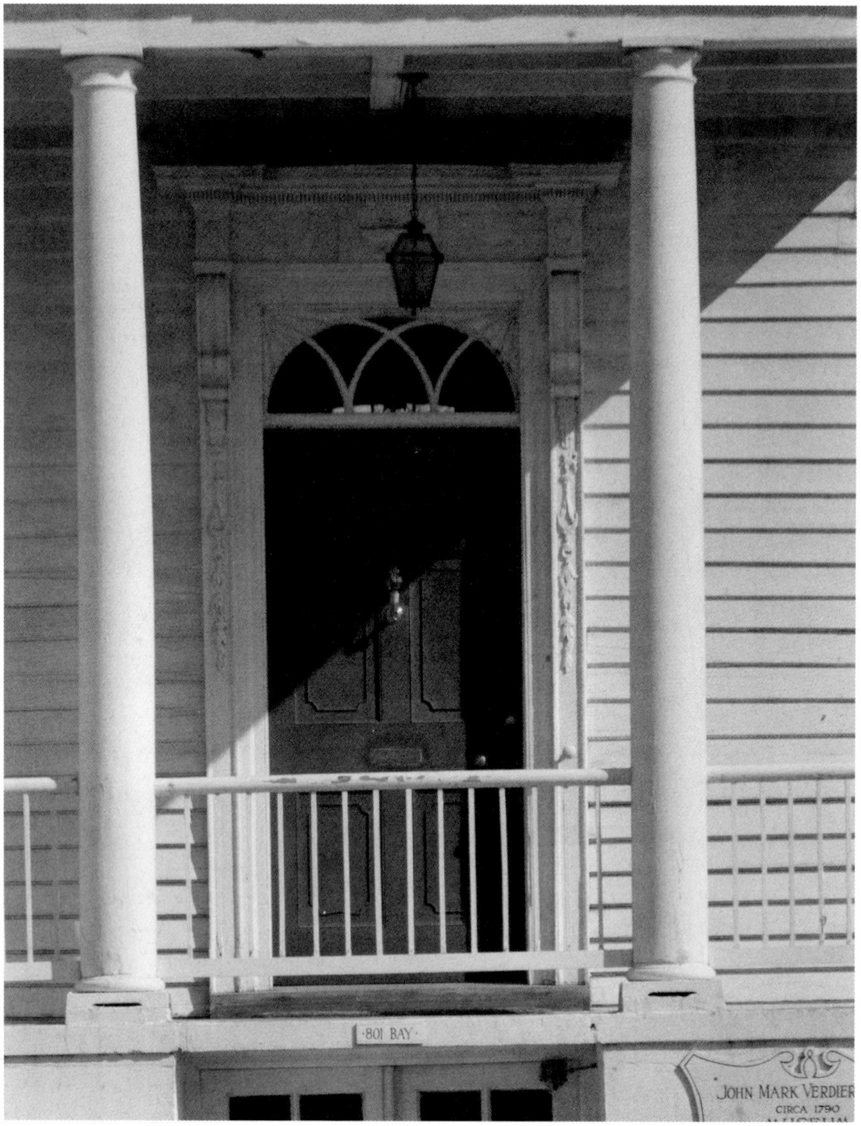

JOHN MARK VERDIER HOUSE

Detail of entry door. As you can see from the sign, the building is now operated as a house museum by the Historic Beaufort Foundation.

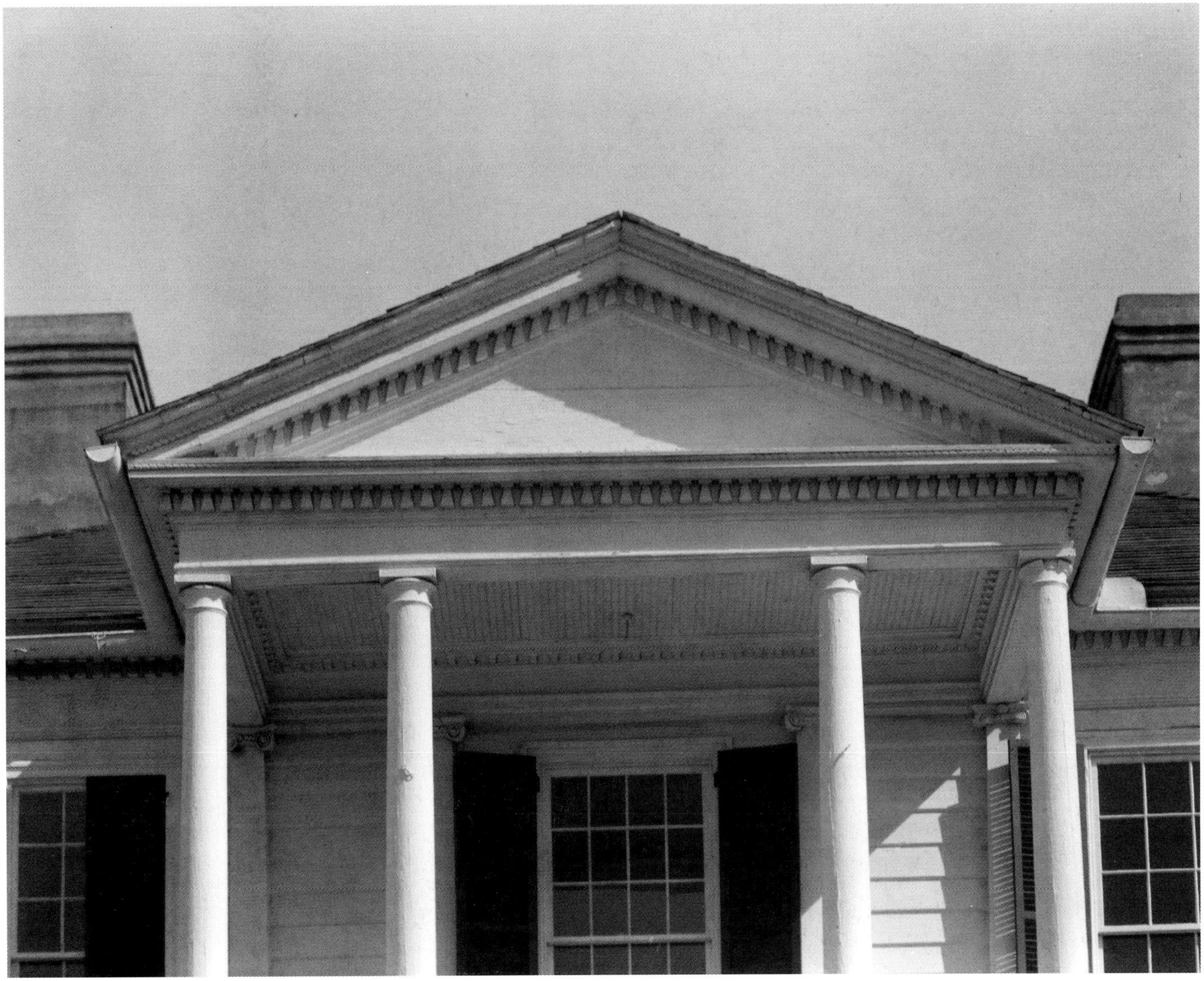

John Mark Verdier House

Detail of portico. Union forces had this as their headquarters. Following the war, the house became a fish market, an icehouse, law offices and a telephone office. In 1942 it was saved from condemnation by concerned citizens.

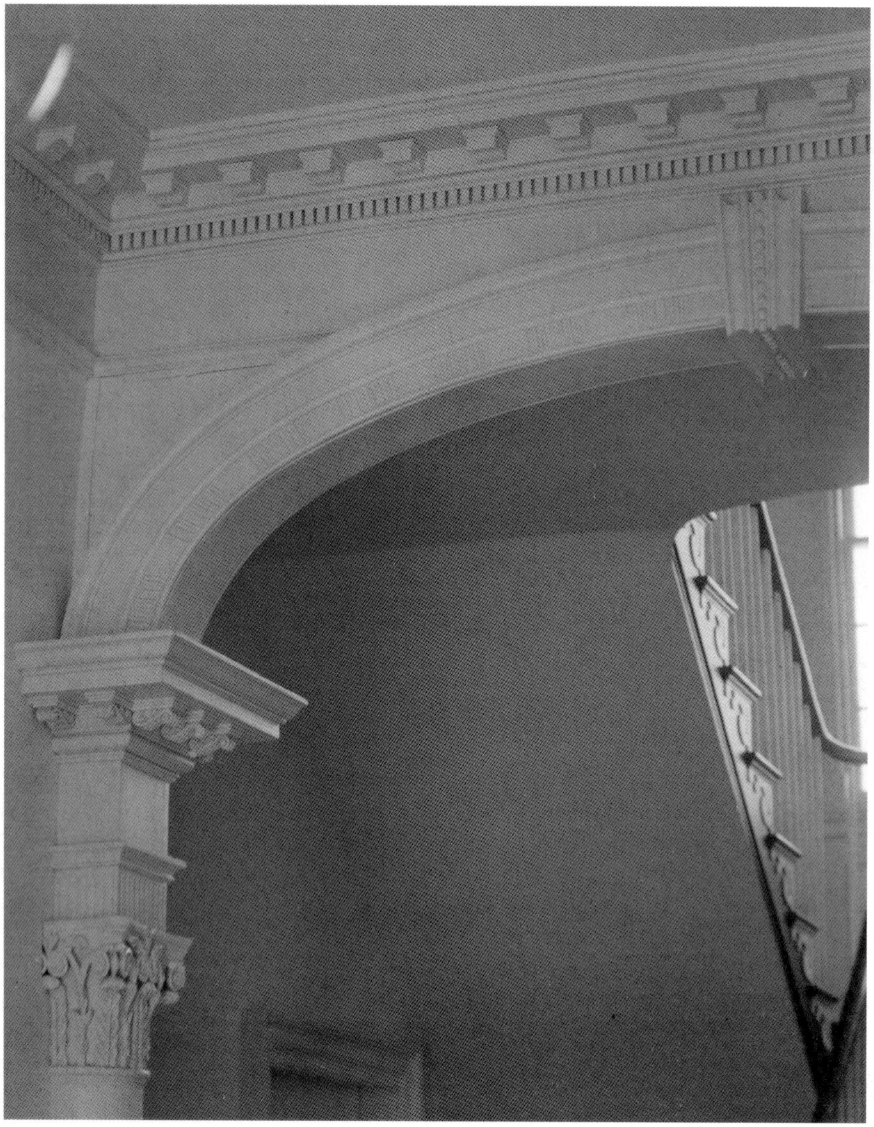

John Mark Verdier House

Detail of interior entry. The Beaufort Historic Foundation acquired the house in 1968 and completed their excellent restoration in 1976.

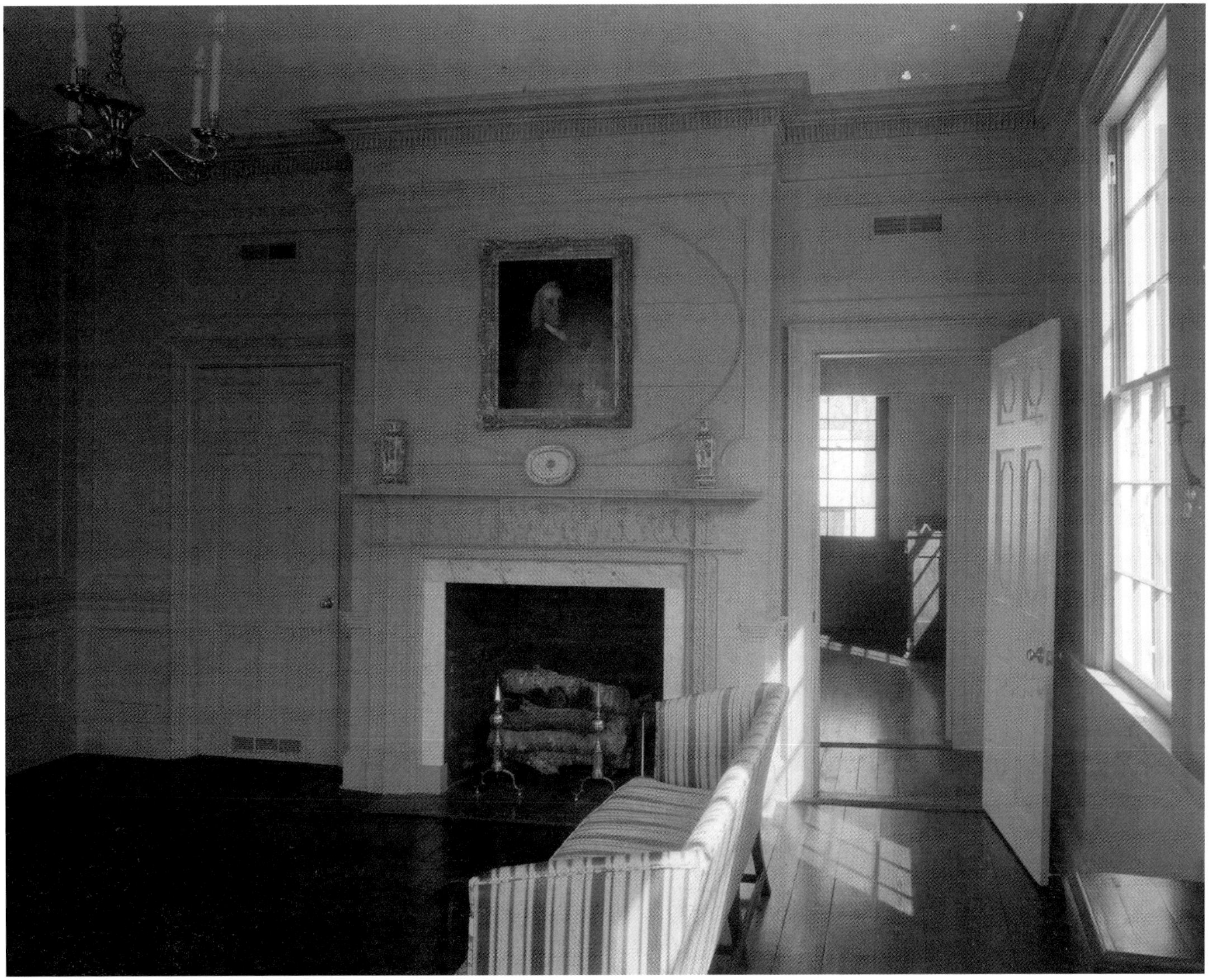

John Mark Verdier House

When this was taken in 1978, the house was being furnished.

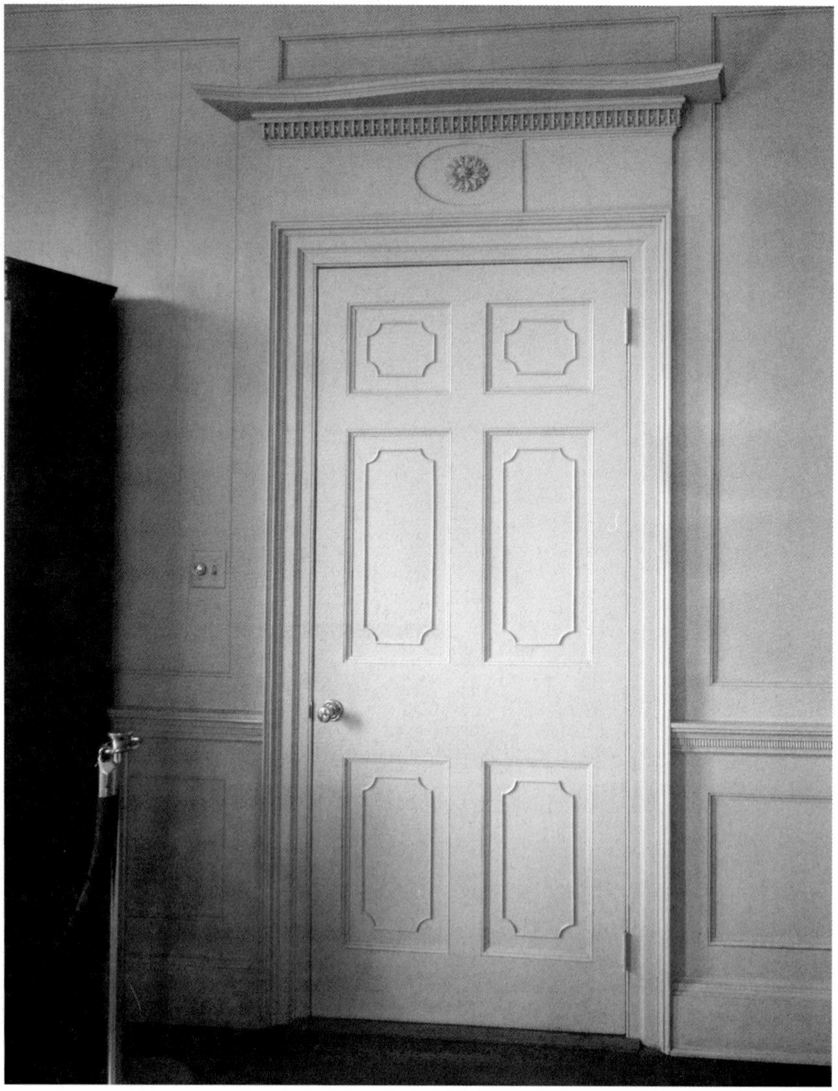

John Mark Verdier House

A typical door treatment—typical in intent. The designs are numerous.

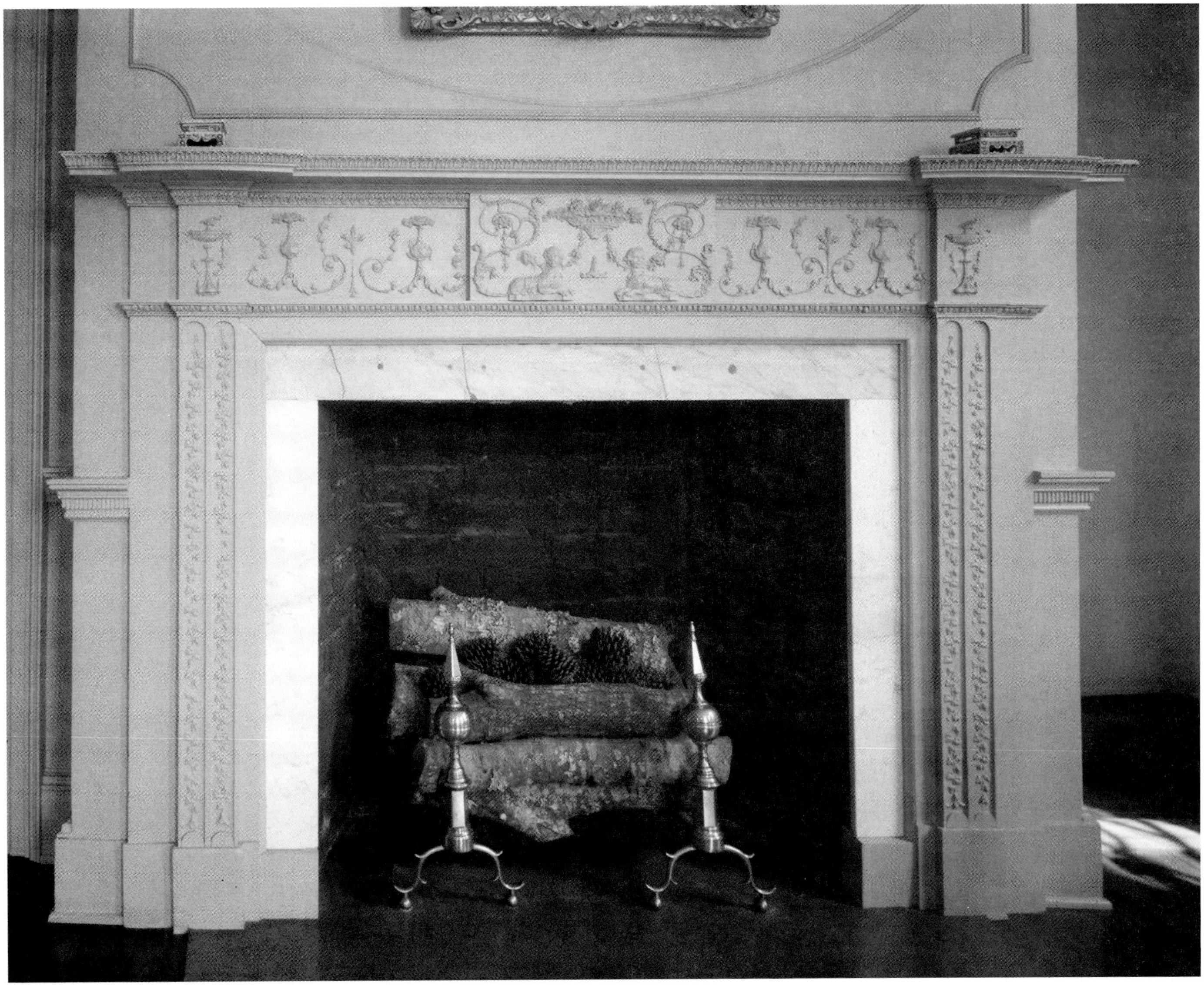

John Mark Verdier House

An ornate Adamesque mantel. One of many.

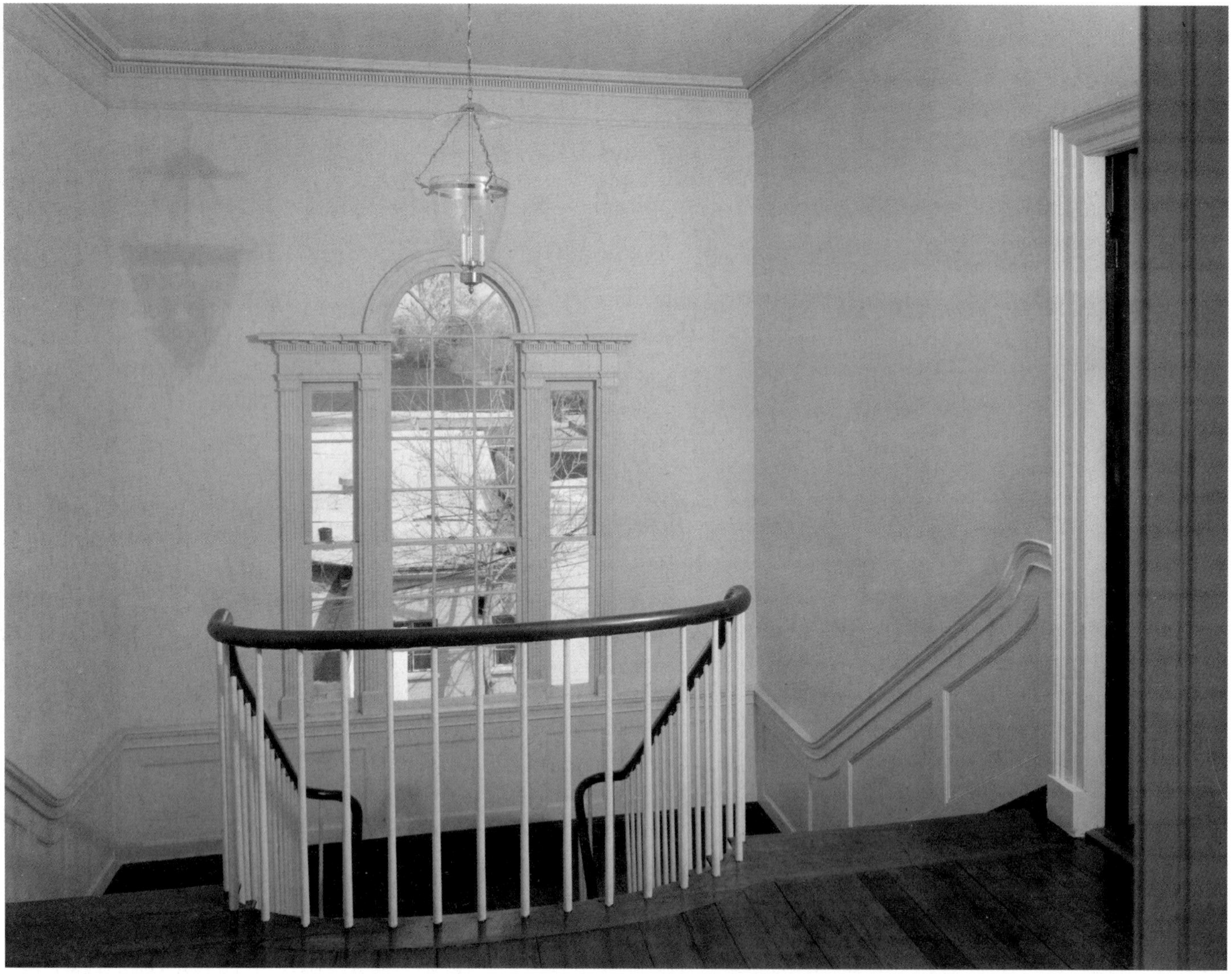

John Mark Verdier House

A Palladian window in the stairwell.

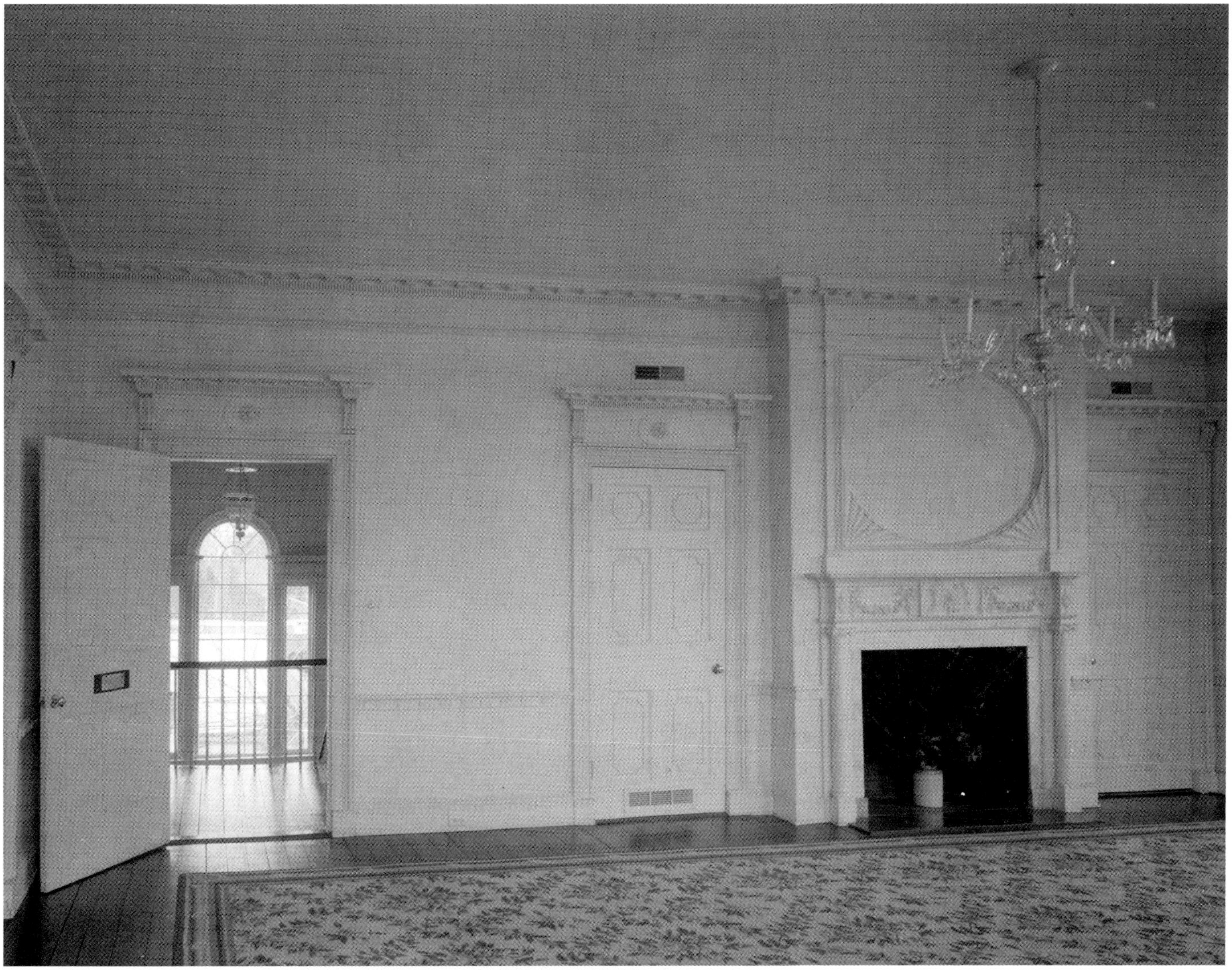

John Mark Verdier House

A second-story ballroom was still common in 1790.

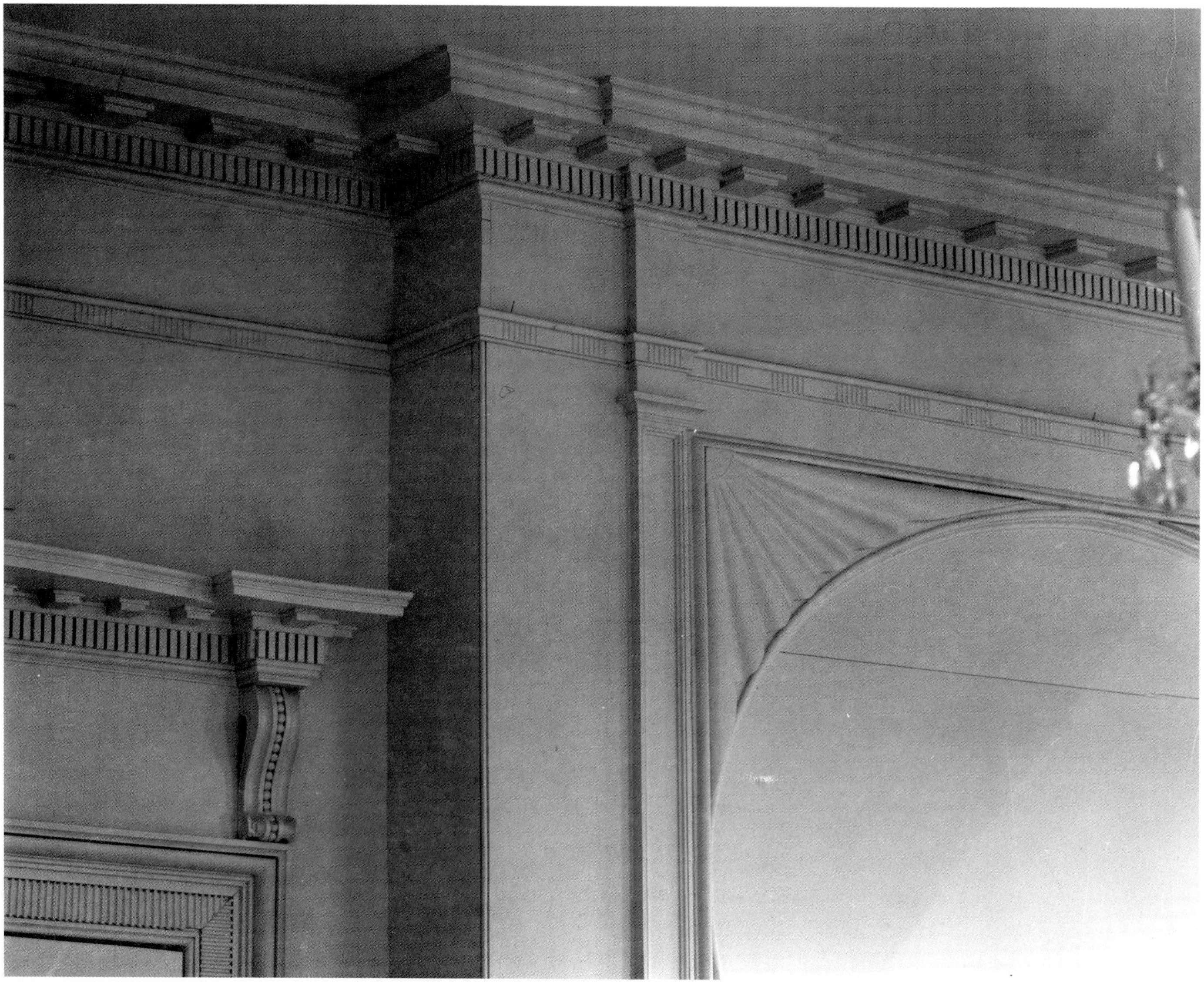

John Mark Verdier House

Detail of overmantel, cornice and door treatment.

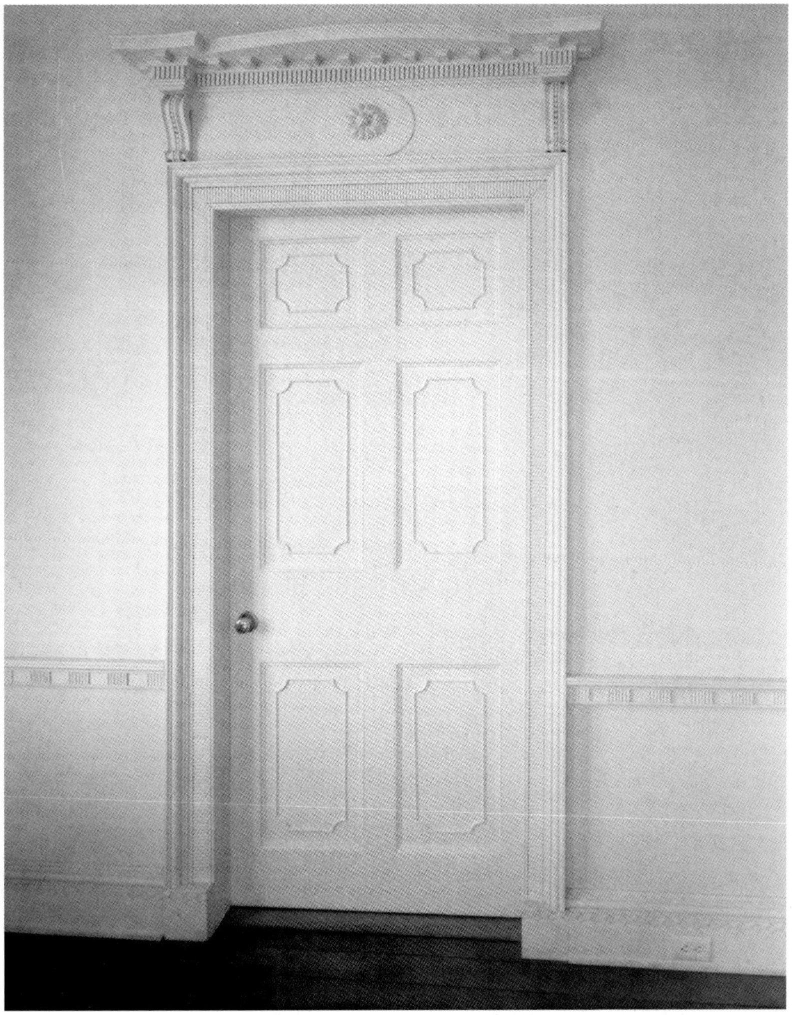

John Mark Verdier House

A typical door. I should say *atypical.*

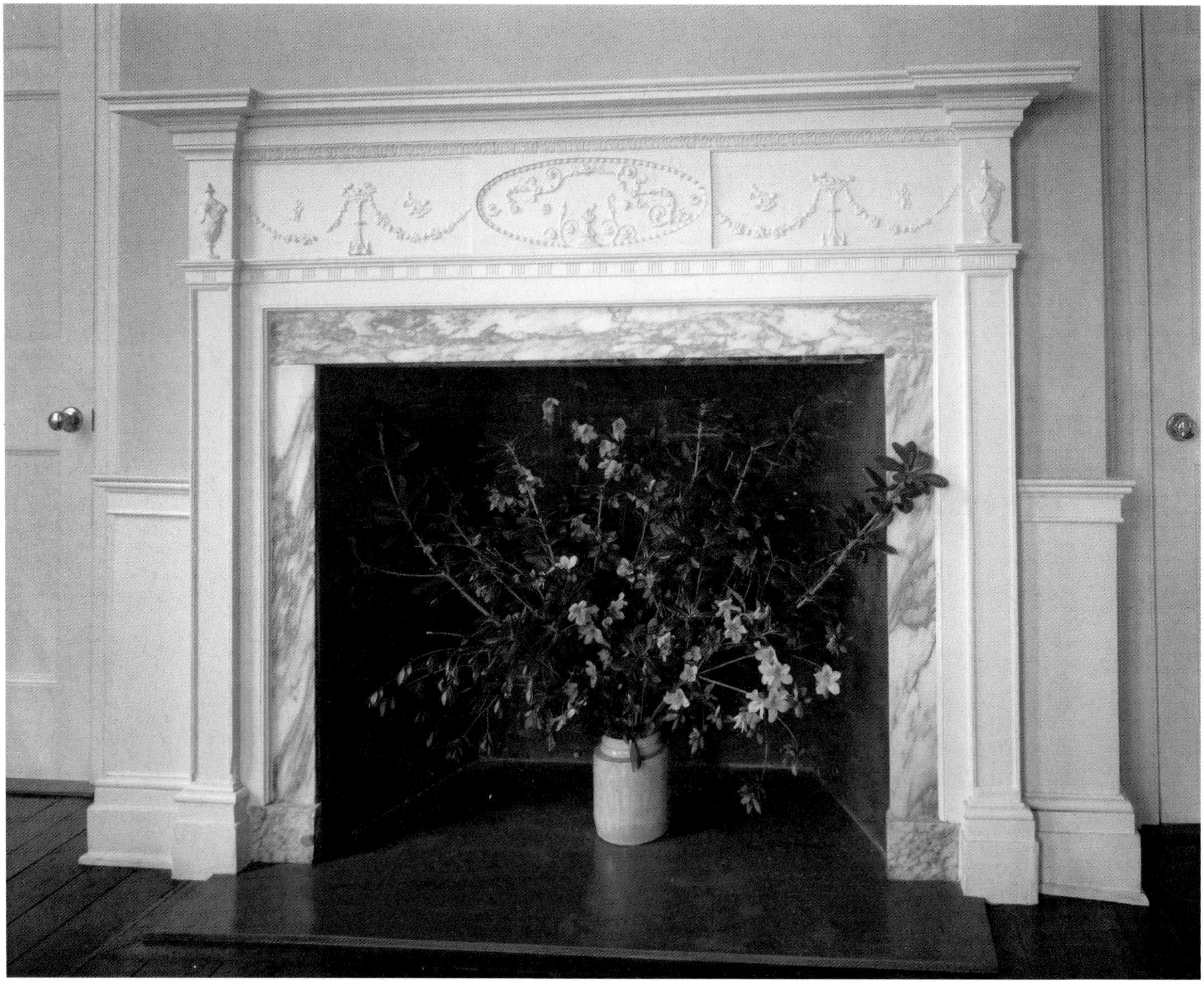

John Mark Verdier House

Another ornate mantel.

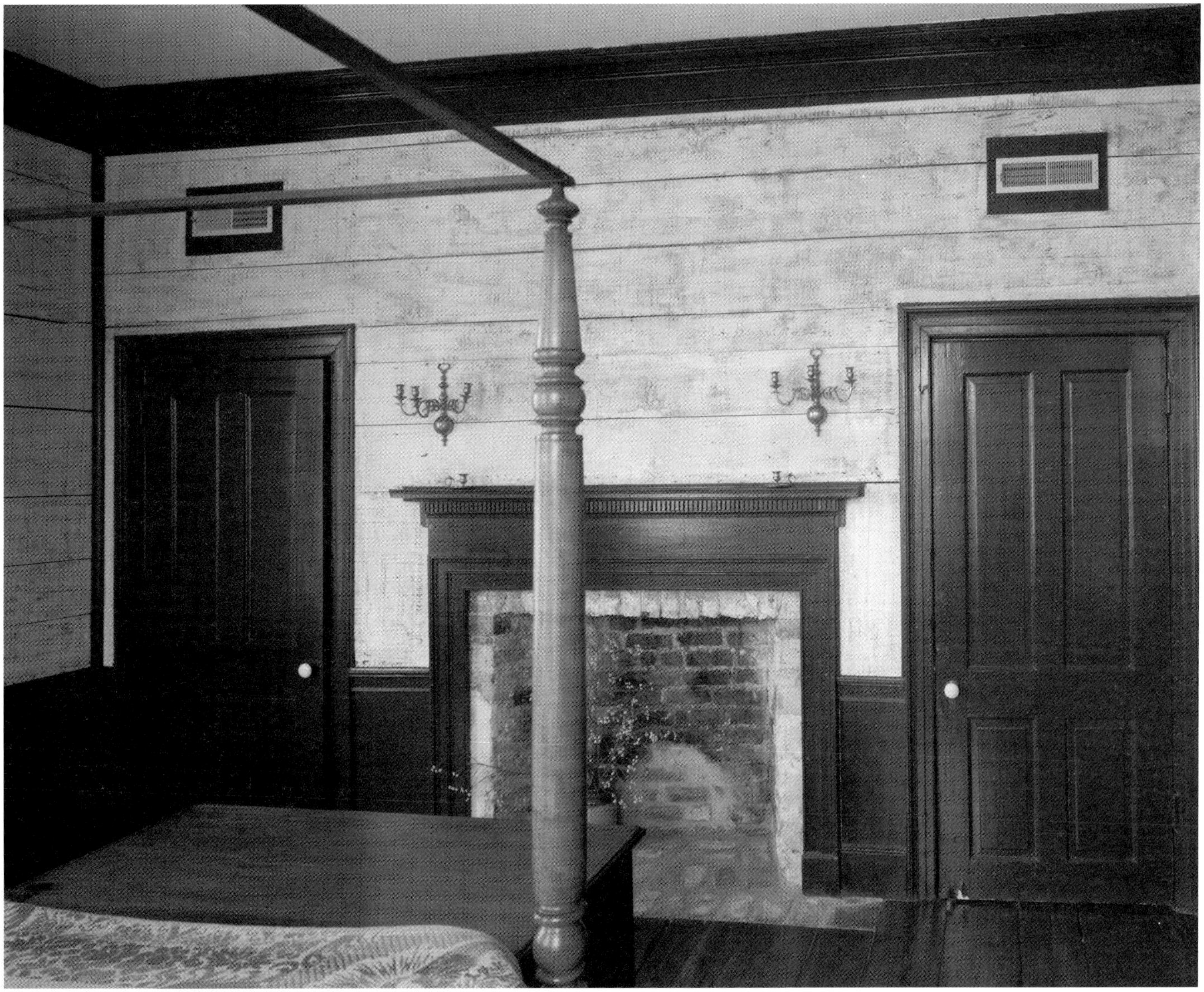

John Mark Verdier House

A second-story bedroom. The boards elsewhere were covered over with wallpaper or plaster.

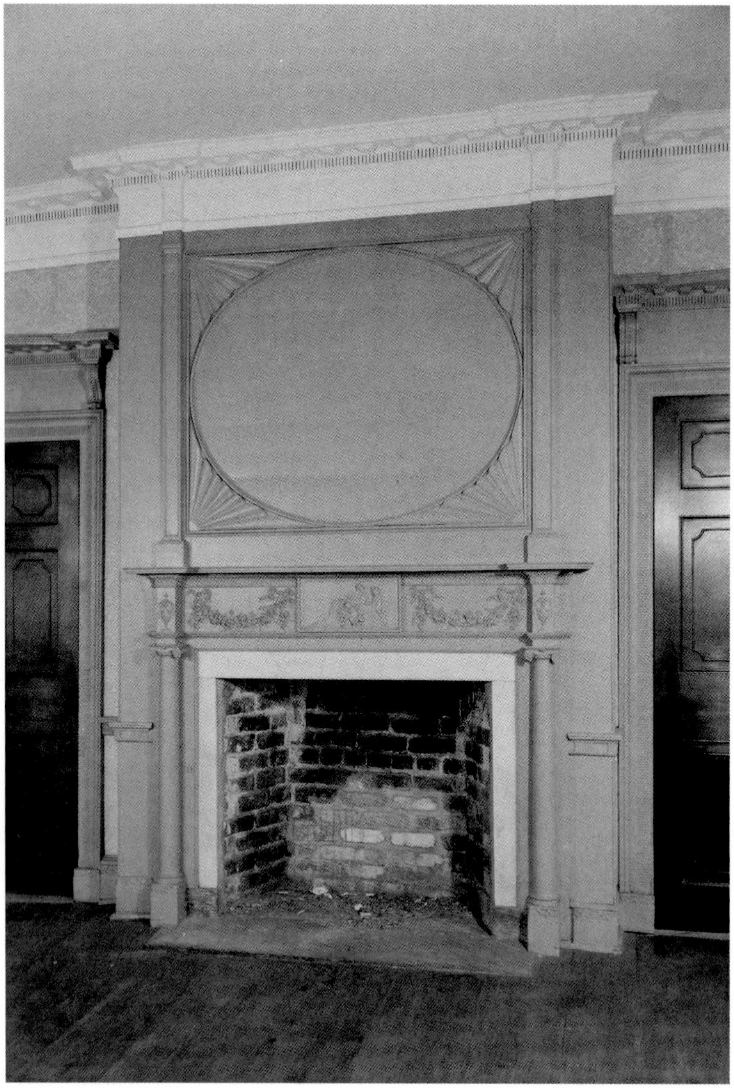

John Mark Verdier House

Mantel and overmantel.

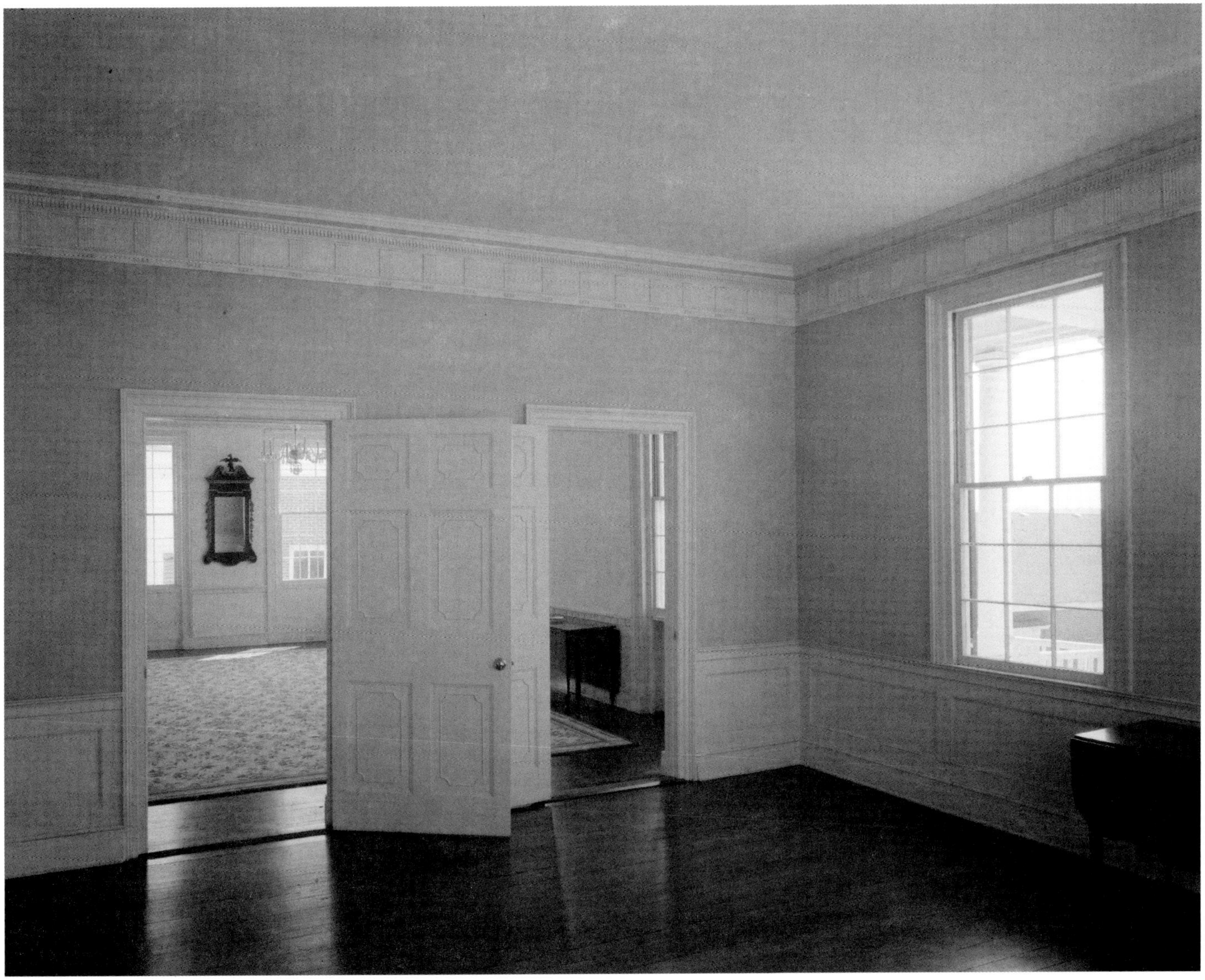

John Mark Verdier House

Looking into the second-story ballroom. Telephone operators once worked here. Fish were sold on the ground floor. And according to Walker Evans's photograph, portrait photographs were taken, notaries notarized and Lafayette spoke here as well.

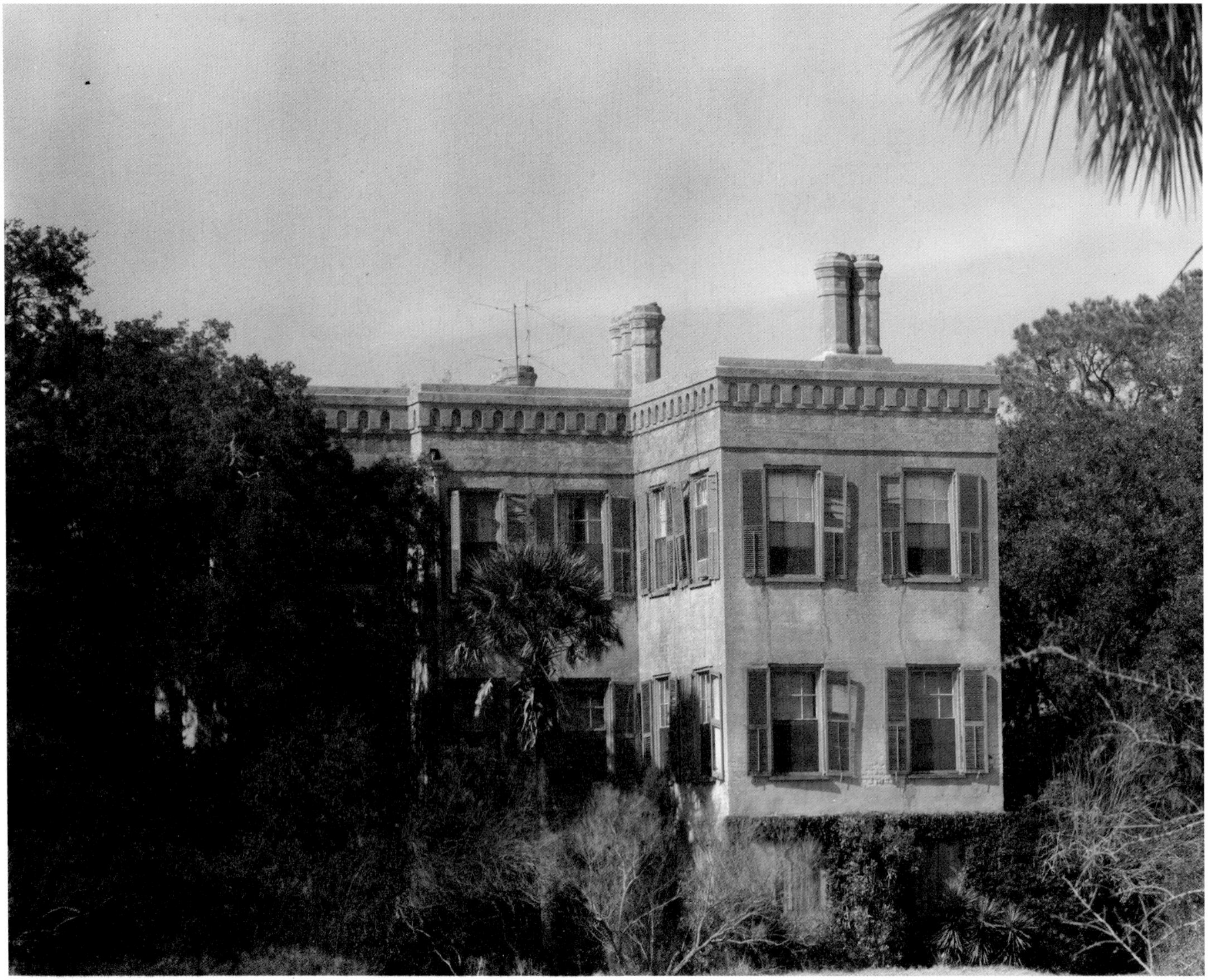

DR. JOHNSON HOUSE

Charles N. Bayless, 1978 (photo series)

Beaufort once had several castles, but this is the only one to survive. A bit of Italianate, Greek Revival and Medieval all mixed together. Built by Dr. Johnson in 1850.

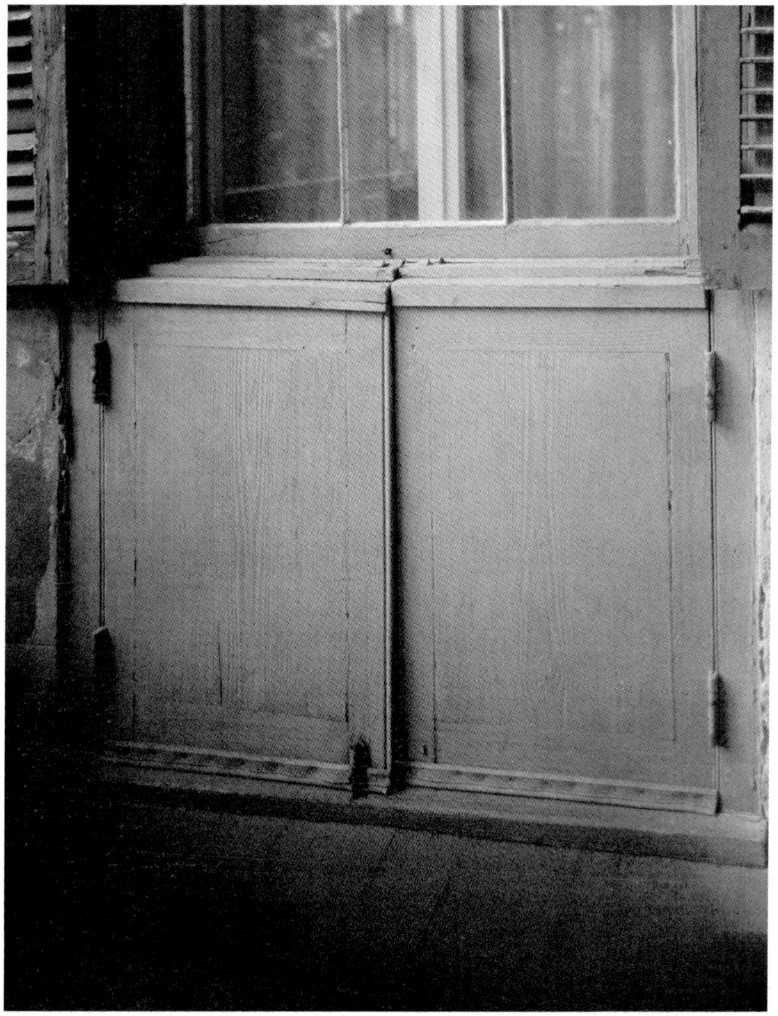

Dr. Johnson House

A jib door gives access to the porch. It's said a ghost lives beneath the house, a dwarf who accompanied the French in the sixteenth century. But only children can see him, and then only at two in the afternoon.

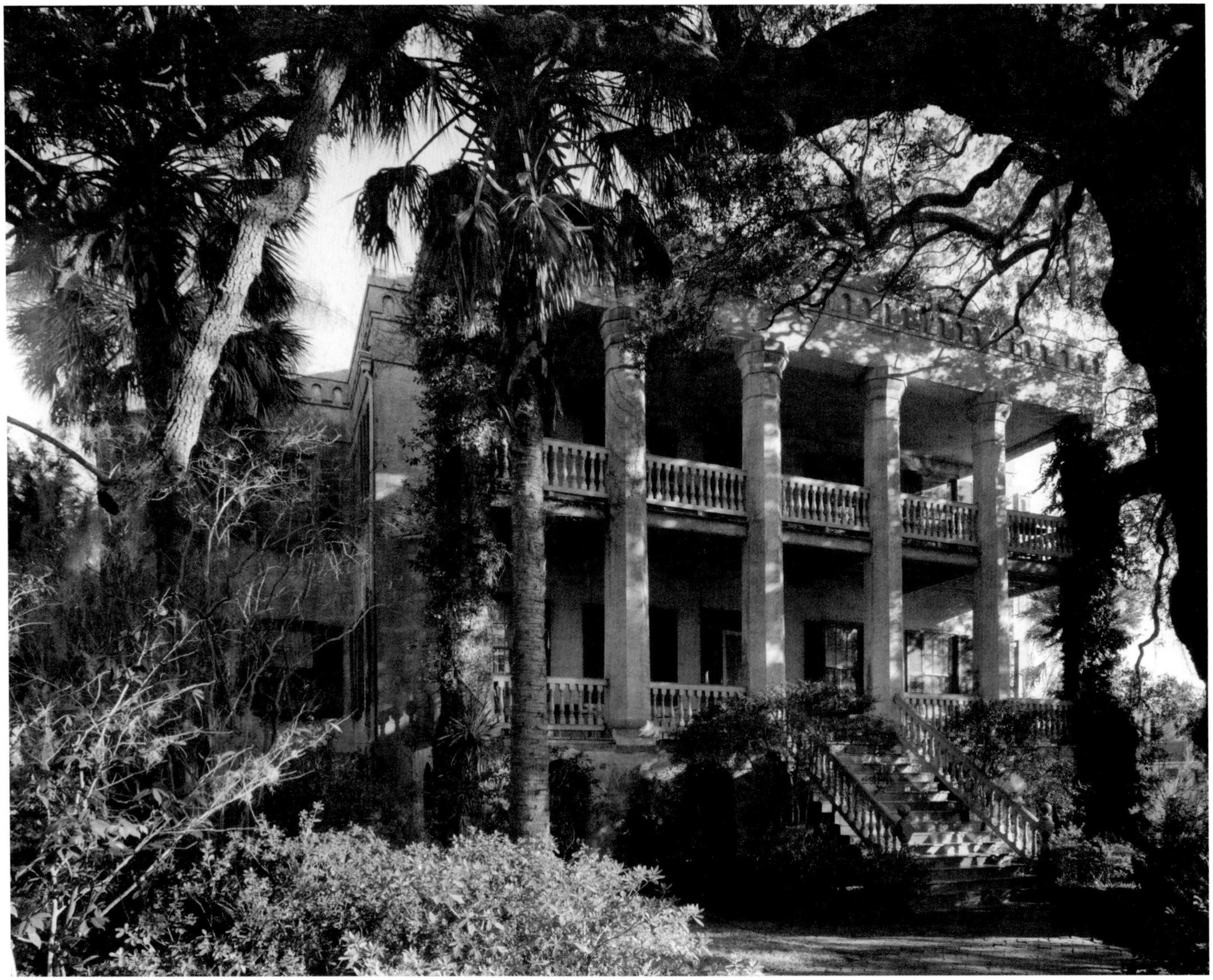

Dr. Johnson House

Six massive hexagonal columns in the company of a massive live oak.

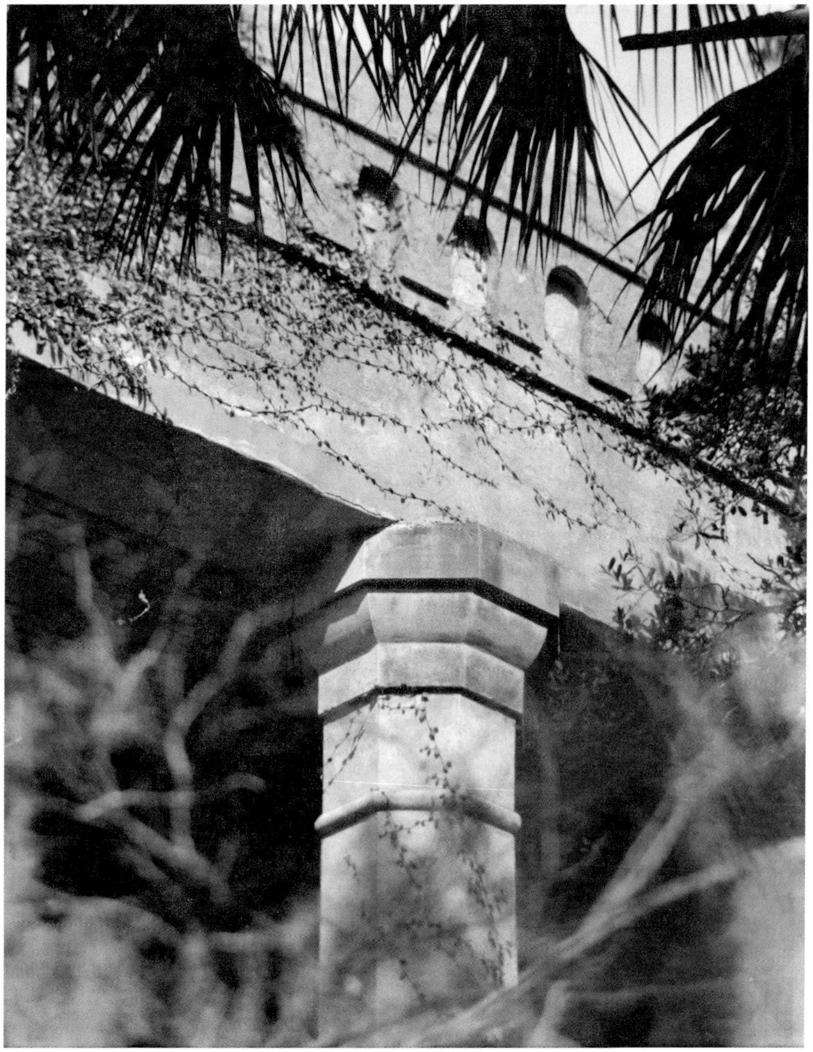

Dr. Johnson House

The stucco of this five-foot parapet changes color with the passing of the sun. Pink to tan to gray.

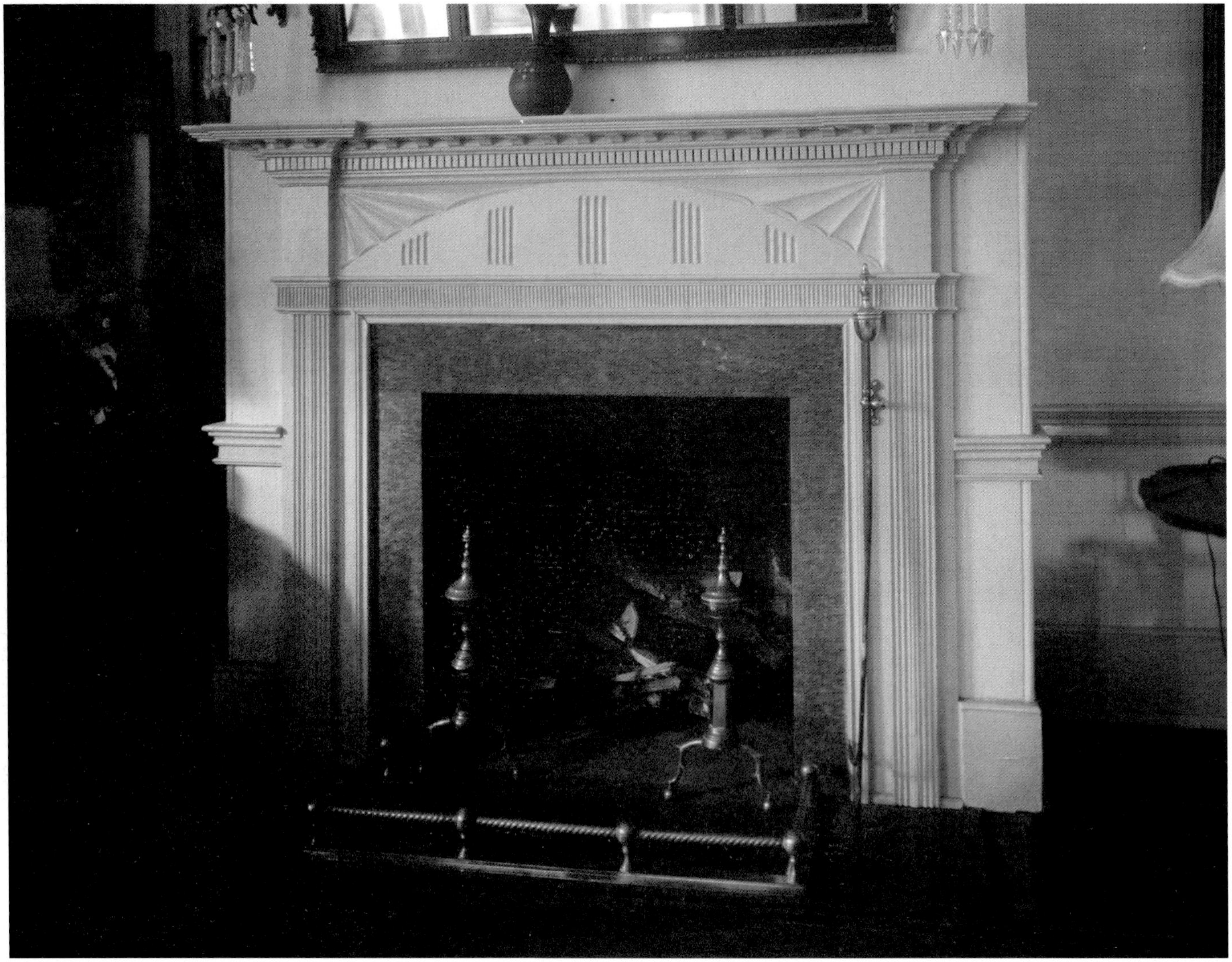

Dr. Johnson House

The mantel is thought to be older than the house.

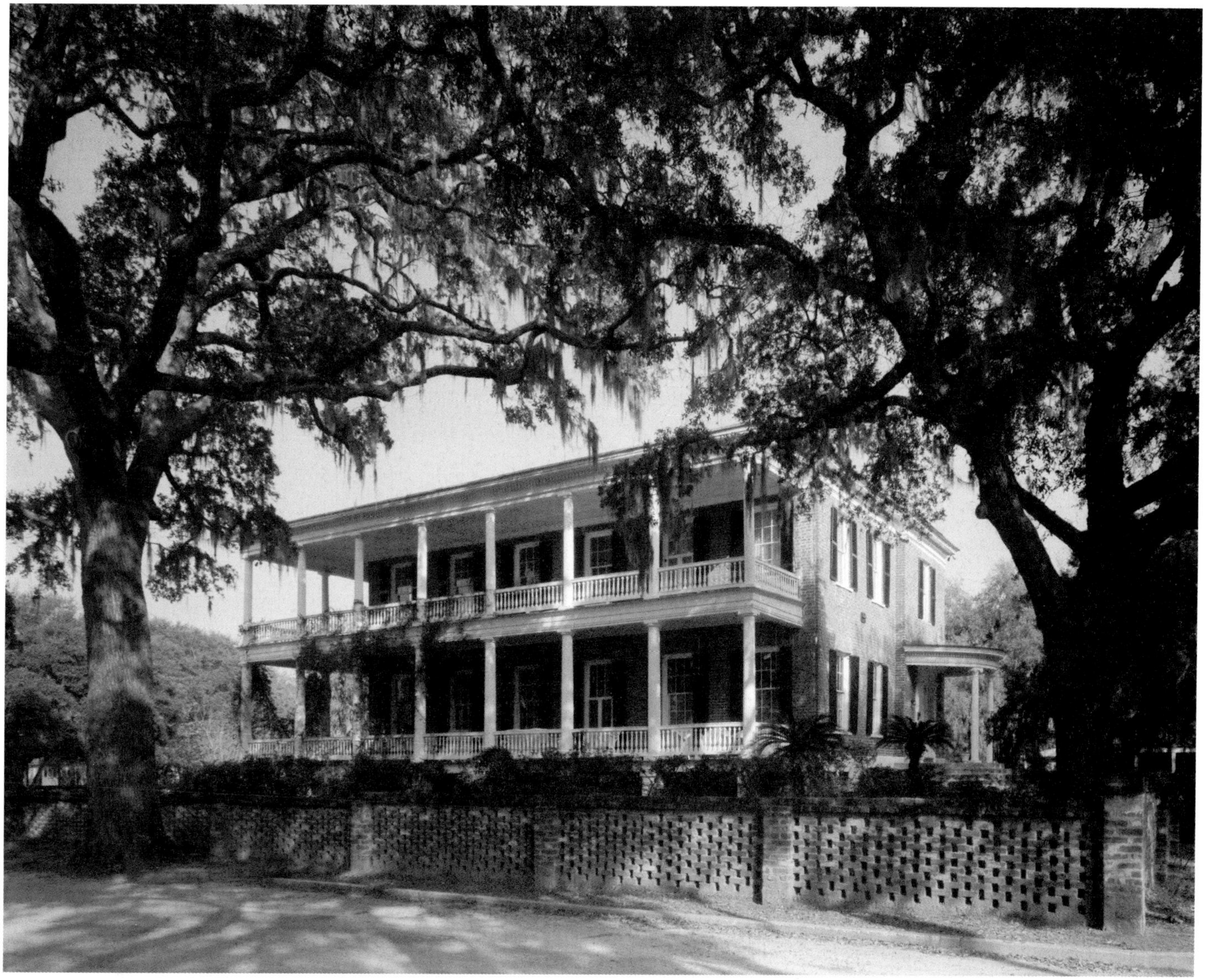

Edward Means House — Charles N. Bayless, 1978 (photo series)

"The splendor of the houses and furniture and the beauty of the place have been exaggerated, but the house of Col. Edward Means would be called handsome in any town of the North." So wrote an occupying Yankee reporter.

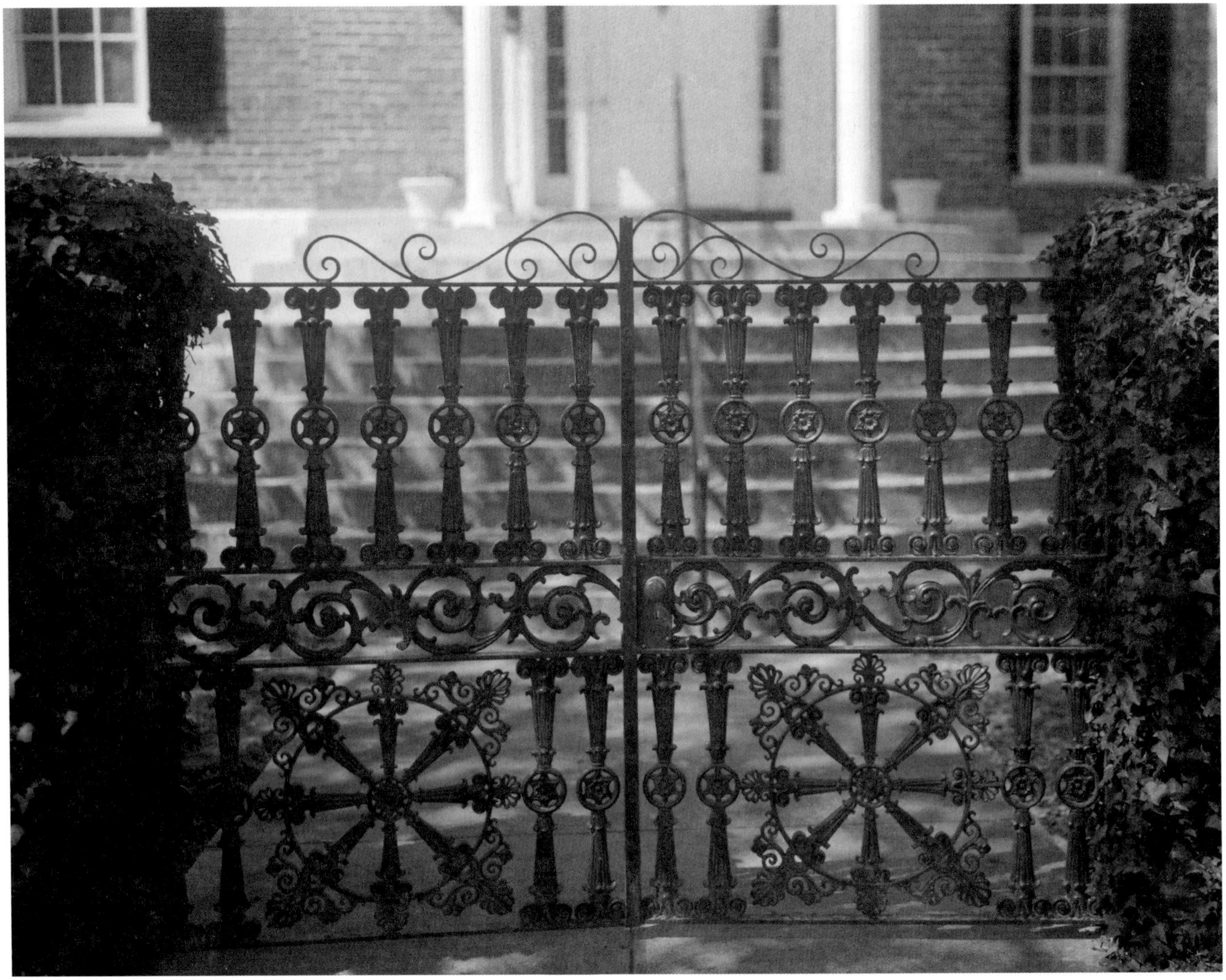

Edward Means House

Ironwork: handsome and distinctive.

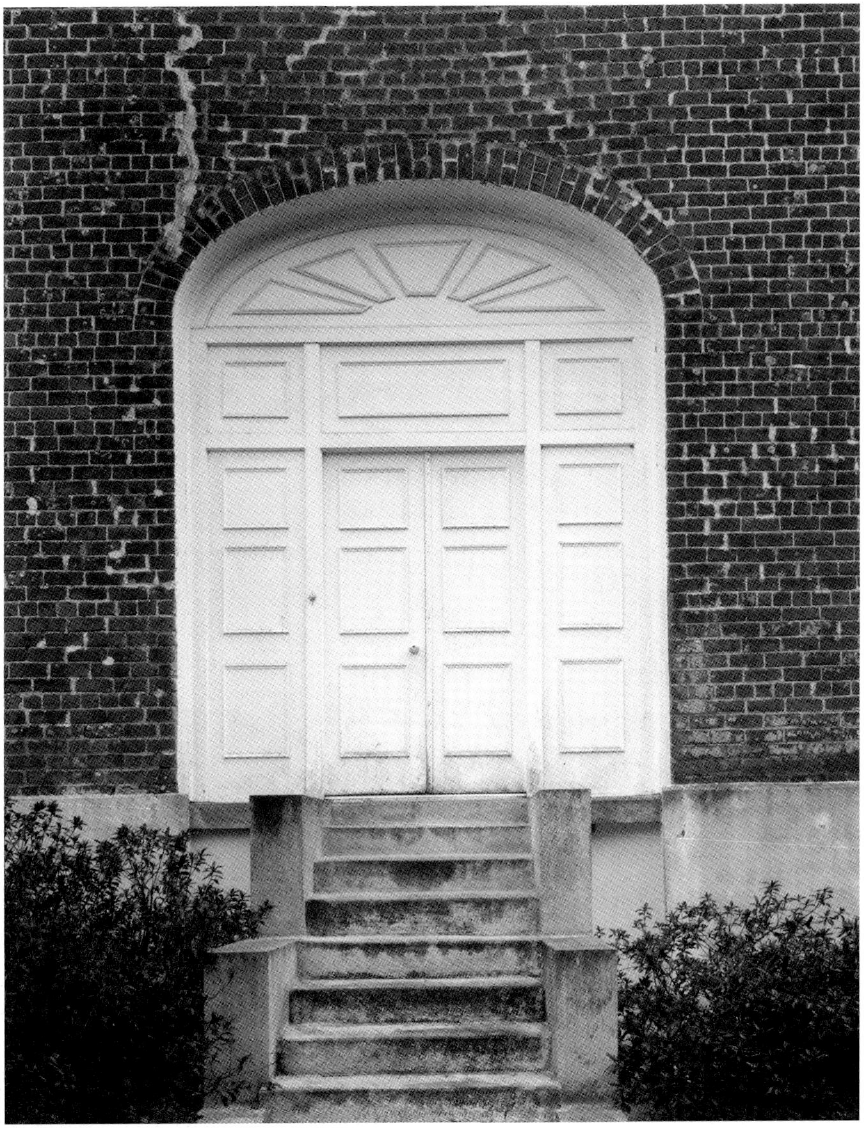

Edward Means House

Clay was scarce but oyster shells and lumber were plentiful. This is one of the few brick houses in the town. A wayward porch entry has left this door stranded.

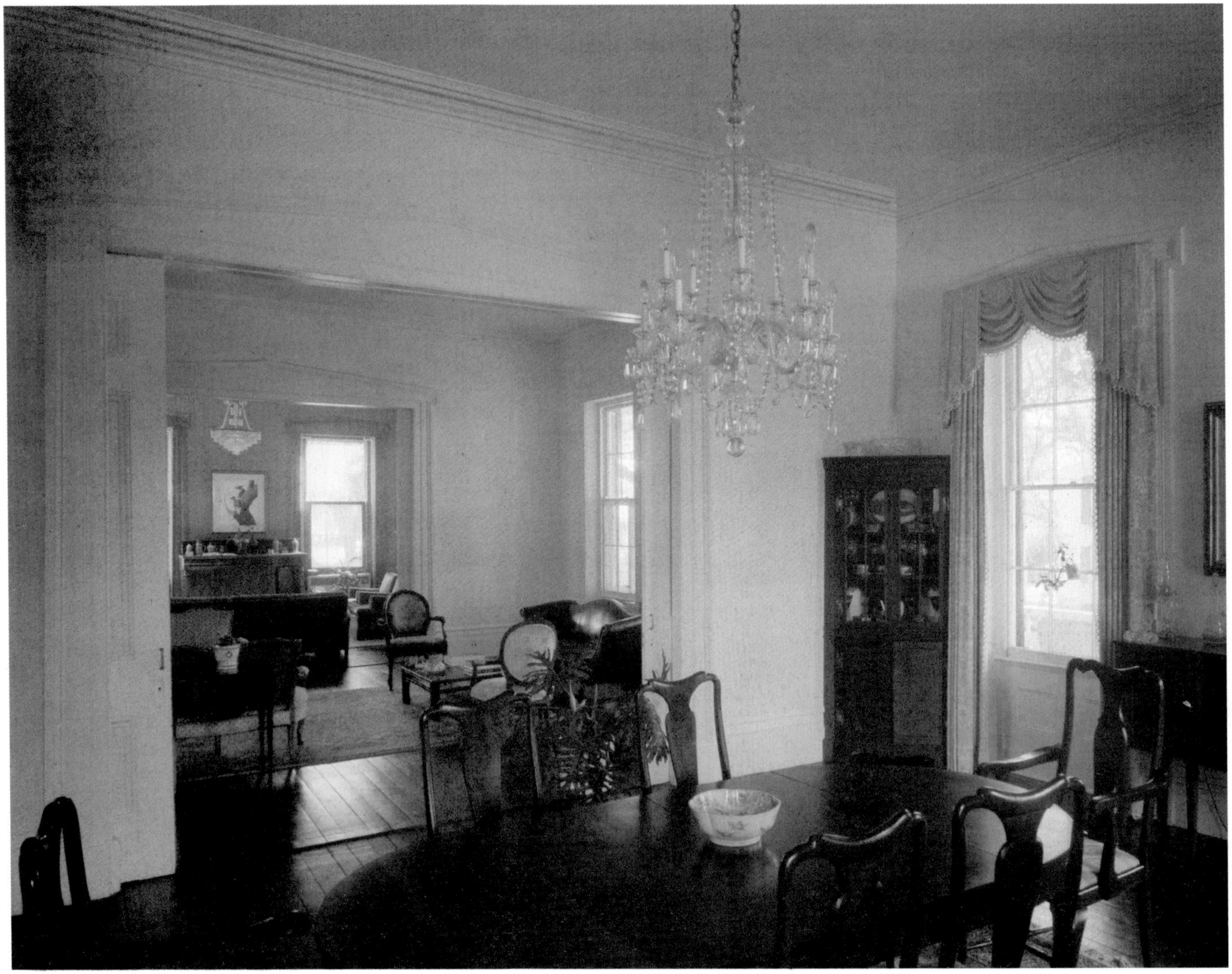

Edward Means House

Massive sliding doors brought privacy to these drawing rooms.

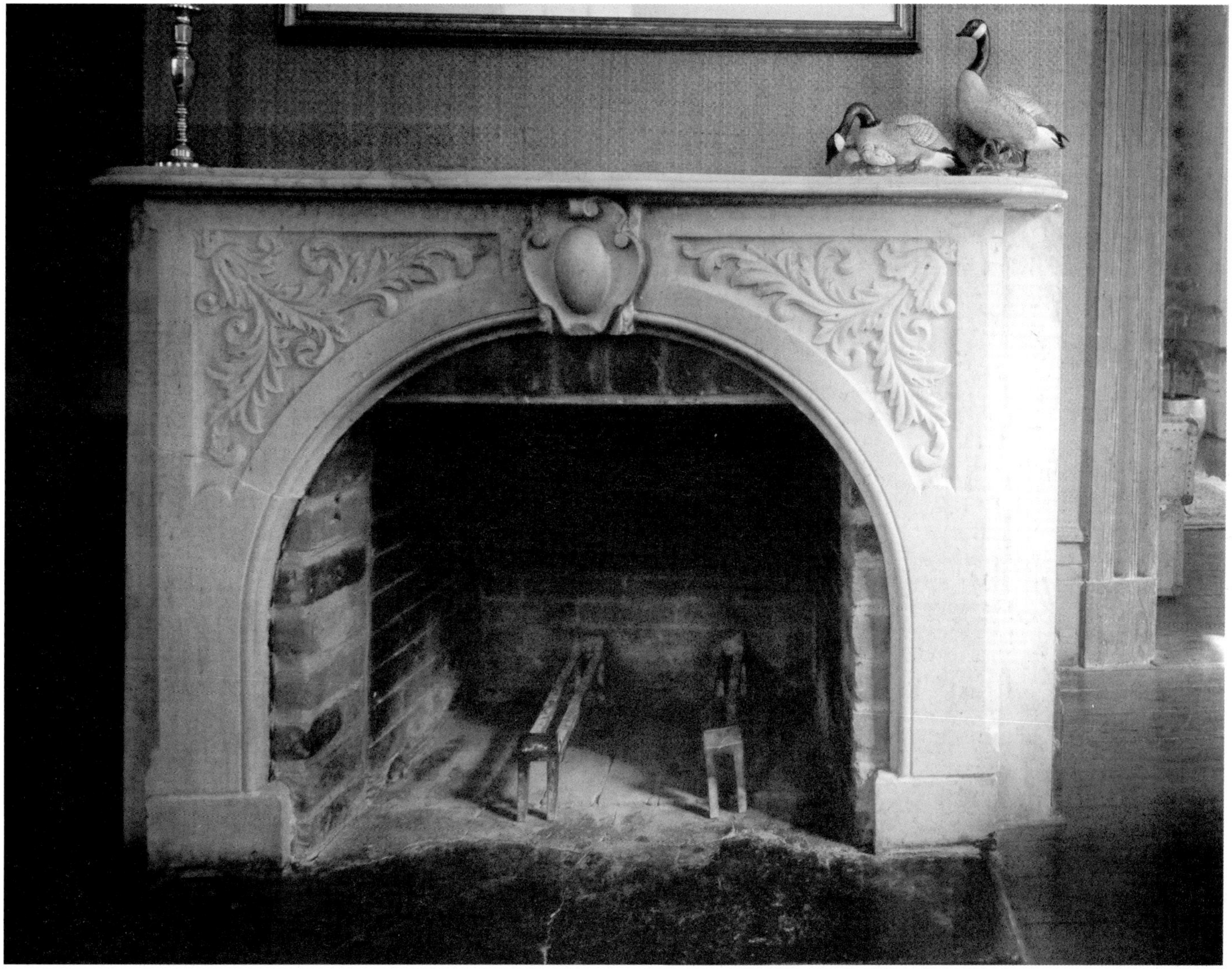

Edward Means House

A marble mantel in keeping with the 1853 construction date.

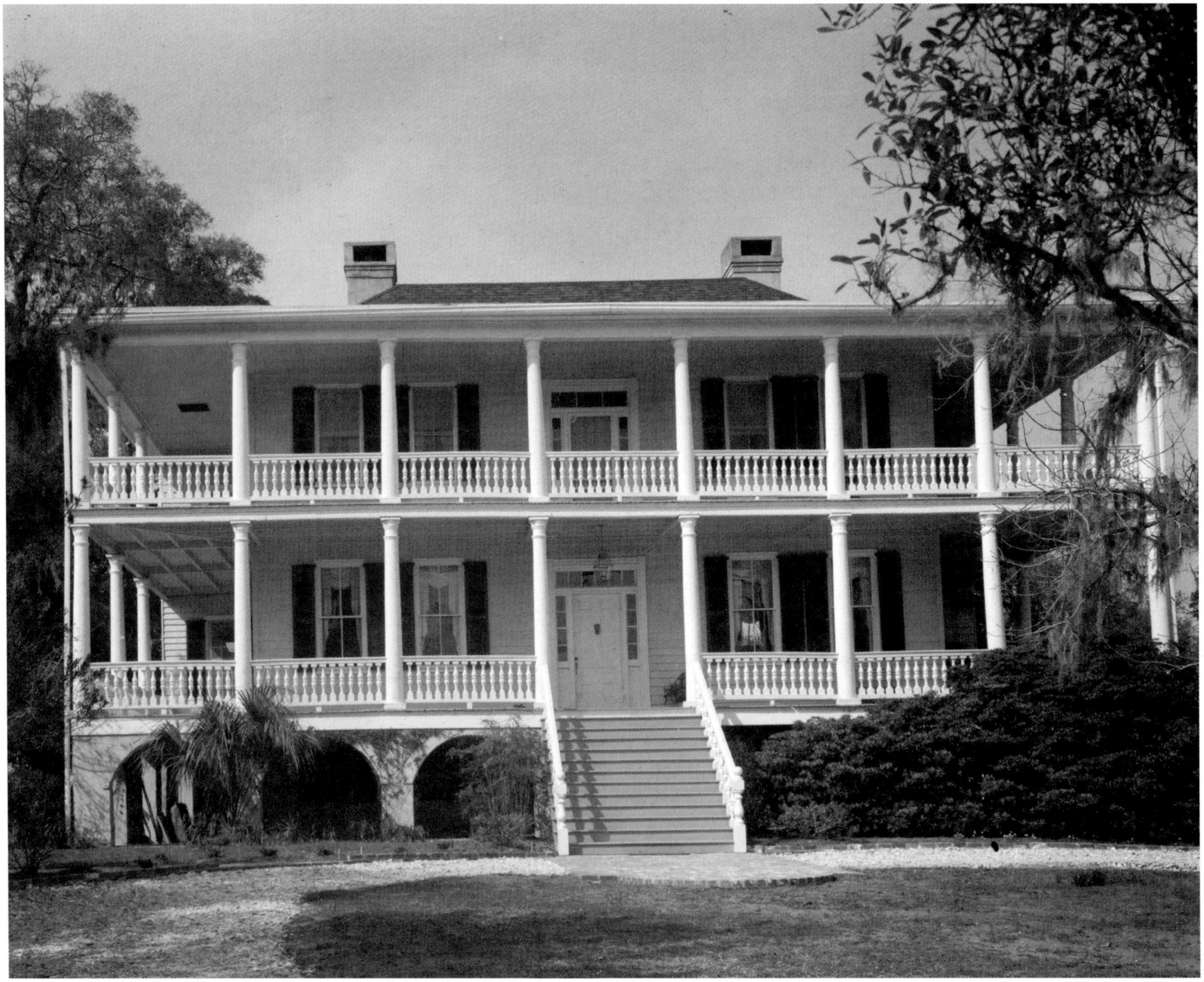

Reverend Thomas Ledbetter House — Charles N. Bayless, 1978 (photo series)

A typical Beaufort-style house to end with.

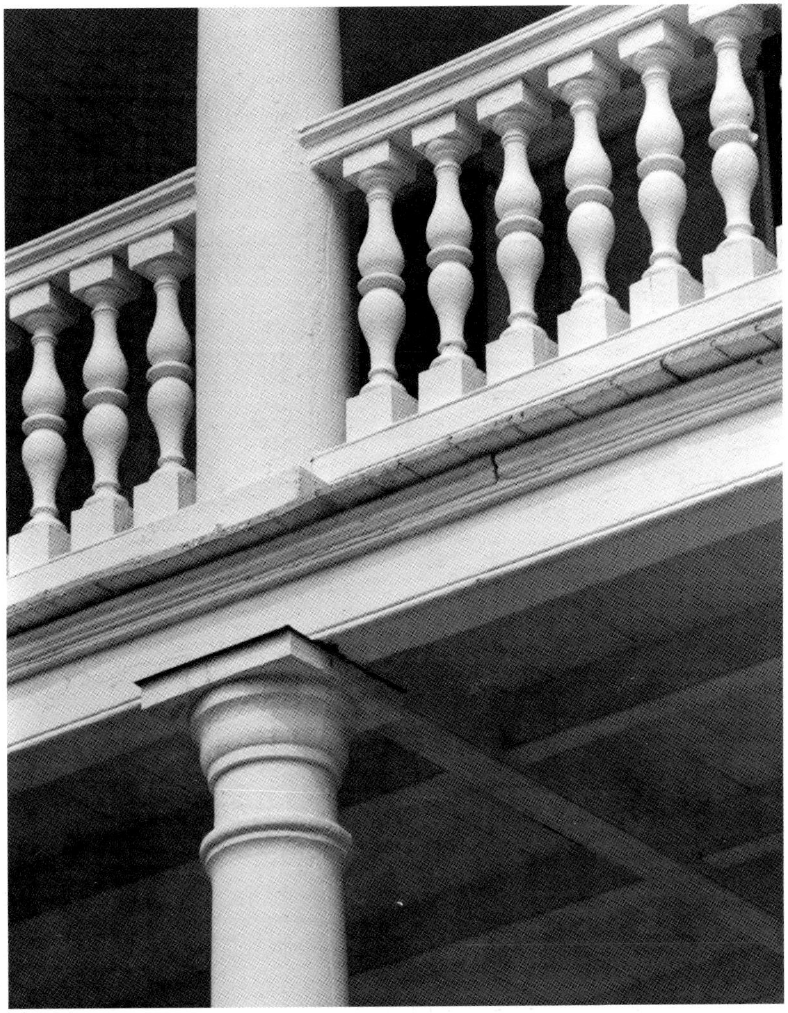

Reverend Thomas Ledbetter House

Piazza detail. Doric columns and turned balustrade.

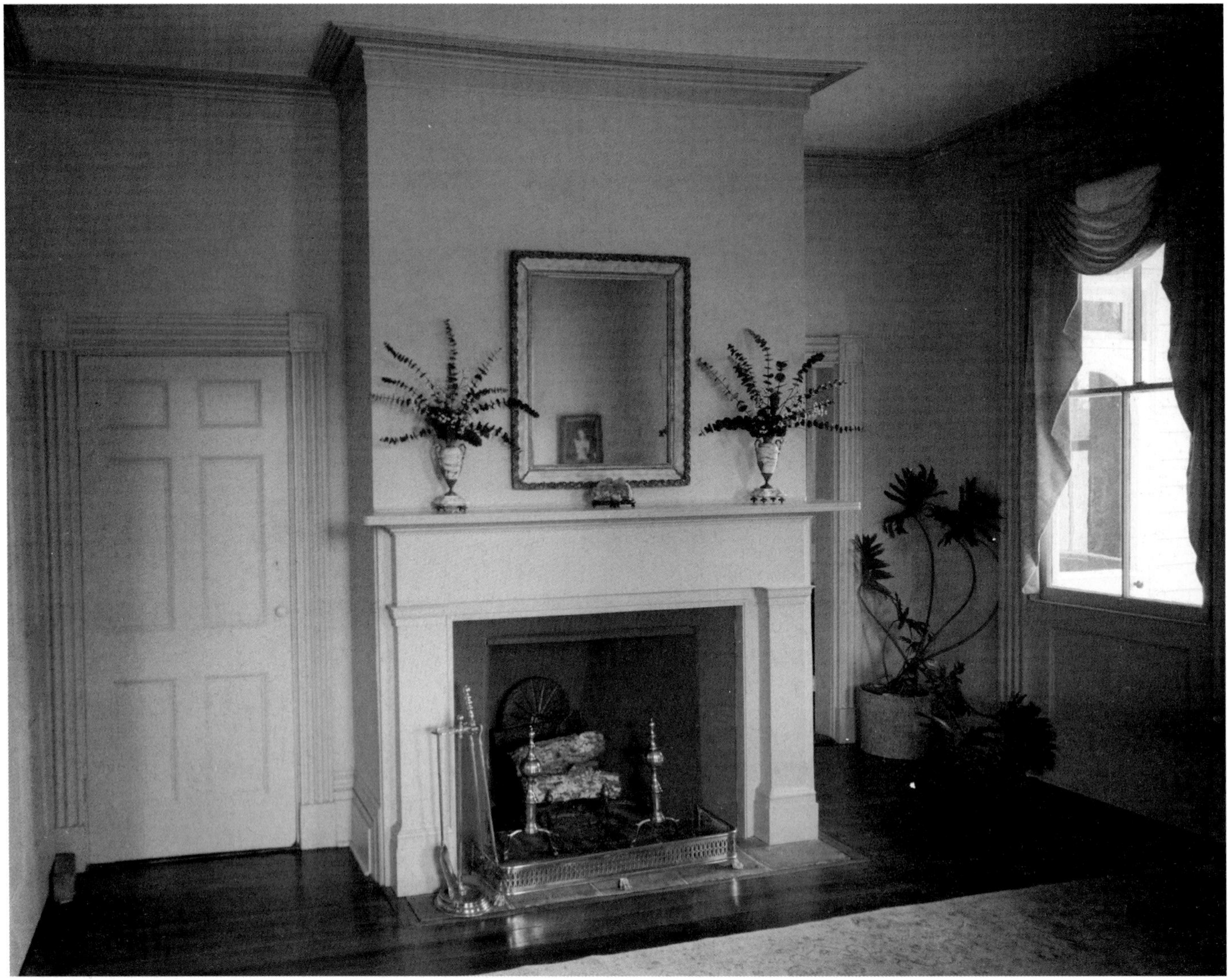

Reverend Thomas Ledbetter House

It's the floral arrangements that drew my attention to this photograph. Those and the glimpse of a painting in the mirror.

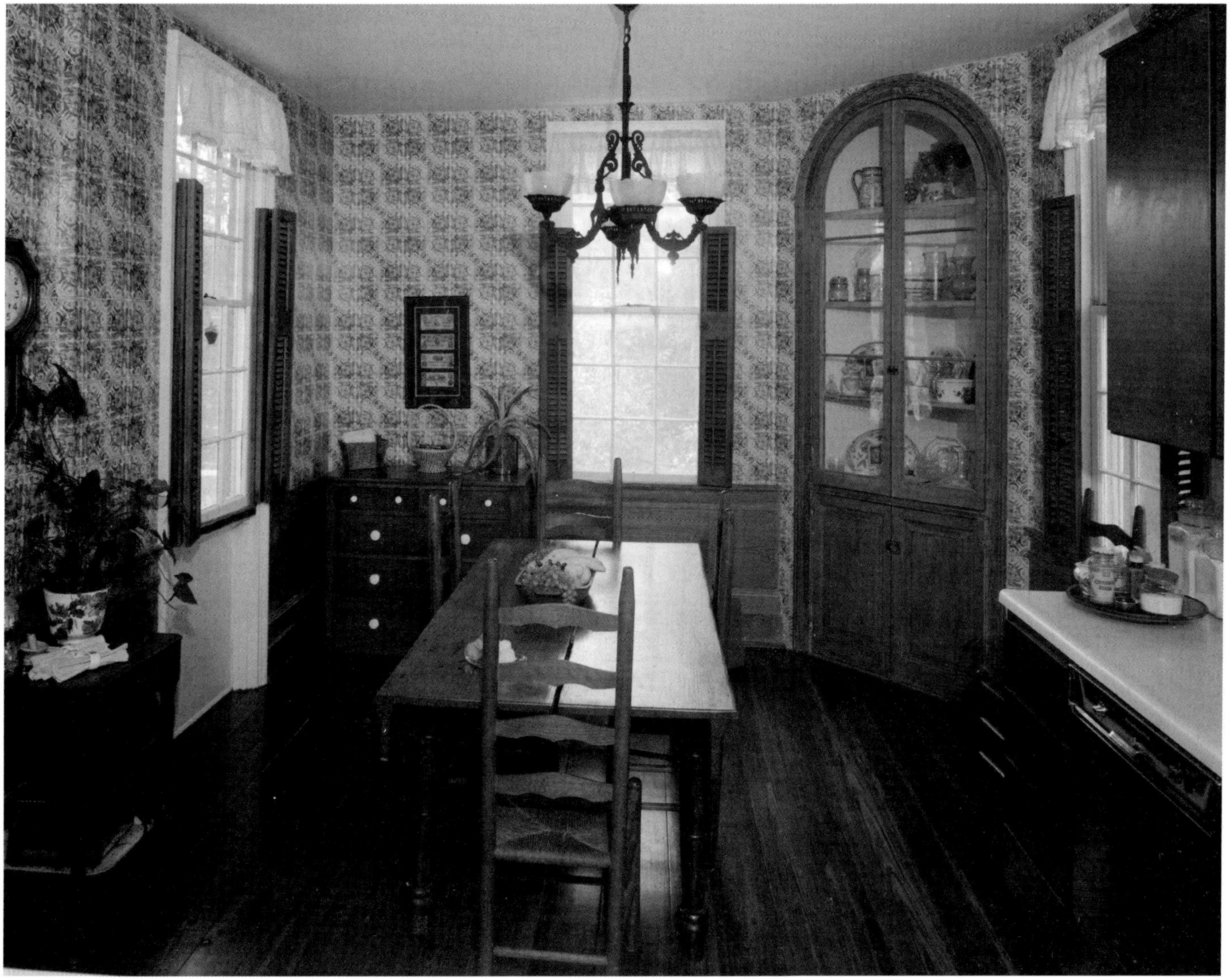

Reverend Thomas Ledbetter House

And it's the promise of domestic quiet that drew me to this photograph. I believe that corner cupboard dates from the time of construction.

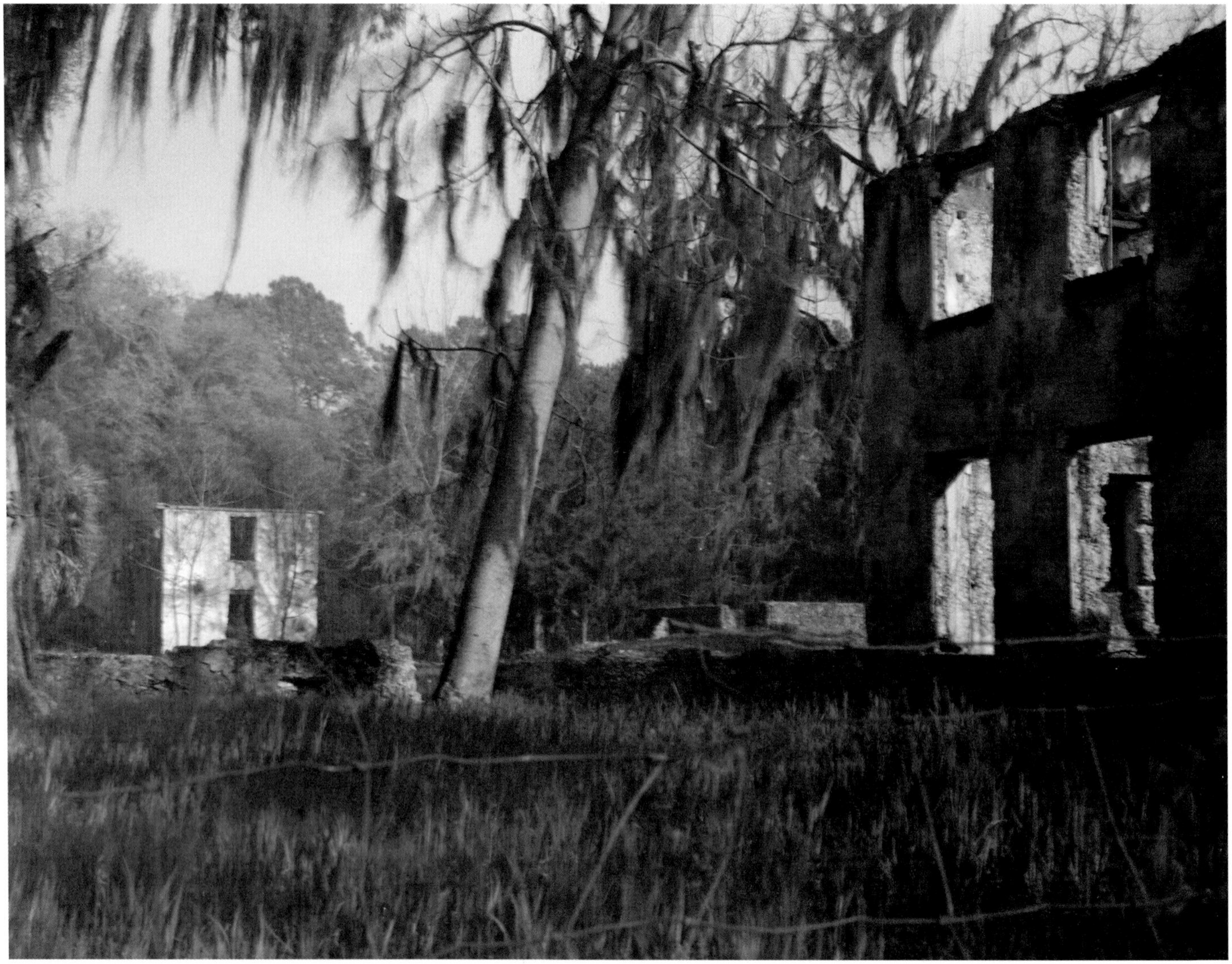

Ladies Island Ruin — Photographer not given

A two-story tabby ruin that's gained a new well-preserved lease on life. The strip of wire fencing is what drew my attention to the photograph.

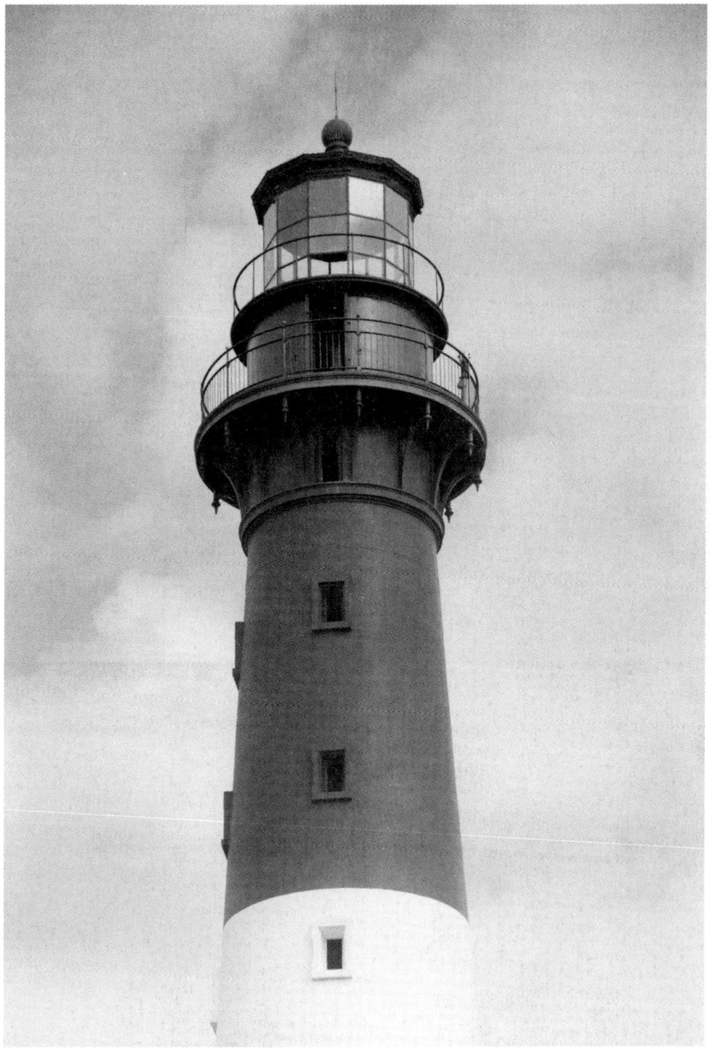

Hunting Island Lighthouse — James E. Boucher, 1987 (photo series)

The designer of this lighthouse, built in 1875, had the foresight to use easily disassembled iron plates. Fourteen years later, the light was moved in from the encroaching ocean.

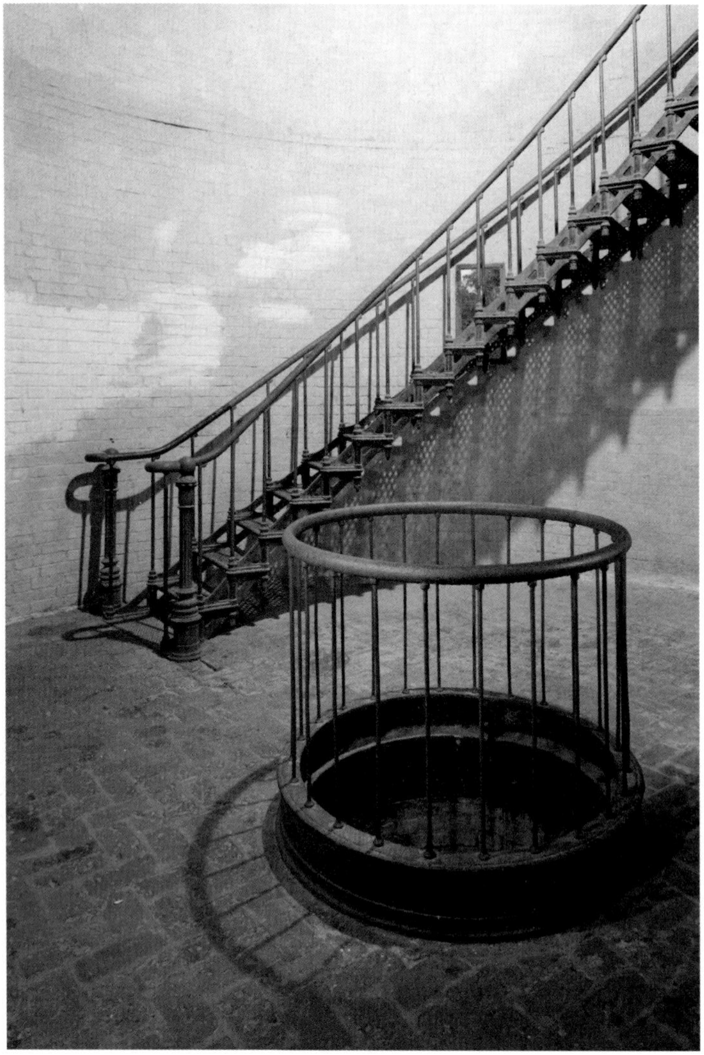

Hunting Island Lighthouse

I climbed these stairs the last time I was here. Barely. And knew I was getting old and that my own parts would not disassemble. The hole in the center was to accommodate the dropping weight that turned the light.

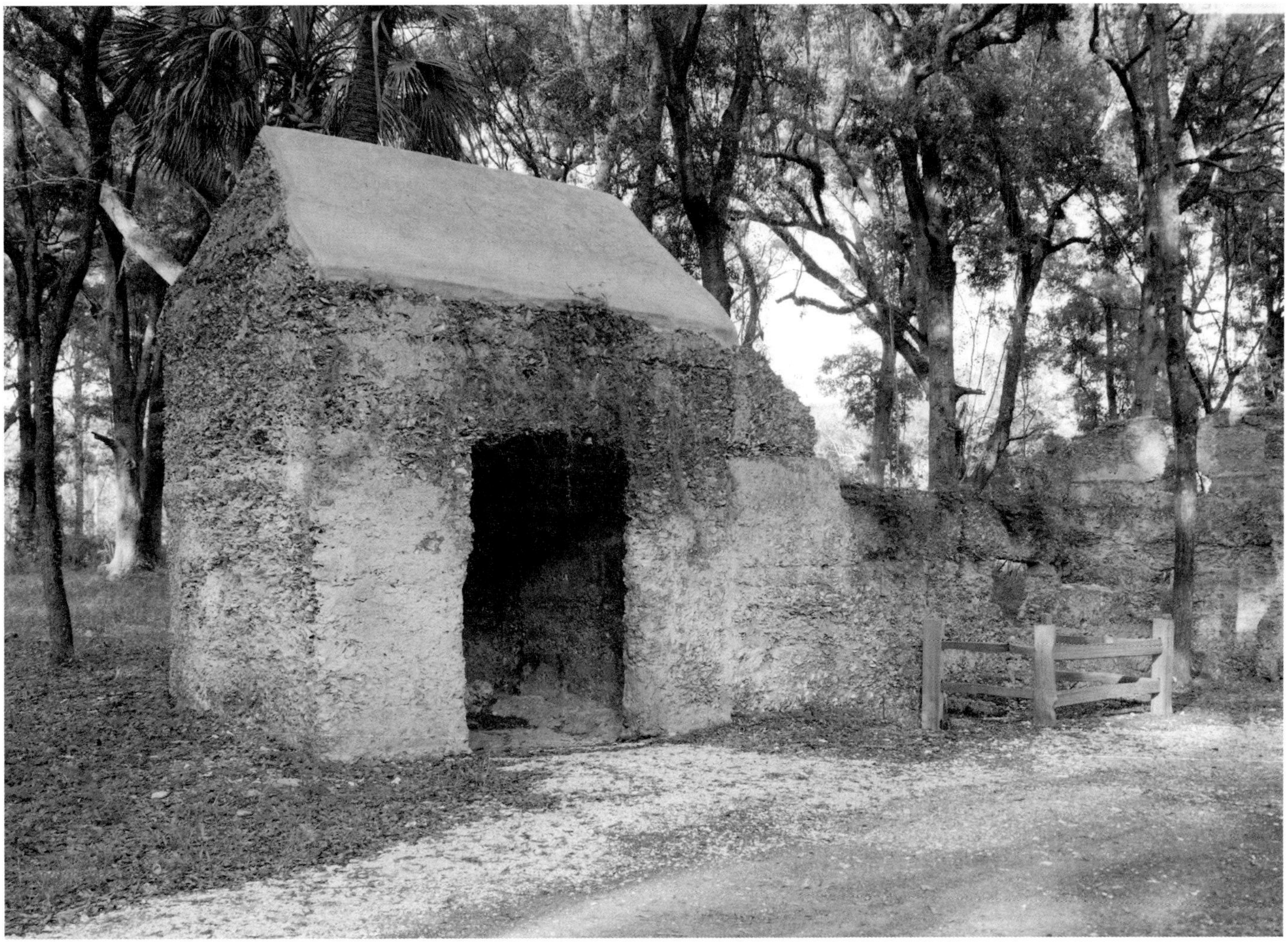

DATAW RUINS — James E. Boucher, 1986

The Sams family and their slave craftsmen were the masters of tabby construction. This is the only tabby roof I know of.

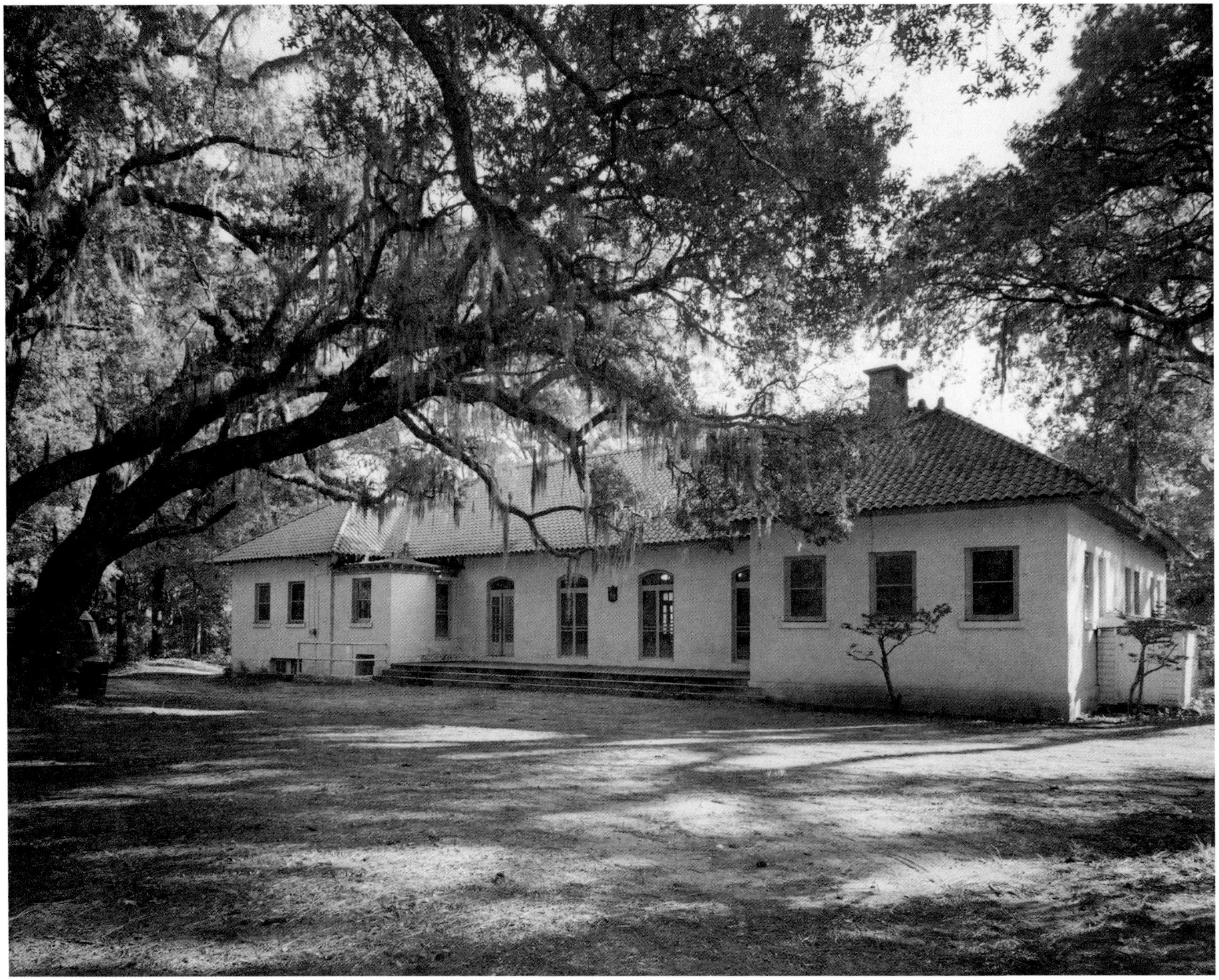

The Penn Center	Gilford Photography, 1985 (photo series)

Tracing its origin back to the freeing of the slaves, today the center concerns itself with improving the living conditions of the poor and related issues. The Frissell House was added to the complex in 1925.

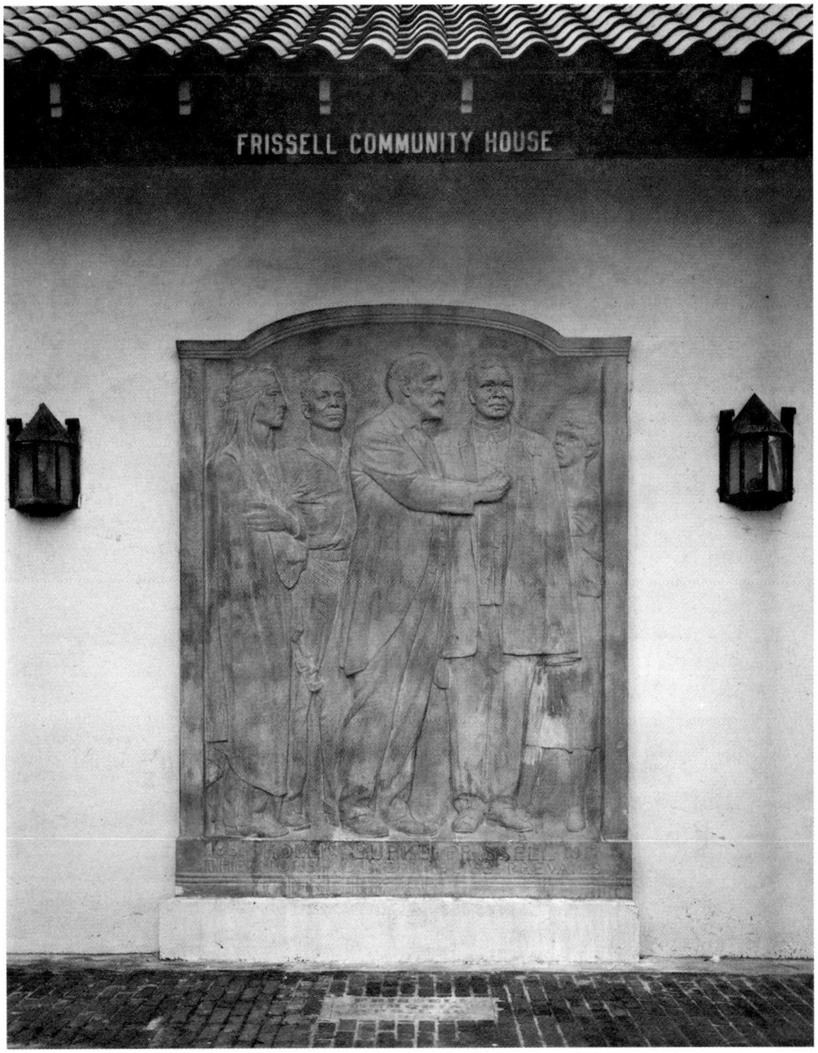

THE PENN CENTER

A bronze plaque honoring men of all races.

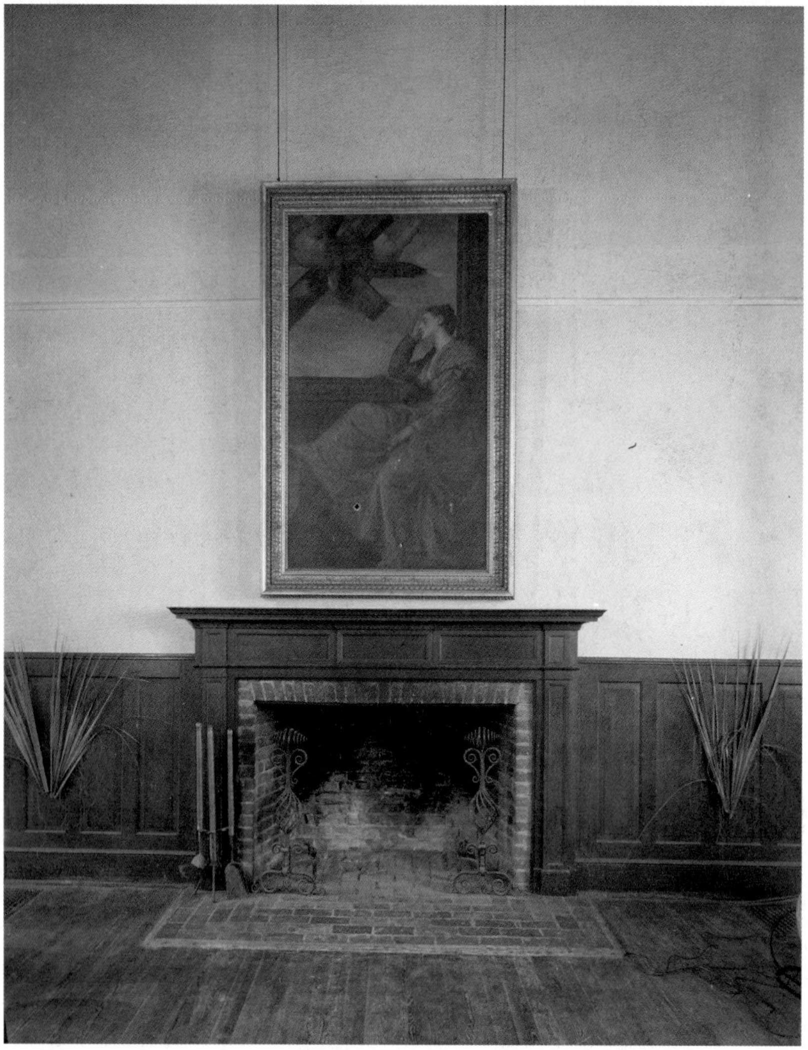

The Penn Center

A painting from the Victorian era. A visitation.

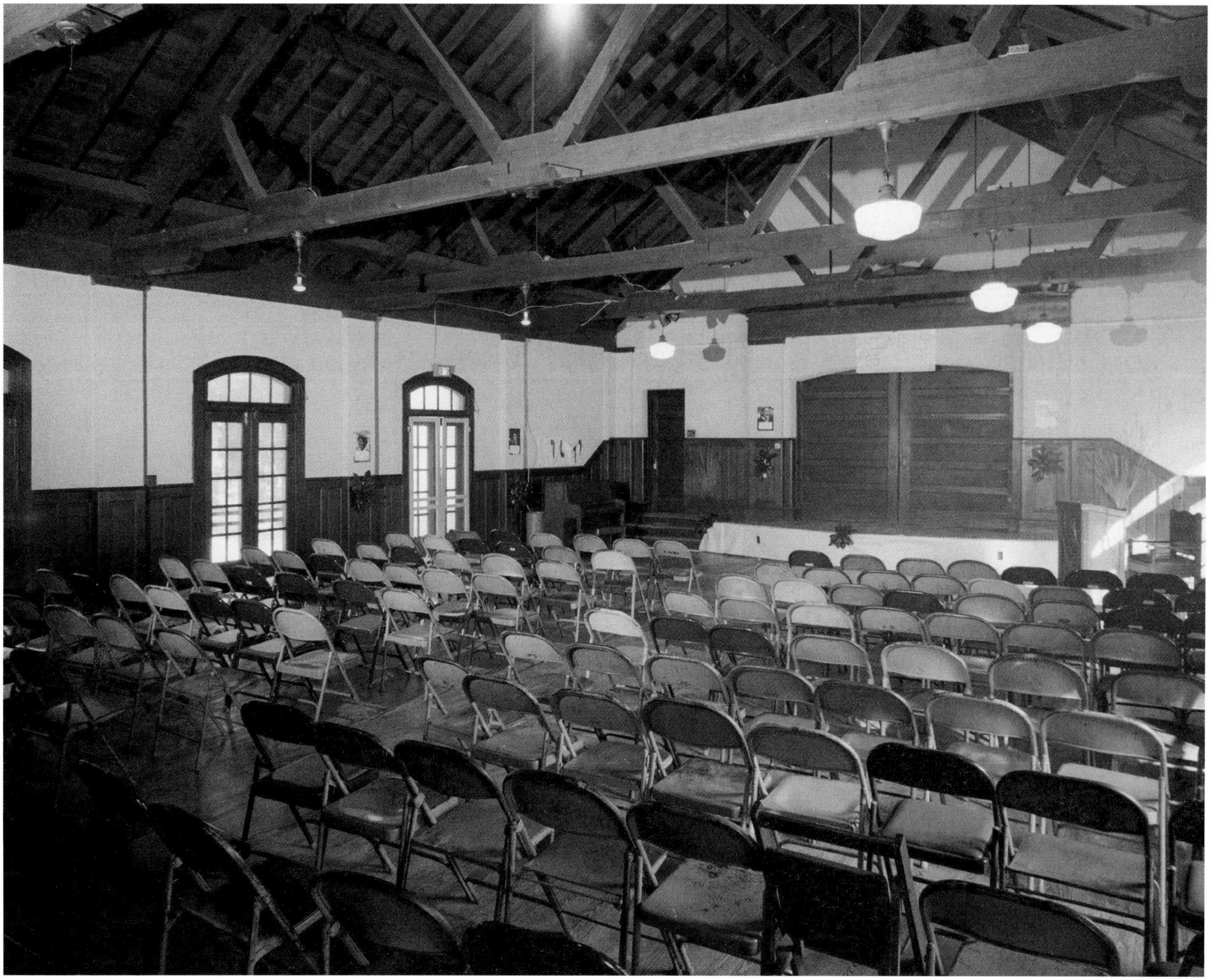

The Penn Center

Since there were few places in the South where blacks and whites could meet, Martin Luther King Jr. used the Penn Center as a retreat during his work in the South. It seems likely that he spoke from this small stage in the Frissell Community House.

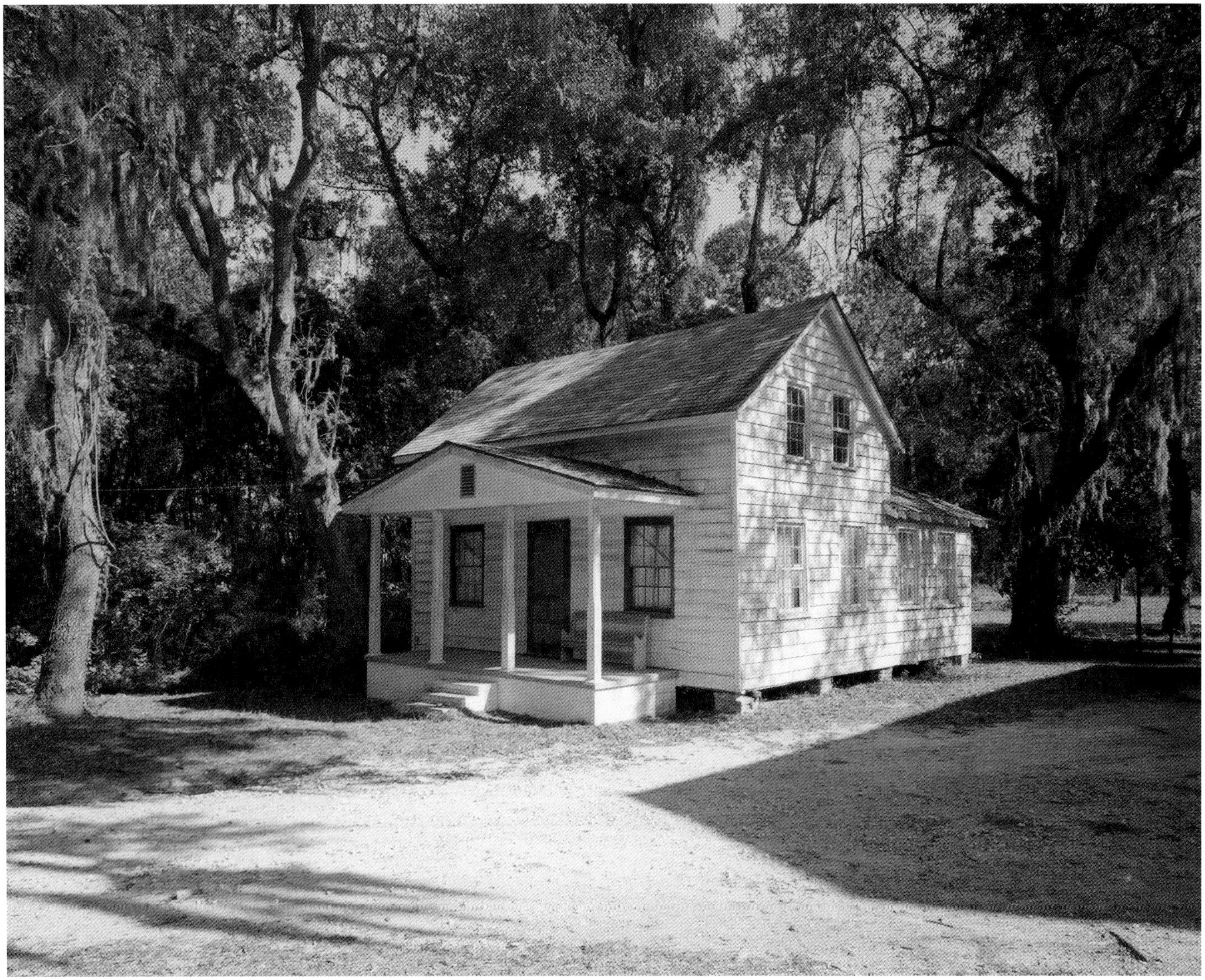

Penn School Historic District — Gilford Photography, 1985

The added portico on this small house next to the Brick Baptist Church disguises the fact that this is a two-story dwelling. The illusionary nature of the architecture is what interested me.

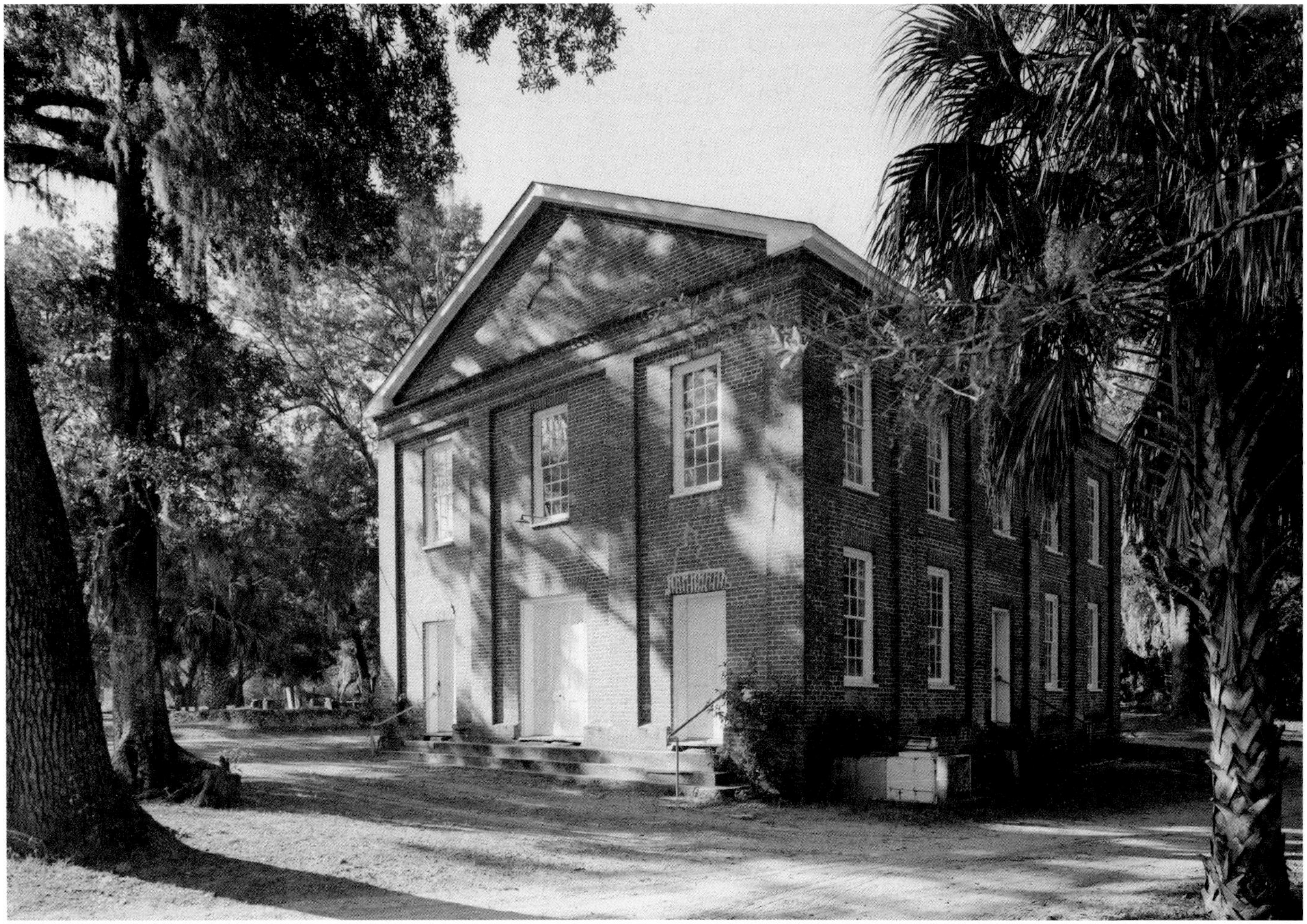

Brick Baptist Church Gilford Photography, 1985 (photo series)

In 1855, island philanthropist "Good Billy" Fripp built this church for a handful of St. Helena whites and a great many slaves. As they had constructed the building, it seems fitting that the slaves, once freed, took it over within a decade.

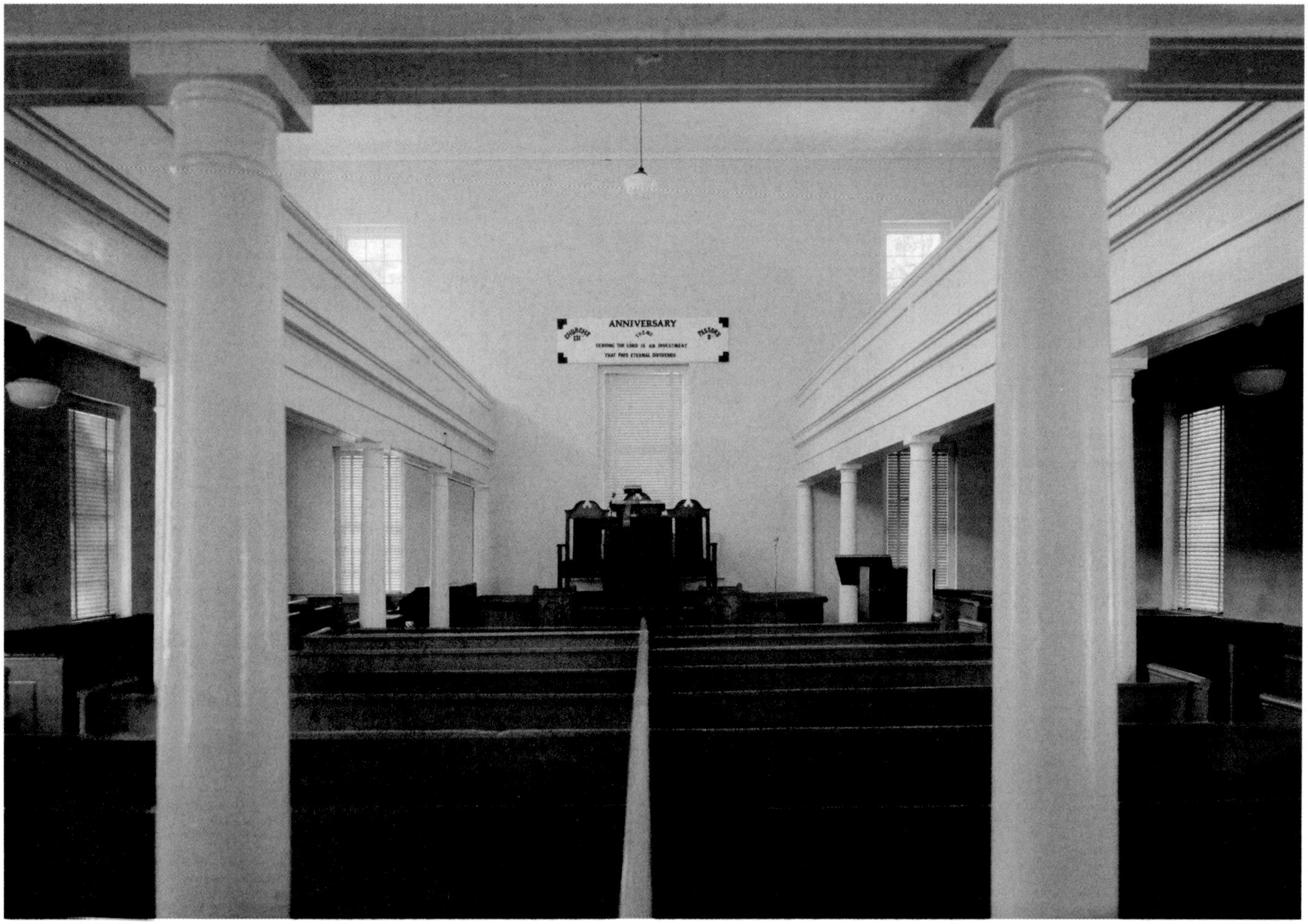

Brick Baptist Church

Slave-built pews.

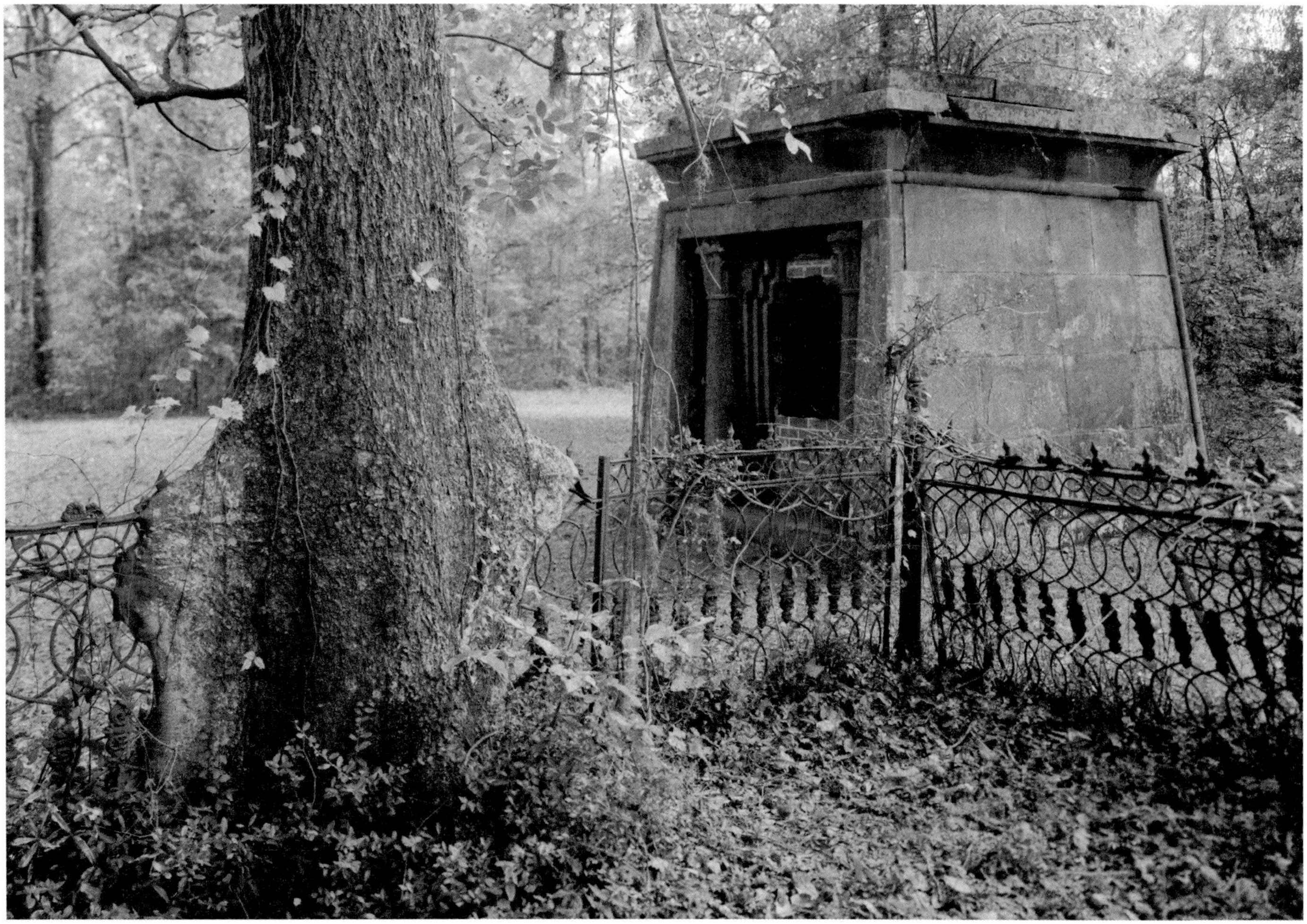

Fripp Mausoleum — James E. Boucher, 1987

Charleston architect William T. White designed the mausoleum in the Egyptian Revival style. I was drawn in by the relationship of fence to tree.

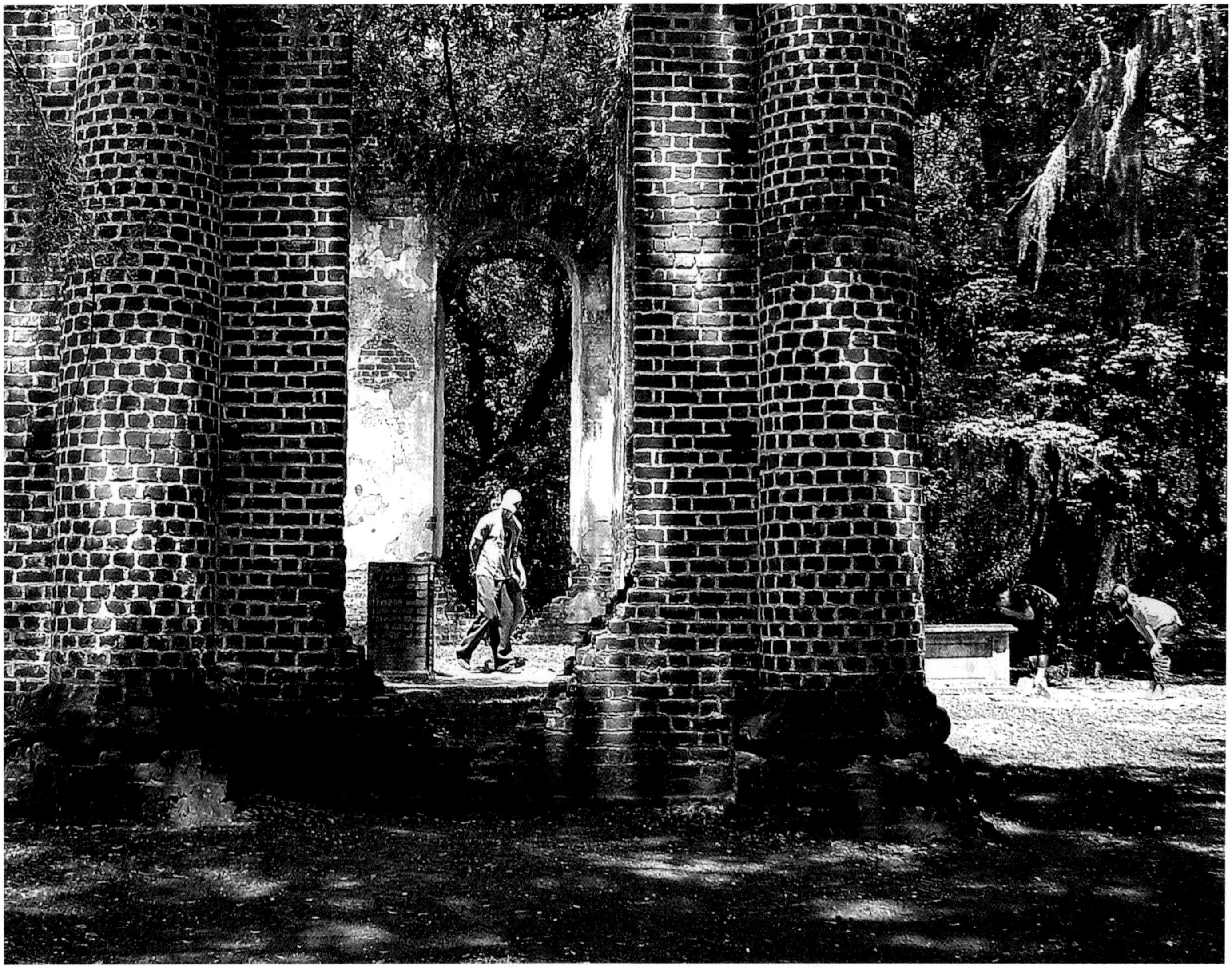

Prince William Ruin — Photographer not given

Seeing is a subjective experience. So is history. Don't let anybody tell you different. "A building more beautiful than St. Philips." British troops burnt the 1751 church and Sherman's troops did the same to the rebuilt version.

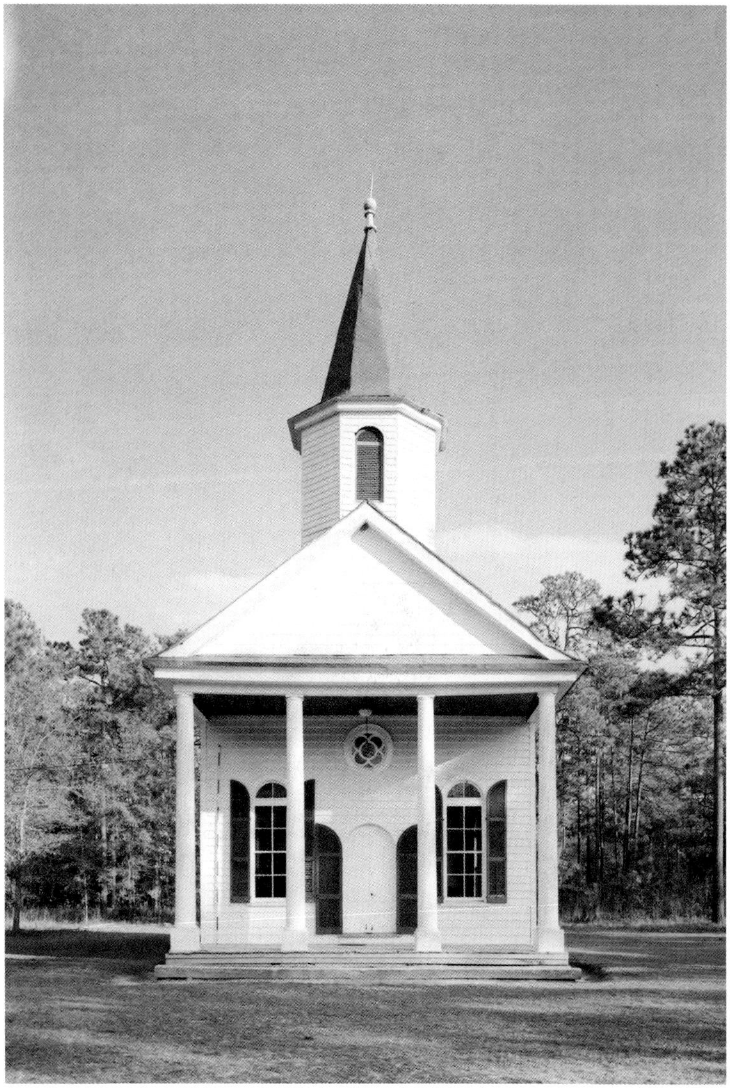

Stoney Creek Presbyterian Church James E. Boucher, 1987 (photo series)

Except for this church, Sherman's troops burnt everything in nearby McPhersonville. In 1908, my grandmother came here and taught school for a year. This is the church she attended.

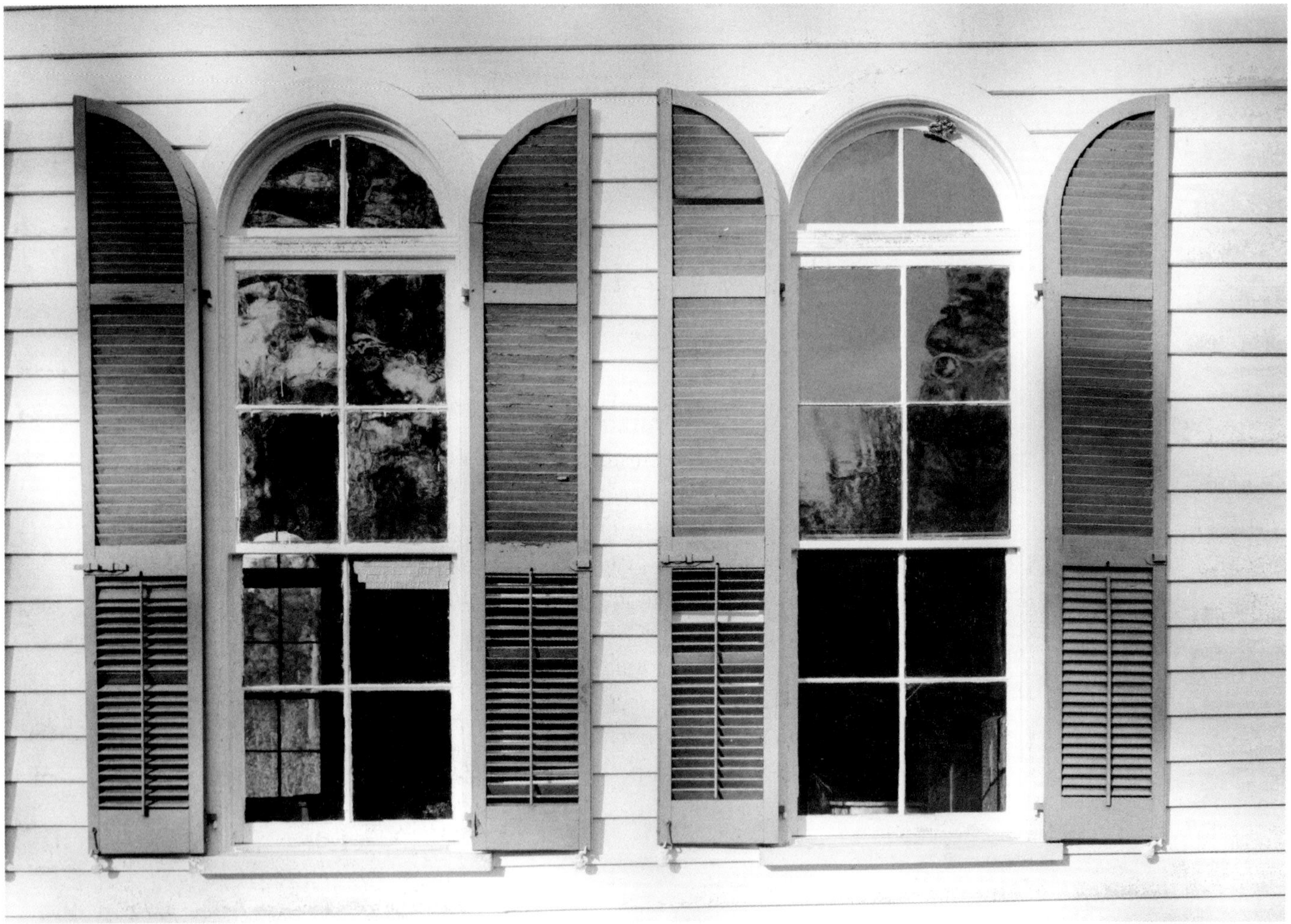

Stoney Creek Presbyterian Church

Then she went home to McClellanville, married my grandfather and through several acts of procreation launched myself and over a hundred others out onto the universe. “Tannic…” Elizabeth had it right. Glass as black as swamp water. What’s up? What’s down?

About the Author

William P. Baldwin is an award-winning novelist, biographer and historian. His novel *The Hard to Catch Mercy* is a past winner of the Lillian Smith Award for Fiction and he is the author of numerous books and articles about the South, among them *Inland Passages: Making a Lowcountry Life, Lowcountry Plantations Today, Plantations of the Lowcountry, Lowcountry Daytrips* and *Mrs. Whaley and Her Charleston Garden.* He is a longtime resident of McClellanville, South Carolina. His most recent novel is *A Gentleman in Charleston and the Manner of His Death.*

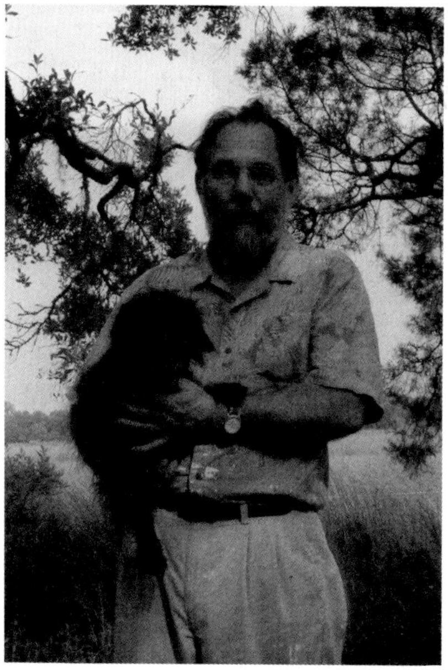

Author photo by John McWilliams.

YOU MIGHT ALSO ENJOY

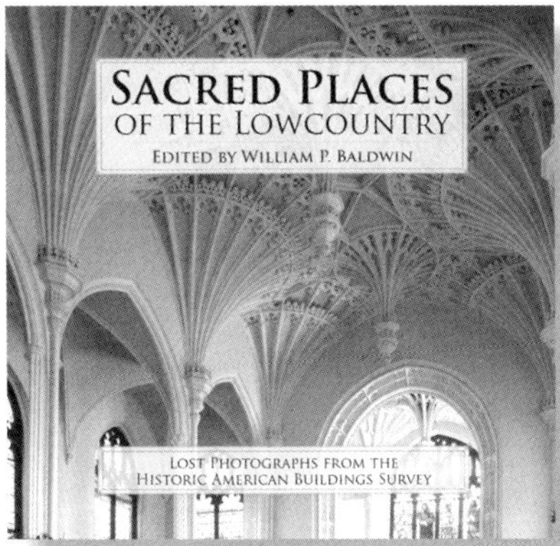

Sacred Places of the Lowcountry
Lost Photographs from the
Historic American Buildings Survey
William Baldwin

978.1.59629.346.5 * $29.99 * Oct. 2007

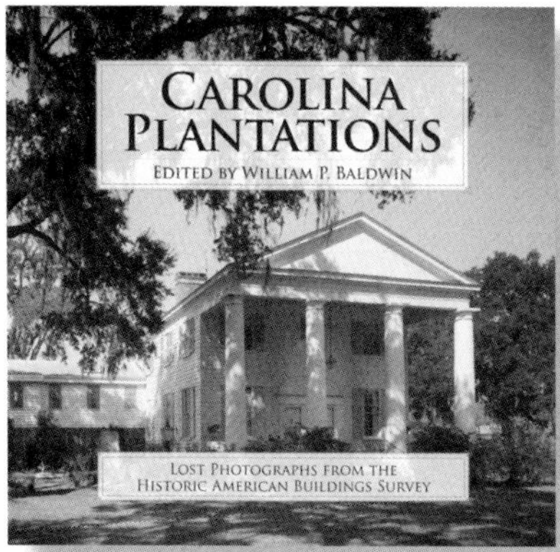

Carolina Plantations
Lost Photographs from the
Historic American Buildings Survey
William Baldwin

978.1.59629.347.2 * $29.99 * Oct. 2007